Aristotle's Practical Epistemology

Aristotle's Practical Epistemology

DHANANJAY JAGANNATHAN

OXFORD
UNIVERSITY PRESS

Oxford University Press is a department of the University of Oxford.
It furthers the University's objective of excellence in research, scholarship,
and education by publishing worldwide. Oxford is a registered trade mark of
Oxford University Press in the UK and in certain other countries.

Published in the United States of America by Oxford University Press
198 Madison Avenue, New York, NY 10016, United States of America.

© Oxford University Press 2024

All rights reserved. No part of this publication may be reproduced, stored in
a retrieval system, transmitted, used for text and data mining, or used for
training artificial intelligence, in any form or by any means, without the
prior permission in writing of Oxford University Press, or as expressly
permitted by law, by license or under terms agreed with the appropriate
reprographics rights organization. Inquiries concerning reproduction outside
the scope of the above should be sent to the
Rights Department, Oxford University Press, at the address above.

You must not circulate this work in any other form
and you must impose this same condition on any acquirer

Library of Congress Cataloging-in-Publication Data
Names: Jagannathan, Dhananjay, 1987– author.
Title: Aristotle's practical epistemology / Dhananjay Jagannathan (Columbia University).
Description: New York, NY, United States of America : Oxford University Press, [2024] |
Includes bibliographical references.
Identifiers: LCCN 2024030483 (print) | LCCN 2024030484 (ebook) |
ISBN 9780197781487 (hardback) | ISBN 9780197781494 |
ISBN 9780197781500 (epub) | ISBN 9780197781517
Subjects: LCSH: Aristotle. Nicomachean ethics. |
Conduct of life. | Knowledge, Theory of. | Wisdom.
Classification: LCC B430 .J34 2024 (print) | LCC B430 (ebook) |
DDC 171/.3—dc23/eng/20240924
LC record available at https://lccn.loc.gov/2024030483
LC ebook record available at https://lccn.loc.gov/2024030484

DOI: 10.1093/9780197781517.001.0001

Printed by Integrated Books International, United States of America

To Paul Woodruff, my teacher

Contents

Acknowledgments	xi
Introduction	1
1. Deflationism about Practical Knowledge	19
2. Ethical Experience in the *Nicomachean Ethics*	35
3. The Nature of the Virtues of Thought	75
4. Practical Understanding and Ethical Science	101
5. Knowledge of Practical Universals	121
6. Political Wisdom	151
Appendix: Further Alternatives to the Practical Epistemology of the Nicomachean Ethics	171
Bibliography	193
General Index	199
Index of Quoted Passages	201

Detailed Contents

Acknowledgments xi

Introduction 1
 I.1 The subject matter and main claim of this book 1
 I.2 Four features of practical wisdom in Aristotle 4
 I.3 Two aspects of Aristotle's method of inquiry 9
 I.4 Outline of the book 16

1. Deflationism about Practical Knowledge 19
 1.1 Practical Knowledge and Uncertainty 20
 1.2 Isocrates on practical knowledge as skillful guesswork 24
 1.3 Deflationism and conventionalism 26
 1.4 Aristotle's rejection of conventionalism and deflationism 29
 1.5 Confronting uncertainty with the help of ethical
  knowledge 33

2. Ethical Experience in the *Nicomachean Ethics* 35
 2.1 A new vision of method in ethics 37
 2.2 The practical contribution of experience 43
 2.3 Political experience in *NE* X.9 58
 2.4 Experience and technical knowledge 68

3. The Nature of the Virtues of Thought 75
 3.1 Practical wisdom as an exceptional achievement 75
 3.2 Practical wisdom amidst the virtues of thought 82
 3.3 Virtues of thought and the possession of truth 92

4. Practical Understanding and Ethical Science 101
 4.1 The superiority of understanding 101
 4.2 The exercise of understanding 106
 4.3 Ethics as a special science 116

X DETAILED CONTENTS

5.	Knowledge of Practical Universals	121
	5.1 Knowledge of principles in ethics	121
	5.2 Justice as a virtue of character	130
	5.3 The unity of practical wisdom	144
6.	Political Wisdom	151
	6.1 The political character of Aristotelian practical wisdom	151
	6.2 The identity of political and practical wisdom	152
	6.3 Practical wisdom as the ruler's excellence	158
	6.4 Practical universals in political life	164
	6.5 Political deliberation as ethical deliberation	167

Appendix: Further Alternatives to the Practical Epistemology of the Nicomachean Ethics ... 171
Bibliography ... 193
General Index ... 199
Index of Quoted Passages ... 201

Acknowledgments

Thinking through the ideas in this book has been the work of many seasons, and I am pleased to say that it has been anything but lonely. I began to think in earnest about Aristotle's practical philosophy as a student in Oxford, chiefly in tutorials with Jessica Moss on the *Nicomachean Ethics* and in a thesis supervised by Terry Irwin on the *Politics*. I carried this work forward into my studies at Cambridge and at the University of Chicago, where I wrote a doctoral dissertation on Aristotle's views of practical wisdom and deliberation entitled "The Labors of Wisdom" under the supervision of Gabriel Richardson Lear and Martha Nussbaum, who served as co-chairs, as well as Richard Kraut. I came to think that the approach I took in the dissertation was insufficiently systematic to resolve the central issues with which I was concerned, and I therefore largely abandoned the project. Still, I gratefully acknowledge the many teachers, friends, and colleagues who saw me through this first phase of my thinking about the topic, not least those mentioned above.

A few years later, I began to take up aspects of Aristotle's practical epistemology that I had not previously investigated, such as the relationship between the views articulated in the *Eudemian* and the *Nicomachean Ethics* and Aristotle's engagement on this topic with Plato's *Statesman* and with Isocrates. I presented some early ideas on these topics in a graduate seminar on the *Nicomachean Ethics* co-taught with Karen Margrethe Nielsen and Terry Irwin in Oxford in Trinity Term 2019. I am grateful to them, as well as to the other participants in that seminar, for their critical engagement on that occasion. This contextual thinking led me back to my original

xii ACKNOWLEDGMENTS

question: What *kind* of knowledge is practical wisdom? I began to see that the concept of a distinctly practical form of understanding could help me past the difficulties that had led me to abandon my dissertation.

Buoyed by this thought, I presented draft material from this project to audiences at Columbia University (in March 2020), where Amogha Sahu and Iakovos Vasiliou kindly served as commentators; at Stanford University (via Zoom in January 2021); at the University of Notre Dame (in March 2022); and at Durham University (in May 2022). Thanks to the members of all of these audiences for their questions and comments, especially Katja Vogt, Wolfgang Mann, Michele Moody-Adams, Christopher Bobonich, Leif Wenar, Christopher Shields, Robert Audi, Sean Kelsey, Thérèse Scarpelli Cory, Joel David Hamkins, Giulia Bonasio, and Phillip Sidney Horky.

In October 2022, a one-day workshop on my book manuscript was held at Columbia, an invaluable occasion where several draft chapters received detailed comment. My departmental colleagues Wolfgang Mann, Christia Mercer, Achille Varzi, and Katja Vogt served as session chairs, while Marta Jiménez, Hendrik Lorenz, Jessica Moss, and Susan Sauvé Meyer served as the commentators. I express my profound gratitude to all of them, as well as to the others who attended the workshop, for their care in reading my work and the time they devoted to helping me to improve it. Thanks also to Robert Howton for providing me written comments on the manuscript. I gratefully acknowledge financial support for the workshop from a Faculty of Arts & Sciences Lenfest Junior Faculty Development Grant and from the Department of Philosophy at Columbia University.

I am grateful also to two anonymous reviewers for Oxford University Press, who pressed me to refine my thinking and my presentation of my ideas throughout the manuscript, and to my editor Peter Ohlin for his perceptive guidance in shepherding the project toward its completion. Abigail Breuker was not only an able research assistant but also a thoughtful interlocutor as I completed the revisions on the manuscript.

Finally, I am pleased to acknowledge my greatest debt, in this as in all my academic work, to Paul Woodruff, my undergraduate advisor and mentor. I regret that I cannot present him with a copy, but I remain grateful for his friendship.

INTRODUCTION

I.1 The subject matter and main claim of this book

Phronēsis, conventionally if imperfectly translated "practical wisdom," is among the central concepts of Aristotelian ethics. The *Nicomachean Ethics* (*NE*), which is generally taken to offer Aristotle's most mature statement of his views about the good life for human beings, makes *phronēsis* its central excellence, since the two happy lives described in *NE* X.6–8, the contemplative life and the political life, both depend on the exercise of *phronēsis*. If we accept that the books that are transmitted as common to the *Eudemian* and to *Nicomachean Ethics* belong properly to both treatises, then *phronēsis* is likewise central to the *Eudemian* ethical ideal, though it is ultimately subordinated to the master virtue of nobility (*kalokagathia*; literally, 'being-noble-and-good') at the end of that treatise. In the *Politics*, moreover, *phronēsis* is identified as the distinctive excellence of the political ruler, a fulfillment of the remark in a common book of the ethical treatises that political wisdom (*politikē*) and *phronēsis* are the same state of soul.

Despite its centrality to Aristotle's ethical and political inquiries, not to mention the considerable labors of scholars and commentators over the centuries, the concept of *phronēsis* remains poorly understood.[1] It is clear enough that *phronēsis* is closely

---

[1] It is perhaps worth noting here that I do not take progress in the history of philosophy to be a given. The numerous cultural and intellectual transformations that stand between the composition of Aristotle's works and our own time have furnished, with each generation of readers, not only new opportunities for engagement but also the possibility of loss and distortion. We do not come naïve to these enormously influential texts. Moreover, the intellectual horizon to which they originally belonged is not fully recuperable in our own time. Nevertheless, we can do a better or worse job of interpreting these texts. My views here are indebted to Hans-Georg Gadamer's idea that textual

---

Aristotle's Practical Epistemology. Dhananjay Jagannathan, Oxford University Press.
© Oxford University Press 2024. DOI: 10.1093/9780197781517.003.0001

2 ARISTOTLE'S PRACTICAL EPISTEMOLOGY

connected to excellence in deliberation and is exercised in paradigmatic cases of virtuous action. But one of the key debates in the recent scholarly literature has been over whether *phronēsis* is more like a skill or a facility for intuitively discerning the correct action to perform in varying circumstances, or whether *phronēsis* is instead more like scientific knowledge, a grasp of what is good for human beings and why that can be brought to bear on deliberative questions. The very nature of *phronēsis* remains in dispute.

The main contention of this book is that neither model or interpretive strategy is on its own fully adequate to explain the various aspects of Aristotle's conception of *phronēsis*. Rather, as I argue, *phronēsis* only comes into view when we see it as practical (or ethical) understanding.[2] As practical understanding, it is *both* the knowledge by which we deliberate and choose the actions that the virtues of character demand in particular circumstances *and* a virtue of thought that counts as an understanding of the human good by contrast to more ordinary forms of ethical knowledge that fail to be comprehensive.

Aristotle's argument in the ethical treatises, then, depends on the possibility that there exists a kind of knowledge that is both practical and an intellectual perfection. Such an intellectual perfection is the best epistemic state one can be in with regard to the

---

interpretation involves a fusion of horizons in *Truth and Method*, 2nd ed. (Sheed and Ward, 1989).

[2] I will move back and forth between describing this understanding as "practical" or as "ethical"; ethics, for Aristotle, is the domain of *praxis* or action in a narrow sense that excludes much of what we would readily describe as practical, e.g., the exercise of technical abilities or skills. For Aristotle, the mark of ethical action in this narrow sense is that it aims at our overall well-being in life rather than any specific or partial good, such as health or wealth (*NE* VI.5, 1140a25–30). What we need to properly inquire into ethical matters is experience of the actions that make up our lives (*NE* I.3, 1094b27–95a6). Roughly speaking, the language of "practical understanding" is especially helpful when considering Aristotle's epistemological contrasts between practical knowledge on the one hand and theoretical and productive knowledge on the other, while the term "ethical understanding" is useful in connection with Aristotle's normative ethical and political views in the *NE* and the *Politics*.

INTRODUCTION 3

particular, contingent, and variable subject matter of human action and success. To make this case, Aristotle develops, both implicitly and explicitly, a distinctly practical epistemology whose contours have not been fully mapped. My goal in this book is to bring to light this distinctive approach to practical knowledge, in order both to show the unity of a range of Aristotelian claims about the nature of ethical and political life and to elucidate a position that is worthy of our consideration in ongoing philosophical reflection on the demands of virtue, the interconnections between ethics and politics, and the nature of practical knowledge.

The rest of this Introduction is divided into three sections. In §I.2 I consider the range of claims that Aristotle makes about *phronēsis* and show how proponents of each of the interpretive strategies I identified above tend to construe these claims, emphasizing some at the expense of making the best sense of others. In §I.3, I develop two ideas that together shape the method of inquiry into the nature of *phronēsis* that I follow in this book. The first of these ideas is that Aristotle is especially concerned in the *Nicomachean Ethics* to establish that the subject matter of ethics allows for knowledge, and the second is that *phronēsis* is the best knowledge we can have in the ethical domain, i.e., the domain of human action. I show how these two ideas lead to the core claims of my account of *phronēsis* as practical understanding, which is superior to more ordinary forms of practical knowledge precisely insofar as it involves a comprehensive grasp of the human good, but which is equally practical in character, meaning that it is exercised in deliberating about and choosing particular actions. Finally, in §I.4, I provide a plan of the rest of the book and a summary of its chapters. As I describe there, I defend my thesis that *phronēsis* is practical understanding in two stages, setting up Aristotle's distinctive theory of ethical experience as a preeminent type of ordinary practical knowledge, from which *phronēsis* develops, before giving my positive account of *phronēsis* as practical understanding.

4 ARISTOTLE'S PRACTICAL EPISTEMOLOGY

I.2 Four features of practical wisdom in Aristotle

Much of the difficulty in understanding what Aristotle says about *phronēsis* can be traced to the sheer range of claims he makes about it. How could a single state meet all these criteria or satisfy all these features?[3] In this section, I outline four core features that any account of *phronēsis* must explain. I then show that these features, taken as a set, are only imperfectly explained by each of the interpretive strategies that I mentioned above in §I.1.[4] These core features are not independent of one another but emerge from the core argument of the *Nicomachean Ethics*. Still, they are not always juxtaposed by interpreters.

Apart from a few passing mentions in Book I, we first encounter *phronēsis* in an argumentative context in the *Nicomachean Ethics* in the definition of virtue of character at the start of *NE* II.6. There, Aristotle defines virtue to be a "state issuing in choice and consisting in an intermediate, relative to us, which is specified by reasoning (*logos*), namely, the reasoning the practically wise person would determine (*horiseien*)" (1106b36–1107a2).[5] This remark expands on Aristotle's earlier claims that virtue—and virtuous action—must accord with correct reasoning (II.2, 1103b31–34). He adds here in II.6 that the reasoning is what a practically wise person *would* determine. In other words, practical wisdom sets limits for the exercise of virtue.[6]

---

[3] A reflection of this difficulty may be seen in the fact that *prudentia* in the medieval Latin Aristotelian tradition, which translates the Greek *phronēsis*, came to signify a set of distinct, though interconnected states. See, e.g., the various senses of *prudentia* described in William of Ockham's *De connexione virtutum*, art. ii, dist. 1.

[4] For ease of exposition, I have provided citations to the relevant passages in the *Nicomachean Ethics* without quoting the texts or analyzing them in detail. I return to many of these passages in later chapters, however. As I am mainly trying to frame the question of what *phronēsis* is, I do not mean for my descriptions of the text to be controversial.

[5] All translations are mine unless otherwise noted.

[6] The word I have here translated 'determine' (*horiseien*) is cognate with *horos* (limit), a term that features prominently in *NE* VI.1 (*EE* V.1), where the focal analysis of practical wisdom begins. Hereafter, I will cite the Common Books of the *NE* and the *EE* as if they

INTRODUCTION 5

Aristotle returns to this intertwining of practical wisdom and the exercise of the virtues of character in *NE* VI.12–13, where he argues that one cannot have practical wisdom without fully having the virtues of character and vice versa.[7] The reason is that these qualities are exercised together, with the virtues ensuring that our goal in acting is correct and *phronēsis* ensuring that we choose the correct actions that advance that goal (*NE* VI.12, 1144a6–9).[8] The first mark of *phronēsis*, then, is that it is the quality by which we are able to intelligently exercise the virtues of character in particular situations. That is why Aristotle says in *NE* VI.5 that the work of *phronēsis* simply is *acting successfully* (*eupraxia*), which we can think of as the aspect of happiness that is up to us (1140b4–7).

As I discuss in detail in Chapter 3, the whole inquiry of *NE* VI is meant to situate *phronēsis* among the intellectual virtues or (as I will typically call them) the virtues of thought, one of the two kinds of human excellence that Aristotle proposes for analysis in *NE* I.13 (1103a3–10). *Phronēsis*, then, is not simply an intellectual ability but specifically an intellectual excellence or perfection. In particular, it is the excellence of the part of the soul that concerns contingent things, things that can be otherwise and hence are capable of change, including, crucially, change through our intervention (VI.2, 1139a3–15). We will not fully understand *phronēsis* until we can explain why, for instance, it is superior to craft (*tekhnē*), which also concerns contingent things. This explanation will be found in an account of what it means to be a virtue of thought and what sort of virtue of thought *phronēsis* in particular is meant to be. The

belonged simply to the *NE*. I return to some of the central differences between the two ethical treatises in the Appendix (§A.2).

[7] As I argue in Chapter 3, the added point being made here is that one cannot rely on the *phronēsis* of others in order to act virtuously. Nevertheless, I defend the view that Aristotle allows for the possibility that we can act *as the virtues require* without having *phronēsis* ourselves.

[8] See Jessica Moss, "'Virtue Makes the Goal Right': Virtue and Phronesis in Aristotle's Ethics," *Phronesis* 56 (2011): 204–261, for an explanation of the significance of this division of labor between the two kinds of virtue relevant for acting well.

6 ARISTOTLE'S PRACTICAL EPISTEMOLOGY

second mark, then, is this: *phronēsis* is not merely any intellectual quality but specifically, a virtue of thought, a perfection of a human capacity to cognize the world.

What part of the world, then, does *phronēsis* grasp? In a passage of *NE* VI.5, where Aristotle is concerned specifically to distinguish *phronēsis* from *tekhnē*, he claims that people of practical wisdom understand what is good for human beings as such, i.e., for their lives as a whole (1140a25–30). By contrast, the various crafts are intelligent ways of realizing particular human goods (*agatha kata meros*), ranging from the most mundane craft-objects such as tables and chairs to the exalted aim of human health (1140a26–27). It is not just any sort of contingent thing, then, but the whole range of human goods that is the purview of *phronēsis* and indeed *the* human good as such. The third mark, then, is this: *phronēsis* is a grasp of the human good as such, not just particular goods.

How, then, do the various particular human goods fit together into a single view of the human good? In Aristotle's analysis, human goods converge in and are governed by the highest good, which is the subject matter of political inquiry (*NE* I.2, 1094a24–28). The political community, as the most comprehensive form of human association, regulates the pursuit of each good (*NE* I.2, 1094a28–b3). Moreover, political wisdom or understanding is the state that aims at bringing about the highest good (*NE* I.2, 1094b4–10). Aristotle says that *phronēsis* and political wisdom are the same state of soul, though they can be formally distinguished (*NE* VI.8, 1141b23–24). I take this to mean that they constitute the same understanding, that is, these two states are understanding of the same thing (i.e., the human good). So, the fourth mark is this: *phronēsis* is political in nature and, indeed, is equivalent to political wisdom.

Let us now put these four marks or features of *phronēsis* together. From a relatively straightforward reading of the texts, we can be confident that Aristotle takes *phronēsis* to be the following: the virtue of thought concerned comprehensively (and, hence, also politically) with the human good as such, by which we act virtuously

INTRODUCTION   7

on particular occasions. Above in §I.1, I described two basic interpretive strategies: one tends to assimilate *phronēsis* to an intuitive skill, and the other tends to assimilate it to a body of scientific knowledge.[9] In this section I will refer to these interpretive strategies simply as the skill view and the scientific view. Can views that favor one of these strategies fully account for the four marks or features of *phronēsis* that I have identified? I will argue that they cannot, before going on to present the outline of my own view.

[9] I do not mean to suggest that every prior interpretation of Aristotle's practical epistemology, many of which are highly sophisticated, falls into one of two camps. Interpreters tend to have *something* to say about the aspects of Aristotle's view that do not neatly fit the model their view favors. The most straightforward example of the skill view among recent influential interpreters can be found in Sarah Broadie's *Ethics with Aristotle* (Oxford University Press, 1991), esp. Chapter 4, "Practical Wisdom," while the most straightforward example of the scientific view among recent influential interpreters can be found in C. D. C. Reeve's *Practices of Reason* (Clarendon Press, 1992). I will use their interpretations as exemplars of the two strategies I have identified. One of the main fault lines in the divide between these interpretations is the role for universal or general principles in practical thought.

John McDowell's interpretation, found in a series of papers on deliberation and practical reasoning in Aristotle, offers another version of the skill view that emphasizes the uncodifiability of ethical principles; see "Eudaimonism and Realism in Aristotle's Ethics," "Deliberation and Moral Development in Aristotle's Ethics," and "Incontinence and Practical Wisdom in Aristotle," all of which are reprinted in *The Engaged Intellect: Philosophical Essays* (Harvard University Press, 2009), 23–40; 41–58; and 59–76, respectively. A. W. Price generally follows Broadie's and McDowell's line of thinking but identifies a small role for general principles in practical thinking, such as prohibitions that apply without exception; see *Virtue and Reason in Plato and Aristotle*, esp. Part C2, "Aristotle on Practical Reasoning," 188–250.

Deborah Achtenberg—in *Cognition of Value in Aristotle's Ethics: Promise of Enrichment, Threat of Destruction* (State University of New York Press, 2002)—offers another version of the skill view that focuses mainly on the cognition of particulars, while identifying "good" as a sort of analogical universal that applies across different practical situations. However, Achtenberg does acknowledge a role for generalizations that hold good for the most part while falling short of rules. I will argue that practical universals, for Aristotle, always have this feature, which helps bring into view the role of *understanding* in practical wisdom, emphasized by proponents of the scientific view.

Finally, recent interpreters who have emphasized a role for scientific knowledge in ethics include Terry Irwin, Karen-Margrethe Nielsen, and Joseph Karbowski, though none endorses the full extent of Reeve's scientific view. See Irwin, "Ethics as an Inexact Science: Aristotle's Ambitions for Moral Theory," in *Moral Particularism*, ed. Brad Hooker and Margaret Little (Oxford University Press, 2000), 100–129; Nielsen, "Aristotle on Principles in Ethics: Political Science as the Science of the Human Good," in *Bridging the Gap between Aristotle's Science and Ethics*, ed. Devin Henry and Karen Margrethe Nielsen (Cambridge University Press, 2015), 29–48; and Karbowski, *Aristotle's Method in Ethics* (Cambridge University Press, 2018).

8 ARISTOTLE'S PRACTICAL EPISTEMOLOGY

The skill view emphasizes, above all, the first mark I noted above, namely, that *phronēsis* enables us to act well on particular occasions. The proponents of the skill view can also draw on analogies between *tekhnē* (craft) and *phronēsis* throughout the *NE* to interpret its status as a virtue of thought (the second mark) on their interpretation.[10] But the third and fourth marks pose more difficulties for the skill view. Its proponents must interpret the claim that the person of practical wisdom has a grasp of the human good (the third mark) as a *distributive* claim, i.e., that such a person grasps what is good on any given occasion without necessarily having a view to the overall good for human beings. But this interpretation of the third mark makes it difficult to see how proponents of the skill view can account for the fourth mark, the political character of *phronēsis*. Some proponents of the skill view resort to distinguishing types of *phronēsis*, the sort that concerns action in ordinary circumstances and some more comprehensive or political type of *phronēsis* that takes a view to the overall human good.[11] The textual evidence for such a distinction is weak. Moreover, as I will show, Aristotle does have a conception of ordinary ethical knowledge, but he identifies such knowledge with experience (*empeiria*), not *phronēsis*, in the *Nicomachean Ethics*.

---

[10] See Tom Angier, *Technē in Aristotle's Ethics: Crafting the Moral Life* (Continuum, 2010), for an attempt to read Aristotle's analogies as offering a model of virtue as a sort of *technē*. See Julia Annas, *Intelligent Virtue*, for a constructive philosophical account of virtue as skill in a broadly neo-Aristotelian spirit (Oxford University Press, 2011). There are, of course, significant questions about how *technē* itself should be understood in Aristotle and how it relates to the other virtues of thought, especially scientific knowledge (*epistēme*). See the essays by Ursula Coope and Robert Bolton in Thomas Kjeller Johansen, ed., *Productive Knowledge in Ancient Philosophy: The Concept of Technê* (Cambridge University Press, 2021): Coope, "Aristotle on Productive Understanding and Completeness," 109–130; and Bolton, "*Technê* and *Empeiria*: Aristotle on Practical Knowledge," 131–160.

[11] This strategy is adopted by Broadie, *Ethics with Aristotle*, 179–198. I discuss this aspect of Broadie's view in detail in Chapter 5, §5.1.

INTRODUCTION 9

The scientific view fares well just where the skill view falls short. The comprehensiveness—and even the political character—of *phronēsis* are easily accounted for on the scientific view, since these are systematic aspects of *phronēsis*.[12] Likewise, it is relatively easy to explain why Aristotle takes *phronēsis* to be a virtue of thought (the second mark) on the scientific view, though it is harder to explain the sharp distinction Aristotle makes between virtues of thought that grasp contingent things—the category to which *phronēsis* belongs—and those that grasp necessary things, such as scientific knowledge (*epistēmē*) and theoretical wisdom (*sophia*). The main difficulty for the scientific view lies primarily in the difference between, on the one hand, demonstrative and other theoretical activities, which are the exercise of scientific understanding, and, on the other hand, deliberation and choice, which are the exercise of *phronēsis*. Deliberation and choice concern particulars, while scientific knowledge primarily concerns universals. These claims can be reconciled by stretching and modifying Aristotle's conception of science to include the possibility of scientific reasoning about contingent and particular matters.[13] But the gap between such scientific reasoning and deliberation, the work of identifying a particular as a *means* to some end, remains. As I will argue, this gap is unbridgeable.

I.3. Two aspects of Aristotle's method of inquiry

In §I.2 I argued—roughly and in outline, to borrow Aristotle's words—that neither the skill view nor the scientific view can bring together all the key features of *phronēsis*. In this section I argue that,

---

[12] This aspect of *phronēsis* is crucial to Nielsen's interpretation, for instance: "Aristotle on Principles in Ethics: Political Science as the Science of the Human Good," in Henry and Nielsen, *Bridging the Gap*, 29–48.

[13] See Reeve, *Practices of Reason*, esp. Chapter 1, "Demonstration and Dialectic," 7–66. I engage with Reeve's view in more detail in Chapter 4, §4.2.

10 ARISTOTLE'S PRACTICAL EPISTEMOLOGY

in order to make sense of this difficult exegetical and philosophical terrain, we are helped by taking note of two aspects of Aristotle's method of inquiry that he foregrounds in the *Nicomachean Ethics*. These methodological claims have no parallel in the *Eudemian Ethics* (*EE*). It is reasonable to suppose that, at the time he composed the *NE*, Aristotle had a special interest in these problems. If the *NE* was composed after the *EE*, as most interpreters suppose, we can also plausibly claim that these methodological claims are a response to problems or difficulties that Aristotle came to think his own earlier view faced.[14]

The first of the two methodological concerns I will discuss is Aristotle's special interest in establishing that knowledge is *possible* in ethics. The basic concern to which Aristotle is responding is that the sphere of action and advantage is so contingent, so various and continually changing, that no stable knowledge can be had in this domain (*NE* I.3, 1094b14–19). Aristotle grants to his skeptical interlocutor that the sphere of action and advantage concerns contingent things, things that could be otherwise.[15] He even grants that this sphere is marked by patterns of variation that are extreme, which makes a stable grasp of it especially challenging to achieve. Nevertheless, he holds that ethical knowledge is possible. Indeed, he thinks knowledge of it to be quite widespread and not the preserve of a few experts.[16]

One of my main arguments in this book is that, in the *Nicomachean Ethics*, Aristotle develops a special account of ethical

---

[14] This latter claim is not necessary for my purpose here, so I leave questions of dating aside from here on; should readers be convinced independently of the traditional chronology, then all the better.

[15] In referring to a skeptical interlocutor, I do not mean to import any particular theory of skepticism or to refer to ancient schools that are called skeptical. What I mean is simply that Aristotle engages with a position—which may or may not correspond to particular figures—on which ethical knowledge is impossible for the reasons stated. In Chapter 1 (§1.1), I explore the affinities between this position and that of Isocrates.

[16] I should note here that the main word I am translating as 'knowledge' in this context, e.g. in the claim that ethical knowledge is widespread, is *gnōsis* (along with its various cognates), which is Aristotle's most general word for successful cognition. The English word 'knowledge' is apt to translate *gnōsis* and its cognates (e.g., the verb *gnōrizesthai*, the adjective *gnōrimos*) because it is similarly profligate: we speak, variously, of knowing people, places, facts, theorems, and what certain experiences are like.

INTRODUCTION 11

knowledge on which it is essentially practical.[17] That means not only that it is exercised in acting but also that it cannot be possessed unless one is also motivated to act accordingly.[18] In establishing the mere possibility of ethical knowledge, however, Aristotle speaks more generally, using terms drawn from his general epistemological theory. In any case, what matters is that successful cognition of ethical matters is not only possible but also common, the product of any decent course of ethical formation (which Aristotle generically refers to as *paideia*, education, though his famous theory of habituation is, no doubt, in the background).[19] It may well be rare to be *fully* educated in ethical-political matters. But anyone who has learned to discipline themselves to live according to reason is able to grasp the starting points of ethical argument, which are claims about what it is noble and good for human beings to do, to be, to suffer, and to have (*NE* I.3, 1095a4–9; I.4, 1095b3–8).

I explore Aristotle's argument against the skeptical position in some detail in Chapter 1. For now, what I mean to point out is simply that Aristotle's response to the skeptic is concessive. The features of the ethical domain that lead the skeptic to despair of the possibility of ethical knowledge are ones that Aristotle acknowledges. Human life is indeed always in flux and ethical matters are difficult to describe precisely (*NE* I.3, 1094b19–27; II.2, 1103b34–4a10). Yet a range of kinds of ethical knowledge are nevertheless possible.[20]

[17] Non-practical ethical knowledge does exist, e.g., in the way that a person of practical wisdom will be in a position to know what *others* should do or have done well, but it is parasitic on the paradigmatic case of practical knowledge.

[18] More, of course, needs to be said about how this view accommodates the existence of weakness of will (*akrasia*), which Aristotle takes not to count against the attribution of some types of knowledge to agents.

[19] In attributing the view to Aristotle that ethical knowledge is widespread, I do not mean to say that Aristotle thinks that the *majority* of people have this knowledge, only that it is not a rarity. Indeed, Aristotle's view of the majority of people is quite dim, as we see in *NE* X.9, 1180a1–14.

[20] I have been using the English word 'knowledge' to refer to a range of terms for successful cognition in Aristotle's Greek and will continue to do so, except in contexts where disambiguation is needed. But a few remarks about Aristotle's epistemological vocabulary, with special reference to ethics and politics, will be pertinent here. For recent general discussions of Aristotle's epistemological vocabulary in the scholarly literature, see

12 ARISTOTLE'S PRACTICAL EPISTEMOLOGY

Here, the second of the claims I wish to highlight as a basis for my inquiry comes into view: *phronēsis* is the best form of ethical knowledge one can have. In his methodological remarks at the start of the *NE*, Aristotle indicates that such a superior form of ethical knowledge, which surpasses the ordinary sort, is possible (I.4, 1095a30–b13). Indeed, ethical inquiry is supposed to put us in a better position to acquire one aspect of this knowledge. (As I will argue, the *practicality* of all ethical knowledge entails that ethical inquiry and other modes of refining what we already know can only be a partial help in this process.) It becomes clear over the course of the main argument of the *NE* that this superior form of ethical

Caleb Cohoe, "Knowing in Aristotle Part 1: *Epistēmē, Nous*, and non-Rational Cognitive States," *Philosophy Compass* 17, no. 1 (2022), e12801, and "Knowing in Aristotle Part 2: *Technē, Phronēsis, Sophia*, and Divine Cognitive Activities," *Philosophy Compass* 17, no. 1 (2022), e12799; and David Bronstein, *Aristotle on Knowing and Learning: The Posterior Analytics* (Oxford University Press, 2016), esp. Chapter 1, "Meno's Paradox and the Prior Knowledge Requirement," 16–21.

The English word most naturally corresponds to Aristotle's *gnōsis* and its verbal counterpart *gnōrizein*, which are used generically to indicate a successful cognitive state (see Bronstein, *Aristotle*). For example, Aristotle uses this family of terms in the case of (especially ordinary ground-level) ethical knowledge in *NE* I.3–4, the stretch of the text that I have been discussing here and that I will analyze in more detail in Chapter 1. More exalted states of knowledge across various domains, including craft and ethics, are often picked out by *epistēmē* (as well as verbal constructions with the cognate verb *epistasthai* and *eidenai*). Aristotle uses *epistēmē* in this cross-domain way, which can aptly be translated as both "knowledge" and "discipline," in *NE* I.2 when he asks what discipline or power considers the human good as such. In a narrower sense appropriate only to strict theoretical sciences, whose subject matter is necessary truths about eternal and unchanging things, Aristotle also uses *epistēmē* (to mean scientific knowledge) and contrasts it sharply with practical and productive forms of knowledge in *NE* VI, a topic that I primarily consider in Chapter 4.

As for *empeiria* (experience), I will argue that in *NE* VI and X.9 Aristotle invests the term with cognitive significance, particularly in relation to ethics and politics. In *NE* VI.7, we learn that the person with experience is capable of acting correctly on the basis of a grasp of narrow generalizations, a passage which I study closely in Chapter 2. In *NE* VI.11, Aristotle adds that we should heed the judgments of those with experience, as much as those who have practical wisdom, on the grounds that they see matters correctly (1143b11–14), a point he returns to in X.9, another text I consider in Chapter 2. Some interpreters, like Cohoe in "Knowing in Aristotle Part 1," argue that Aristotle does not elevate *empeiria* to a state by which we grasp generalizations or universals; I discuss this issue in relation to *NE* VI.7–8 in Chapter 2, §2.2.4. I follow a recent consensus that *empeiria* is cognitively sophisticated and rely especially on the passages in the *NE* that have been understudied by comparison to those elsewhere in the corpus. I discuss this issue in more detail in pp. 35–36, fn. 1.

INTRODUCTION 13

knowledge is simply *phronēsis*. The clearest instance of this claim is in the idea that the person of practical wisdom has all the virtues of thought that concern action and advantage (*NE* VI.11, 1143a25–35). Aristotle canvasses these virtues in *NE* VI.10–11, but *phronēsis* emerges as the chief such virtue, the one responsible for the whole domain of contingent things.

If *phronēsis* is the best epistemic state one can be in with regard to matters of action and advantage, then we can begin to make sense of what it is by considering how Aristotle thinks of superior forms of knowledge generally.[21] In one highly general epistemological passage, the first chapter of the *Metaphysics*—which ranges over all three types of knowledge: theoretical, practical, and productive (or craft-like) knowledge—the best form of knowledge in each domain turns out to be knowledge of principles or causes, or knowledge of reasons why, which we can bring under the common heading of *understanding* (A.1, 981a5–b10).[22] Crucially, understanding is essentially different in different domains. More specifically, understanding does not form a single genus, differentiated by its object, but rather varies with the mode of the relevant type of knowledge. For example, the master craftsman's understanding

---

[21] My approach to the superiority of *phronēsis* is, in some respects, similar to that of Hendrik Lorenz and Benjamin Morison in "Aristotle's Empiricist Theory of Doxastic Knowledge," *Phronesis* 64, no. 4 (2019): 431–464, who likewise start from the claim that *phronēsis* is "the optimal state with regard to the domain of action" (463). Lorenz and Morison rightly argue that, although *phronēsis* is the excellence of one part of the rational soul (the calculative part) and so the counterpart of *sophia* on the theoretical or contemplative side, we should not import the *rationalist* concept of knowledge that Aristotle develops in the theoretical domain to the *empiricist* domain of practice. Moreover, as I do, Lorenz and Morison emphasize that the superiority of the person of practical wisdom must rest in their ability to act well on the basis of their practical knowledge, rather than in a grasp of essences. I also agree with Lorenz and Morison that experience is crucial to exercising one's practical wisdom. I depart from Lorenz and Morison's view in arguing that, in addition to a grasp of *situation-specific* goals, the person of practical wisdom has an understanding of ethical universals that enables them to act well where a person with experience alone may falter. I also affirmatively reject the possibility of scientific knowledge of ethical matters, whereas Lorenz and Morison allow that it may exist, though we agree that it would be otiose for practice. I develop my views on these topics in greater detail in Chapters 4 and 5.

[22] I discuss this text in detail in Chapter 4 (§4.1).

14 ARISTOTLE'S PRACTICAL EPISTEMOLOGY

is still *productive* knowledge rather than a kind of detached counterpart of the ordinary craftsman's grasp of how to make or produce the characteristic object of their shared craft.[23]

As I will argue in Chapters 3 to 5, we can carry over this model to the case of ethics, even though Aristotle does not offer us a systematic account of these two levels of ethical knowledge. His theory of ethical knowledge assumes a distinction between ordinary or ground-level ethical knowledge—which includes, centrally, ethical experience (*empeiria*)—and ethical understanding, which turns out to be nothing other than *phronēsis* itself. For this point, I draw on several further claims that Aristotle makes to fill out this basic picture. For instance, in a crucial passage to which I will return several times over the course of my argument, Aristotle notes that *phronēsis* involves both universal and particular knowledge (VI.7, 1141b14–21). Knowledge of universals is frequently identified in other texts with knowledge of principles or causes or the reason why. I argue that Aristotle's description of the shortcomings of the person who has ethical experience (or 'knowledge of particulars') alone, i.e., without knowledge of universals, supports this identification of *phronēsis* with ethical understanding.

These two key claims—that ethical knowledge exists despite the contingent and highly variable domain it concerns; and that *phronēsis* is the best form of such knowledge, by contrast to more ordinary forms of ethical knowledge—are foundational and should form the basis of any investigation of *phronēsis*. Accordingly, I will use these claims both to structure my inquiry into the nature of *phronēsis* in Aristotle's ethical and political writings and to develop my positive account of *phronēsis* as practical understanding. I show that *phronēsis* does not merely originate, as a causal or genetic matter, in a body of ethical experience, but it also develops

---

[23] In the background of this discussion lies an intriguing passage in Plato's *Statesman* where, by contrast, the master craftsman's knowledge is sharply distinguished from the productive knowledge it directs; I take up the contrast between Aristotle's view and that of the *Statesman* in the Appendix, §A.1.

out of such experience, as we refine the universals that we use to deliberate about fulfilling the demands of the character virtues in particular types of circumstances. Just as ethical experience is practical knowledge, so too is *phronēsis*, since both are exercised in deliberating and choosing particular actions. Still, *phronēsis* is a genuine form of understanding because it (unlike *empeiria*) involves a grasp of principles, which are explanatory universals. The explanations in questions are not demonstrative relationships, as the scientific view holds. Rather, as I will argue, the universals are the characteristic goals or ends of the practically wise and virtuous person, which count as principles insofar as they are final causes of their actions.

Many of these claims made above in this section are highly abstract or schematic as stated, not least since I have eschewed detailed discussion of the texts. I expand on my claims in the next section, where I sketch the argument of each chapter, and a full vindication of them will depend on the details of the arguments provided in the body of the book. Let me conclude this section by showing how my view avoids the difficulties highlighted in the previous section for the skill view and the scientific view.

As the skill view emphasizes and as the scientific view wrongly downplays, we must regard *phronēsis* as a form of practical knowledge, exercised in choosing and acting virtuously in particular circumstances. I will show that Aristotle's account of practical reasoning and his metaphysics of the domain of human action both commit him to this view. Yet, as practical understanding, *phronēsis* counts as a virtue of thought that is analogous to theoretical wisdom insofar as the person of practical wisdom has a grasp of universal and explanatory principles. These are claims that the scientific view can accommodate easily, but that the skill view ends up either rejecting or allocating purely to political wisdom as a state distinct from practical wisdom, despite Aristotle's identification of the two states.

I.4. Outline of the book

The argument of *Aristotle's Practical Epistemology* is divided into two stages. In the first two chapters, my focus is on ordinary practical knowledge, especially the view of ethical experience developed in fits and starts in the *Nicomachean Ethics*. The rest of the book is focused on showing why *phronēsis* should be seen as practical understanding and how this view makes good on the desiderata for an interpretation outlined above.

I take up an alternative to Aristotle's own view, against which he situates his own inquiry in the *Nicomachean Ethics*, in Chapter 1. Very few discussions of Aristotle's ethics have taken up the striking connections between the puzzles about practical epistemology with which he begins the *NE* and the views of Isocrates, for whom practical knowledge does not really exist. I show how a consideration of Isocratean deflationism about practical knowledge, and the Protagorean conventionalism about what is good and bad that may help to motivate it, can help us understand the importance of both ordinary and exalted forms of ethical knowledge in the inquiry of the *NE*. (I introduce two other salient alternative views in practical epistemology, in Plato's *Statesman* and Aristotle's own *Eudemian Ethics* in the Appendix, which can be read as an extension of the inquiry of Chapter 1.)

In Chapter 2, I draw on detailed readings of texts from *NE* I.3–4, VI.7–8, and X.9 to defend five claims about Aristotle's theory of ethical experience as a form of practical knowledge. These claims are the following: (1) ethical experience is a kind of practical knowledge, that is, knowledge of how to act in accordance with virtue; (2) ethical experience is a characteristic product of good habituation; (3) ethical experience constitutes a grasp of the *basic facts* in ethics—knowledge of the 'that' and not the 'why' to use Aristotle's own language; (4) ethical experience equips the would-be inquirer with the starting points needed to appreciate and make good use of ethical claims and arguments; and (5) since the person with ethical

INTRODUCTION   17

experience lacks a grasp of the reason why, they fall short of the ethical understanding that belongs to the person of practical wisdom and which it is the task of ethical inquiry to foster. In the rest of the book, I try to show how these features of ethical experience help constrain an interpretation of what *phronēsis* must be.

In Chapter 3 I address the question of why Aristotle's explicit treatment of *phronēsis* is embedded in an inquiry into the virtues of thought in *NE* VI, why, in other words, he treats *phronēsis* as parallel to craft (*tekhnē*) and theoretical wisdom (*sophia*). My answer is that *phronēsis* is an excellence by which we achieve the truth, which is the task of the intellect. To be disposed in this way requires being able to pursue practical truth on one's own, without the guidance of another. The centrality of this Independent Agency Criterion explains both the superiority of *phronēsis* to ethical experience in deliberation and points toward the political dimensions of Aristotle's claims, which I take up again at the end of the book.

I then show—in Chapter 4—why this account of *phronēsis* as a virtue of thought and, indeed, as a type of understanding does not entail that there is ethical science, i.e., ethical knowledge that is scientific or demonstrative in character. I argue against both robust forms of this claim, which identify the universal knowledge that the person of practical wisdom is said to possess with science, as well as weaker forms of the claim, which make ethics a special practical or inexact sort of science. The mark of having scientific knowledge, for Aristotle, is the ability to demonstrate, but the relevant sorts of demonstrative relationships do not hold in ethical matters and in actions. The universal component of *phronēsis*, then, while having a sort of explanatory character, does not amount to scientific knowledge.

I explain what, instead, the practically wise person's grasp of universals must be in Chapter 5. I argue that we can only really make sense of Aristotle's point by immersing ourselves in his theory of the character virtues and the deliberative excellence they demand for their full exercise, by contrast to the deliberative competence

18   ARISTOTLE'S PRACTICAL EPISTEMOLOGY

afforded by ethical experience. In particular, I consider the character virtue of (particular) justice, which helps us resist the tendency to assimilate *phronēsis* to a body of experience or some other more intuitive sort of knowledge. The just person must be reflective in ways that require an understanding of practical universals, including especially the ends for which a just person ought to act. The reason is that Aristotelian justice is not merely an avoidance of a set of proscribed act-types but a positive and discerning orientation toward bringing about justice in one's community. I suggest that a similar approach must be taken to the other character-virtues, as well.

Finally, in Chapter 5, I take up Aristotle's striking identification of practical and political wisdom. The view of *phronēsis* as practical understanding that I have developed up to this point helps us appreciate the import of this commitment. The key idea is that the person of political wisdom has the very same grasp of practical universals that belong to the person of practical wisdom but deliberates about these in relation to the political community as a whole. As someone equipped with the totality of the virtues, the person of practical wisdom has an understanding of the common good, which is the collective flourishing of the citizens, as well as the deliberative excellence needed to bring it about. The simultaneously universal and practical character of the understanding that just is *phronēsis* is therefore clearly displayed in its manifestation as political wisdom.

1

DEFLATIONISM ABOUT

PRACTICAL KNOWLEDGE

The core argument of this book is that, in Aristotle's ethics, practical wisdom must be understood as practical *understanding*. A key component of this interpretation is that, in any domain, understanding is to be contrasted with more ordinary forms of knowledge. Therefore, we can only grasp what Aristotle means by *phronēsis* if we situate it with respect to ordinary practical knowledge. In the *Nicomachean Ethics*, specifically, Aristotle develops an account of ordinary practical knowledge as ethical experience (*empeiria*). In the course of this argument, he draws on an analogy between ethical knowledge and crafts like medicine where experience is a grasp of how to treat types of particular cases that is not only an essential component of the practical skill of the doctor but also the basis from which a deeper, causal understanding develops. The analogy between craft and ethical knowledge, however, is liable to be misunderstood, in part because Aristotle does not present his view of ethical experience systematically.

The goal of this chapter is to head off such misunderstanding by situating Aristotle's view in relation to a salient alternative way of conceiving of ordinary practical knowledge, one that Aristotle was aware of and that he cites explicitly, though briefly in the opening chapters of the *Nicomachean Ethics*.[1] This alternative deflationary

---

[1] It is important to note at the outset that my goal is to highlight the type of ordinary practical knowledge from which *phronēsis* arises. In Aristotle's considered view (in the *Nicomachean Ethics*) on this matter, that ordinary practical knowledge is experience (*empeiria*). But there may well be other types of ordinary practical knowledge that enable people to achieve types of practical success, even on this view. If Aristotle

---

Aristotle's Practical Epistemology. Dhananjay Jagannathan, Oxford University Press.
© Oxford University Press 2024. DOI: 10.1093/9780197781517.003.0002

20 ARISTOTLE'S PRACTICAL EPISTEMOLOGY

view of practical knowledge can be found in the writings of Isocrates and can also be associated with the thinking of the sophist Protagoras.[2]

My aim here is not merely intellectual historical. I also hope to provide an important prophylactic to a serious methodological problem with many discussions of Aristotle's practical epistemology in which a reconstruction from the scattered remains of the text is attempted without an explanation of the philosophical motivations that lie behind a view. The best way to start to get traction on Aristotle's motivations for the practical epistemology of the *Nicomachean Ethics* is to consider a plausible path that he does not take and, indeed, that he explicitly rejects. My inquiry in this chapter, therefore, is primarily philosophical, though I take the historical context to be illuminating.

1.1 Practical Knowledge and Uncertainty

Consider the following intuitively appealing picture of practical wisdom:

thinks that knowledge other than *empeiria*, on his specialized conception of it, might contribute to the acquisition of *phronēsis*, he does not say so. Rather, *empeiria* is the only type of knowledge we are told leads to *phronēsis*. I therefore take this claim to be a central commitment of his practical epistemology. Thanks to Marta Jimenez for pressing me to clarify this point.

[2] To supplement my historical presentation and to illuminate some other dimensions of Aristotle's views about ethical knowledge, I provide a wider survey of alternative views of ordinary practical knowledge in the Appendix, where I contrast Aristotle's views, first, with that found in the opening pages of Plato's *Statesman*—which presents ordinary practical knowledge as intuitive know-how—and, second, with that found in his own treatment of the topic in *Eudemian Ethics* VIII.3—where such knowledge is characterized as mere prudence about what is advantageous for human beings. I do not take a stand on the relative chronology of the *EE* and the *NE*. What matters for my purpose are the differences between the *NE* and the *EE's* conceptions of ethical knowledge and its sources.

Nothing is certain in human life, and little can be known about how the future will unfold. Still, we all have our ideas about how best to live, which we build up through experience. Everyone has to rely on their own opinions, that is, our intuitive judgments, in the face of our common uncertainty and lack of knowledge.

Some people are foolish because they fail to size up the situations they find themselves in or they fail to see how to respond. They make poor use of intuitive judgment. For instance, one kind of folly is recklessness, that is, being heedless of danger and for that reason throwing oneself into hopeless situations. Reckless people often end up squandering what they have for little gain. But one cannot be prudent simply by being cautious or diffident either. Instead, the prudent person weighs the risks and makes a good guess about what they should do.

If people can be prudent not just about risk and danger but about the whole of life, such people deserve to be called intelligent or wise. They are adept at making their way in the world by accurately perceiving how things are and responding effectively. Even intelligent people, of course, make mistakes because everyone alike must use their own opinions, and opinion is a fallible guide to the future.

This picture of practical wisdom has a number of notable features: (i) it seems to realistically capture how difficult decision-making is for everyone, (ii) it nevertheless preserves our sense that some people are better at it than others, and (iii) it explains that superiority in terms of better use of one's intuitive judgment. These features together locate wisdom and folly on a spectrum of use of a single human faculty for understanding our practical world and reacting appropriately to it.

This picture is one that still has some appeal for theorists of practical reason today. Perhaps as a result, aspects of this view, especially versions of (iii) that emphasize practical perception, have made it into popular interpretations of Aristotle. I will argue in this section

22 ARISTOTLE'S PRACTICAL EPISTEMOLOGY

that this view, which I call 'deflationism' about practical knowledge, should instead be attributed to Isocrates, and that Aristotle rejects this view in the *Nicomachean Ethics*, particularly in the opening chapters of *NE* I, where he describes the nature of inquiry into the just and the good (these for Aristotle are the subject matter of politics; for ease of exposition, however, I will refer to this as 'ethical inquiry.') The reason that the view *deflates* practical knowledge is its stress on the unknowability of much of what is relevant to the outcomes of our actions.

The way that the deflationist view is presented in *NE* I is rather crabbed and somewhat complicated, and Aristotle associates it with a view about ethical facts we can call 'conventionalism.' Conventionalism states that what is good and bad is simply what people generally regard as good and bad. That is why, according to the conventionalist, things sometimes turn out so unexpectedly, even to the point of so-called good things being the source of harm to us.

Isocrates himself does not motivate his deflationism by appeal to conventionalism, though Protagoras may well have connected the two thoughts.[3] I will focus on Isocrates because we can more safely identify his influence on Aristotle, but I will also make some remarks about Protagoras to illuminate conventionalism. In any event, though the intellectual lineage of these ideas is not fully clear, it is worth tracing out the shape of a position that Aristotle seems to take his readers to be familiar with and to which he directly contrasts his own. The brevity of his remarks should not be confused for the importance of the topic to his own project.

By showing that Aristotle rejects deflationism in *NE* I.3–4, we will better be able to understand why he goes on to emphasize that practical wisdom is a *virtue of thought* and not just a

---

[3] The reconstruction of Protagoras' views is fraught with difficulty, especially where we depend on the evidence of Plato, but the connection between conventionalism and deflationism can be found in the so-called digression in Plato's *Theaetetus* (172c2–177c2).

DEFLATIONISM ABOUT PRACTICAL KNOWLEDGE 23

capacity, one of the four aspects of Aristotle's theory of *phronēsis* that I highlighted in the Introduction. The contrast between a capacity (*dunamis*) and a virtue as a developed state of soul (*hexis*) is central to Aristotle's analysis of *phronēsis*. While interpreters have often taken note of Aristotle's distinction, in *NE* VI.12–13, between cleverness (*deinotēs*) as a capacity for implementing one's ends and practical wisdom (VI.12, 1144a23–29; VI.13, 1144b1–4), they have seldom identified the underlying motivation for this distinction in Aristotle's broader project in the *NE* or the stakes for Aristotle in drawing it. My hope is that by identifying Isocrates as a plausible philosophical interlocutor for Aristotle in *NE* I and by analyzing a key passage about *phronēsis* from Isocrates, I will be able to do just that. It will turn out that Aristotle's point about cleverness and *phronēsis* is quite central to his whole way of thinking about practical knowledge.

The rest of this chapter is divided into three main sections: a sketch (in Section 1.2) of Isocrates' view of the uncertainty of human life and the character of practical knowledge in one of his late treatises, contemporary with Plato's mature work; an even briefer exposition (in Section 1.3) of Protagorean conventionalism, which Aristotle links to the deflationist view; and an analysis (in Section 1.4) of how Aristotle rejects deflationism about practical knowledge in *NE* I.3–4 and offers the outline of an alternative conception of both ordinary and exalted practical knowledge. I will conclude my discussion with some brief reflections on how the rejection of deflationism points toward Aristotle's account of *phronēsis* as a virtue of thought, which is the subject of Chapter 3. Since Isocrates sees little difference between how ordinary people get by and how the wise do so—all alike use the same faculty of opinion in the absence of real knowledge—my discussion here will discuss both ordinary and exalted practical knowledge.

24 ARISTOTLE'S PRACTICAL EPISTEMOLOGY

1.2 Isocrates on practical knowledge as skillful guesswork

The clearest statement of Isocrates' deflationism about practical knowledge comes from a treatise in the form of a fictional courtroom speech, *Taking My Turn* (*Antidosis*).[4] This text represents Isocrates' defense of his own practice of rhetoric as a human pursuit against competing models of education, including, most notably, Plato's. While the text functions as a sort of advertisement for Isocrates and his life's work, it was written in the aftermath of a major professional and financial setback, a loss in a trial where he was held liable for insufficient public generosity.[5] In the opening of the treatise, Isocrates notes how he was caught off guard by the trial and the unfavorable outcome (15.3–5). While his account of practical knowledge is consonant with what he says elsewhere, especially in his earlier tract *Against the Sophists*, the ideas have a special significance in this personal context.

The passage that best sums up his overall approach to practical knowledge runs as follows:

[T1] For since there is not present in human nature the capacity to attain knowledge by which we might know what we must do or say, I regard as wise (*sophous*) those among the rest who are able to light upon (*epitugkhanein*), generally, what is best by means of their opinions (*tais doxais*), and I take philosophers to be those

---

[4] I explain my unusual translation of this title in the following note.

[5] The title *Antidosis* means, literally, an 'exchange' and refers to the practice in Athens of one wealthy citizen calling upon another to either make a contribution to the commons required of the first (the liturgy, *leitourgia*) or else exchange property. The speech itself constitutes a form of 'payback' for Isocrates (see 15.13 for this idea), but the real meaning of the title lies in his emphasis throughout on the intellectual and not merely material contributions he has made to the polity. Hence, I translate the Greek title *Antidosis* as *Taking My Turn*, since the speech itself is part of this contribution. For this theme of material versus intellectual contributions in the text, see Josiah Ober, *Political Dissent in Democratic Athens: Intellectual Critics of Popular Rule* (Princeton University Press, 1998), 258; and Yun Lee Too, *A Commentary on Isocrates'* Antidosis (Oxford University Press, 2008), 6–7.

DEFLATIONISM ABOUT PRACTICAL KNOWLEDGE   25

who spend their time on such matters on the basis of which they will soonest attain this sort of intelligence (*phronēsin*). (15.271)

Notice that Isocrates identifies what makes someone wise with the capacity to uncover "what we must do or say." He thereby draws on a tradition in Greek literature that goes back to the *Iliad*, where Phoinix describes the education he was meant to provide Achilles as teaching him how to be "a speaker of words and a doer of deeds," that is, preeminent not only on the battlefield but also in assemblies (*Iliad* 9.437–443).[6] On the basis of this picture of the goal of proper education, Isocrates distinguishes two further notions, the philosopher as the pursuer of such wisdom and *phronēsis* as the mastery possessed by someone who merits the honorific 'wise' (*sophos*).[7]

In **T1**, then, we get a succinct statement of the two most important features of Isocrates' view that bear on Aristotle's own. The first is Isocrates' rejection of the possibility that human beings can have secure knowledge of deliberative matters as opposed to mere opinions about them. In this regard, his view has a strong affinity to Plato's suspicion that nothing in the world of change and becoming, including human affairs, is stable enough to allow for the best kind of knowledge, though he does not provide an explicitly

---

[6] Cf. Protagoras' advertisement in Plato's *Protagoras*: "What I teach is good judgment (*euboulia*) in personal affairs, so he can best manage his own household, as well as in city affairs, *so he can both act and speak powerfully* when it comes to his city" (*Protagoras* 318e5–319a2 = DK 80B5). On the education promised here, see Paul Woodruff, "*Euboulia* as the Skill Protagoras Taught," in *Protagoras of Abdera: The Man, His Measure,* Philosophia Antiqua vol. 134, ed. J. M. van Ophuijsen, M. van Raalte, and P. Stork (Brill, 2013), 179–193; and (more speculatively) Nicholas Denyer, "The Political Skill of Protagoras," in *Politeia in Greek and Roman Philosophy,* ed. Verity Harte and Melissa Lane (Cambridge University Press, 2014), 155–167.

[7] I have translated *phronēsis* as 'intelligence' above to capture Isocrates' distinctive view of this mastery, which comes up in other passages of *Taking My Turn.* See esp. 15.207 and the commentary on both passages in David Depew, "The Inscription of Isocrates into Aristotle's Practical Philosophy," in *Isocrates and Civic Education,* ed. Takis Poulakos and David Depew (University of Texas Press, 2004), 157–185, at 162–166. Notice that the adjective *sophos* has a much wider semantic range (both in ordinary Greek and in Aristotle's usage) than the intellectual virtue of *sophia* in Aristotle's specialized sense. In any case, it is not surprising to find Isocrates labeling *phronēsis* as the virtue that makes someone count as *sophos.*

26 ARISTOTLE'S PRACTICAL EPISTEMOLOGY

metaphysical backing for this position as Plato characteristically does.[8] The second is Isocrates' distinction between those who make better use of their opinions as opposed to others who are less well-equipped. While he rejects unshakable knowledge, Isocrates nevertheless identifies an intellectual excellence that belongs to a special few—*phronēsis*—who rise above the crowd in their ability to discover what is best. Notably, the verb *epitugkhanein*, which I have rendered 'light upon,' suggests both success and imprecision in the intellectual activity of the wise.

In sum, these two features together add up to an account of practical knowledge as a capacity for *skillful guesswork*.

1.3 Deflationism and conventionalism

We can locate this Isocratean view within a larger family of conceptions of practical knowledge. Most generally, the deflationist regards the connection between practical knowledge and success as underpinned not by a reasoned *account* of the domain of human action and human life but by an *ability* possessed by those with practical knowledge, independent of the possibility of such an account.

---

[8] A key text for this view is *Republic* V, 479d2–480a1, where Socrates establishes that the things that people generally regard as beautiful roll around between unreality and genuine reality and so cannot be known but only the object of opinion. This sort of view has deep roots in Greek philosophy before Plato. Consider Xenophanes fragment DK B34 (= Laks and Most D49, vol. III, 55): "And thus there has never been any man, nor will there ever be one, Who knows what is clear about the gods and what I say about all things. For even if he happened most to say something perfect, *He himself nonetheless does not know: opinion is wrought upon all*" (trans. Laks and Most, with the crucial final line emphasized and modified). Xenophanes speaks elsewhere of his own wisdom (*sophiē*), e.g., fragment DK B2 = Laks and Most D61, vol. III, 65–66) and suggests here that he himself is able to speak well "about the gods and . . . all things." The question of what sort of knowledge of human affairs is, according to Plato, possible for us in this life is a difficult one. See Katja Vogt, *Belief and Truth: A Skeptic Reading of Plato* (Oxford University Press, 2013), esp. Chapter 2 on the *Republic*; and Jessica Moss, *Plato's Epistemology: Being and Seeming* (Oxford University Press, 2021).

DEFLATIONISM ABOUT PRACTICAL KNOWLEDGE 27

Isocrates, specifically, grounds his deflationist view of practical knowledge on the unknowability of the contingencies of life. A different way to motivate deflationism is to focus on the *instability* of our judgments about good and bad, that is, what is on balance beneficial and harmful to us. For example, if these judgments are not simply difficult to make but also bottom out in the way that things appear to us (rather than a set of facts about the world), then we have all the more reason to give up on the possibility of finding anything more than intuition to guide us. Some further reflection on the court case that led Isocrates to pen *Taking My Turn* can shed light on this alternative.

One reaction to the trial, Isocrates' own, is to suggest that anyone else similarly positioned would have been equally unfortunate (15.6–7). After all, Isocrates points to his own rhetorical skill as a powerful safeguard on which he could ordinarily have relied. An unexpected combination of circumstances thwarted his attempted defense, but by his own telling his strategy was sound and the education he promises to others retains its value in the face of occasional setbacks such as these. The plain implication is that others would have been even more poorly equipped to fend off such a clever attack on their life and career.

Another possible reaction to the trial is to identify rhetorical skill as itself essentially fallible. Just as we might see Socrates' philosophical refutation of his prosecutors in Plato's *Apology* as grist to their mill—the basis for the charge being that Socrates was dangerous as opposed to the official accusation of impiety—so too we can see how Isocrates' cleverness might have turned the Athenian *dēmos* against him. Isocrates himself adverts to this worry near the opening of *Taking My Turn* (15.4–5), which is why he proposes to set down a more lasting defense of himself in this very text.[9]

---

[9] The Platonic resonances are clear. Socrates, too, undertakes a second defense of his life after his trial and conviction in the *Phaedo*, this time before the more favorable audience of his friends and companions in prison (*Phaedo* 63b1 ff.)

28 ARISTOTLE'S PRACTICAL EPISTEMOLOGY

If even rhetorical skill can lead to ruin, one might be led to think that nothing is good or bad in itself but rather that goodness or badness depends merely on convention. Skillful speakers seem to us to flourish, so we conventionally regard their skill as good. In reality, it is not good or bad but only seems so to us. This position was, if we can trust the evidence of the Platonic dialogues, held by Isocrates' fifth-century predecessor Protagoras who was known for his famous dictum that "a human being is the measure of everything, of what is that it is and of what is not that it is not" (DK 80B1). Let us call this view *conventionalism*.

Conventionalism about good and bad clearly helps to motivate deflationism about practical knowledge because there is no objective basis on which to found secure knowledge about what is good or bad, beneficial or harmful to us. All that is left is our best surmise about how things will seem to us and to others. The latter is of course notoriously unstable territory. Indeed, there is a deep and interesting puzzle about how to connect conventionalism on the level of individuals (how things seem to *me* here and now) with the collective judgment of many (how things seems to *us*) and why Protagoras, like Isocrates, promised to teach rhetorical skill, despite what might seem like pessimism about there being anything secure in human life.[10] I leave this puzzle aside here in order to turn now to my main topic, Aristotle's own engagement with deflationism in *NE* I.3–4.

---

[10] For a resolution of this puzzle and further discussion, see Lauren Apfel, *The Advent of Pluralism: Diversity and Conflict in the Age of Sophocles* (Oxford University Press, 2011), esp. Chapter 2, "Pluralism and Protagoras: The Plurality of Truth."

DEFLATIONISM ABOUT PRACTICAL KNOWLEDGE   29

1.4 Aristotle's rejection of conventionalism and deflationism

In the course of outlining his methods and what is needed for the inquiry into the highest human good that was proposed in the opening arguments of *NE* I.1–2, Aristotle turns in *NE* I.3 to consider a deflationist position about practical reason akin to Isocrates' account of *phronēsis* as a capacity for skilled guesswork motivated by an appeal to something like Protagorean conventionalism about the good. Addressing deflationism is crucial for Aristotle, because, if such a capacity is all to which we can aspire in the domain of human action, his inquiry is a nonstarter.

> [T2] The things that are noble and just, which are the concern of a political inquiry, admit of great variation and deviation; hence, they are thought purely conventional and not natural. Goods, too, admit of some deviation of this kind, since harms come to many people as a result of them. For there have been cases of people who are ruined by wealth, others by courage. Hence, one must be content (*agapēton*) to reveal the truth roughly and in outline (*pakhulōs kai tupōi*) when one speaks about such things and on the basis of such facts—that is to say, when one speaks about what holds good for the most part (*peri tōn hōs epi to polu*) and on the basis of what is like this, [one must be content] also to draw conclusions of this kind. (*NE* I.3, 1094b14–22)

As happens so often in Aristotelian treatises, the dialectical structure of this passage is covered over by subtle shifts in voice, and the conventionalist position to which his own is opposed is described in passing and rebutted with the irenic expression 'one must be content' (*agapēton*).

What is in fact going on in **T2** is the following: Aristotle accepts the basic claims about human life and fortune used by the conventionalist—that good things sometimes lead to bad

30 ARISTOTLE'S PRACTICAL EPISTEMOLOGY

outcomes, or to use Aristotle's own terms for it, that what is good by nature may not be good *for* someone—but he rejects the inference to conventionalism about the good and the corresponding deflationism about ethical knowledge. It is not true that good and bad lose their absolute meaning because of the instability of human life and the possibility of reversals. We can still make progress in ethical inquiry and thereby achieve understanding in ethics, which in the following chapter Aristotle calls knowledge of 'the why' (*to dioti*), that is, the reason things are as they are.

In his reply to the deflationist, which is the first step toward providing his positive view of the nature of human affairs and inquiry into them, Aristotle invokes a doctrine from his philosophy of nature in order to defend the cogency of his inquiry into the highest human good. In the sublunary sciences of nature, principles often explain what happens *for the most part* (*hōs epi to polu*), that is, what would happen if the principle could operate unimpeded. (The notion is not, as the verbal expression and its English translation suggest, the same as what happens with the greatest statistical frequency.) Just so, in ethics, claims about what is good in human life must be made for the most part, which is no bar to the existence of principles.[11]

It is crucial to place this notion of what happens for the most part against the background of Aristotle's explanatory theory of scientific knowledge. The explanatory connection between a principle and a fact that it explains can hold good even if, in similar circumstances, another outcome obtains. In the latter, deviant case, a further explanation must be sought in some interfering condition. Even in such a case, the principle still has an explanatory

---

[11] Note that I am speaking here of Aristotle's notion of a principle (*arkhē*), not the modern notion of a principle as a generalization, exceptionless or otherwise, though there are important connections between these two notions. See Georgios Anagnostopoulos, *Aristotle on the Goals and Exactness of Ethics* (University of California Press, 1994) for a detailed treatment of Aristotle's notion of precision or exactness (*akribeia*) in relation to theory.

DEFLATIONISM ABOUT PRACTICAL KNOWLEDGE   31

relevance; it is the principle relative to which an interfering condition counts as interfering.

As my brief discussion indicates, being 'for the most part' is an *epistemological* as well as an ontological notion, since it expresses how facts are linked in explanatory relationships.[12] The conventionalist, like a modern anti-realist in metaethics, thinks that apparently factual statements in ethics do not correspond to anything like a mind-independent ethical *reality*. Aristotle rebuts this metaphysical and semantic claim by offering an alternative: ethical statements are made 'for the most part,' which prevents them from dissolving in the face of counterexamples. Courage really is good for the courageous person, even though such a person may be exposed to death precisely because they exercised their courage, and even though death is bad, both in general and for this person. The vulnerability of the virtuous life—the fact that the virtues do not (or do not seem to) make us immune from harm—has been widely disputed by moral philosophers from antiquity to the present, so Aristotle's use of this challenging example sets up his analysis in the next chapter of the *goal* of ethical inquiry, understood as dealing with 'for the most part' conclusions.

[T3] We should not overlook the fact that arguments from first principles and arguments toward first principles differ. For Plato also rightly puzzled over and inquired whether the path led from first principles or to them, as from the judges to the turning post in a stadium or the other way round—[rightly] since we must begin from what is knowable to us, and this [sc. knowable] has two senses, some things being knowable to us, and others knowable simply speaking. Perhaps, then, we at least must begin from what is knowable to us. That is why one must be raised with noble habits if one is to be a capable student of the noble and the just

---

[12] Because knowledge, for Aristotle, touches reality, whose structure is reflected in that knowledge, ontological and epistemological considerations are mutually implicating.

32 ARISTOTLE'S PRACTICAL EPISTEMOLOGY

and politics in general. For the starting point is what is so (*to hoti*) and if this is sufficiently apparent, there is no need in addition for the reason why (*to dioti*): someone in this position either has or could easily get the starting points. (*NE* I.4, 1095a30–b7)

Here, Aristotle has more to say about his alternative to the deflationist approach to practical knowledge than in the previous chapter. In particular, he establishes two critical points. First, he notes that—provided we have received a suitable upbringing—we are already in possession of some practical knowledge before ethical inquiry begins (i.e., 'what is knowable to us' about the noble and the just), which in fact serves as the starting point for such inquiry. Second, beyond such knowledge lies genuine understanding ('the reason why'), which ethical inquiry can help us achieve.

The example of courage bringing ruin, which the deflationist would drawn on to establish that robust practical knowledge is impossible, can be located within this framework. We know, from experience, that a good character is no defense against certain types of deprivation. Whether in the form of examples or a rough general characterization such as I have just provided, knowledge of this fact makes up part of 'what is knowable to us.' But such a striking fact calls out for an explanation, which is the work of practical philosophy to provide.[13] Inquiry involves a search for such explanations, and it is unsurprising that Aristotle goes on to describe an account of the highest good for human beings as a kind of first principle for ethics (*NE* I.7, 1098b34–99a8), for which he has provided an outline sketch in the first half of *NE* Book I.

---

[13] Aristotle himself explores the relationships among deprivation, good character, and happiness in *NE* I.9, 1100a4–9; I.10, 1100a31–1101a19. The topic was a staple of reflection in ancient Greek popular morality and philosophy. See Martha Nussbaum, *The Fragility of Goodness: Luck and Ethics in Greek Tragedy and Philosophy* (Cambridge University Press, 1986).

1.5 Confronting uncertainty with the help of ethical knowledge

I have provided, in the previous section, a sketch of Aristotle's alternative to deflationism about practical knowledge, though I will return to these two passages in *NE* I.3–4 in more detail in the next chapter because they reveal much about his conception of ordinary ethical knowledge. Aristotle characterizes ethics as concerned with 'for the most part' regularities, which allow us to escape the pessimistic inference to conventionalism. There really can be things that are good or bad *in their own right* and not simply with reference to how things seem to us. Hence, the subject matter of ethics can be the object of knowledge, not merely skillful guesswork. First, even our preliminary grasp of how things stand in matters of action and advantage is a kind of knowledge, namely, ethical experience. Second, through inquiry we can aspire, on the basis of experience, to a more secure and well-founded type of knowledge.

I do not take myself to have answered some major questions that have already begun to arise about Aristotle's view. First, how can experience be differentiated from guesswork or the use of merely intuitive judgment? Isn't experience just another name for such judgment? Second, how can experience be transformed by *ethical inquiry*? Doesn't inquiry concern theoretical matters? I will take up these questions in the next chapter of this book.

I do hope to have provided a sharp contrast between Aristotle's views and the deflationist in order to show that, right from the outset of the inquiry, Aristotle has important commitments about the shape of ethical knowledge, including the ordinary ethical knowledge by which most of us live. These commitments, in turn, help us see why it is central to Aristotle's conception of *phronēsis* that it is a virtue of thought, which is a state of soul (*hexis*) and not merely a capacity (*dunamis*).

Recall that, for the deflationist, (i) decision-making is difficult for everyone, (ii) all the same, some people are better at it than

34   ARISTOTLE'S PRACTICAL EPISTEMOLOGY

others, and (iii) the superiority of some turns on their capacity for better intuitive judgment. Aristotle agrees, in a certain sense at least, with (i) and (ii), but he rejects (iii). Aristotle grants that some people are good at identifying ways of accomplishing the goals they have, whatever they happen to be, and in a certain sense the exercise of practical wisdom involves identifying the correct ways of accomplishing the right goals (since the goals we are to pursue are given by the character-virtues). Nevertheless, the wise person and the crafty vicious person do not share a single capacity for cleverness, which is put to different uses (*NE* VI.12, 1144a23–29). Rather, the wise person has a store of knowledge of what is good and bad for human beings that they use in deliberating well about what to do. The starting point for the development of such knowledge is not a bare capacity for reasoning but rather the ethical experience that we acquire in the course of a good upbringing that fosters a love of what is genuinely good and makes us basically capable of orienting ourselves toward it.[14]

---

[14] On the need for a love of what is noble and how it is instilled, see *NE* X.9, 1179b4–16.

2

ETHICAL EXPERIENCE IN THE

NICOMACHEAN ETHICS

I argue in this chapter that Aristotle articulates a distinct conception of ordinary practical knowledge in the *Nicomachean Ethics*: ordinary practical knowledge is ethical experience (*empeiria*), that is, experience in and regarding the actions we ought to do. Aristotle first gestures toward this idea in two passages on the proper method for ethical inquiry in *NE* I.3–4 (which I discuss in §2.1) before developing it more substantively in his discussion of *phronēsis* in *NE* VI.7 (§2.2). Strong confirmation for the interpretation I favor is found in a passage on the appropriate method for inquiring into politics in *NE* X.9 (§2.3). Because the subject matter of the *NE* also belongs to politics, we can readily make use of the more precise details offered about *empeiria* in X.9. I conclude by taking up an objection that purports to show that *empeiria* is not necessarily virtuous (§2.4).

Taking these passages together yields the account of *empeiria* contained in the following five claims.[1] As I build my account from

---

[1] *Empeiria* is a seriously neglected notion in the study of Aristotle's ethics, which has hindered a grasp of his distinctive practical epistemology. It has received more attention in the study of his general epistemology, given its appearance in two key passages that reflect Aristotle's empiricism, *Metaphysics* Alpha 1 and *Posterior Analytics* II.19. On the philosophical topic of Aristotle's empiricism as a whole, see Marc Gasser-Wingate, *Aristotle's Empiricism* (Oxford University Press, 2021). On empiricism in Aristotle's view of practical knowledge specifically, see Hendrik Lorenz and Benjamin Morison, "Aristotle's Empiricist Theory of Doxastic Knowledge," *Phronesis* 64, no. 4 (2019): 431–464. For a cogent analysis of *empeiria* that surveys the use of the notion in the corpus as a whole, with a brief coda on Aristotle's ethics, see Pieter Sjoerd Hasper and Joel Yurdin, "Between Perception and Scientific Knowledge: Aristotle's Account of Experience," *Oxford Studies in Ancient Philosophy* 47 (2014): 119–150. Other recent work on this

---

Aristotle's Practical Epistemology. Dhananjay Jagannathan, Oxford University Press.
© Oxford University Press 2024. DOI: 10.1093/9780197781517.003.0003

36 ARISTOTLE'S PRACTICAL EPISTEMOLOGY

interpreting the passages individually, I will refer to these claims as they are numbered here and by the abbreviated labels I also supply as mnemonics.

i. Ethical experience is a kind of practical knowledge, that is, knowledge of how to act in accordance with virtue. (PRACTICAL KNOWLEDGE)

ii. Ethical experience is a characteristic product of good habituation, a process that is, essentially, a shaping of the non-rational soul—desires, emotions, pleasures, and pains—to conform to reasoning but which also must equip the learner in virtue to reason well about the situations that demand the exercise of virtue. (HABITUATED KNOWLEDGE)

iii. Insofar as ethical experience is a grasp of how to respond to kinds of situations, it is what Aristotle describes as knowledge of 'the that' with respect to the just and the noble, by contrast to knowledge of the reason why. Put in plainer terms, ethical experience constitutes a grasp of the *basic facts* in ethics. (BASIC FACTS)

iv. Since, in any given domain, reflective inquiry demands knowledge of the basic facts of the domain, ethical experience equips the would-be inquirer with the starting points needed to appreciate and make good use of ethical claims and arguments. (STARTING POINTS)

v. Since the person with ethical experience lacks a grasp of the reason why, they fall short of the ethical understanding that belongs to the person of practical wisdom and that it is the task of ethical inquiry to foster. (ORDINARY KNOWLEDGE)

---

topic has tended to focus exclusively or almost exclusively on *Metaphysics* Alpha 1 and *Posterior Analytics* II.19 (e.g., Pavel Gregorić and Filip Grgić, "Aristotle's Notion of Experience," *Archiv für Geschichte der Philosophie* 88 [2006]: 1–30). Still this work, too, confirms the recent consensus, exemplified and defended in Hasper and Yurdin's paper, that *empeiria* is cognitively sophisticated. I rely on this general point while developing my own interpretation of what ethical experience must be.

ETHICAL EXPERIENCE IN THE *NICOMACHEAN ETHICS*   37

In this chapter, I rely on Aristotle's explicit remarks about *empeiria* in the *Nicomachean Ethics,* which, despite their importance, have not caught the attention of the majority of interpreters concerned with practical wisdom.[2]

2.1 A new vision of method in ethics

2.1.1 The education needed for ethical inquiry (*NE* I.3)

I have already made note of Aristotle's preoccupation in the *Nicomachean Ethics* with the proper method for inquiry into the human good. These reflections on method are deeply intertwined with the distinct practical epistemology of the treatise, and, for that reason, they deserve further investigation here as a preliminary to laying out further features of that epistemology.

We have already encountered several of the most relevant claims in the texts I discussed in Chapter 1, where I showed how Aristotle rejects the Isocratean conception of ethical knowledge (§1.4). One

---

[2] On the importance of *empeiria* for understanding practical wisdom, I agree entirely with the assessments of Marta Jimenez, "*Empeiria* and Good Habits in Aristotle's Ethics," *Journal of the History of Philosophy* 57 (2019): 363–389, and Rosalind Hursthouse, "Practical Wisdom: A Mundane Account," *Proceedings of the Aristotelian Society* 106 (2006): 285–309. Jimenez, in particular, is concerned, as I am, to point to a prominent role for *empeiria* in the specific kinds of knowledge that one must acquire in order to be practically wise. The central difference between our views, as I will discuss in detail below, turns on the relationship between *empeiria* and the process of habituation. Jimenez holds that habituation is responsible for the production of habits while *empeiria* is gained through other means. By contrast, I hold that the single process of habituation characteristically leads to our gaining *empeiria*, while accepting the distinction between the shaping of the non-rational soul that is essential to habituation and the acquisition of knowledge in the rational soul that is merely concomitant to it (HABITUATED KNOWLEDGE). The difficulty facing Jimenez's view is that *empeiria* is rendered an unstable category, which includes both *empeiria* relevant for virtue and *empeiria* that is not. By contrast, on my view, Aristotle isolates a specific kind of *empeiria* in the key passages in the *NE* that is a form of practical knowledge, by which one is able to act in accordance with virtue (PRACTICAL KNOWLEDGE; BASIC FACTS). This knowledge is not simply *potentially* relevant for virtuous action, as is true on both Jimenez's and Hursthouse's view of experience, but is exercised in reasoning about how to act well.

38 ARISTOTLE'S PRACTICAL EPISTEMOLOGY

of these claims is the idea that without experience, ethical inquiry cannot be undertaken (point iv above—Starting Points).

> [T4] Each man judges well what he knows, i.e., in these matters he is a good judge. Hence, on a given topic it is the educated man who judges well, and overall it is the man educated on all subjects. For this reason, a young man is not an appropriate student of politics, since he lacks experience in the actions that make up life and arguments on this subject start from and concern these [actions] (*apeiros gar tōn kata ton bion praxeōn, hoi logoi d' ek toutōn kai peri toutōn*). Besides, being inclined to follow his passions, he will listen to no purpose or benefit, since the goal [of such inquiry] is not knowledge but action (*to telos estin ou gnōsis alla praxis*). (*NE* I.3, 1094b27–95a6)

In this passage, Aristotle makes an argument about what is needed to make good judgments when presented with claims about the human good, which he had earlier established is the subject matter of politics (*NE* I.2, 1094a26–b11). The argument of the passage runs as follows. In any domain, knowledge or education specific to that domain is needed to judge well. Hence, there must be a specific kind of knowledge or education that allows one to judge well about the human good. Aristotle then adverts to the relevant sort of knowledge or education as experience of actions, though for now the identification is preliminary, with a fuller account to come in the following chapter.

Despite its being preliminary, this passage is central to appreciating the distinctive approach to ethics articulated in the *NE*, so it will be useful to draw out a few points from this argument carefully. First, although Aristotle passes freely between speaking of knowledge and speaking of education, the difference between these notions is important in the dialectical context. The reason is that Aristotle's aristocratic audience would have bristled at the suggestion that one needed, e.g., to be a doctor to evaluate arguments

ETHICAL EXPERIENCE IN THE *NICOMACHEAN ETHICS* 39

about medicine. The doctor is the person who has medical knowledge, which is a craft (*tekhnē*), but one can be educated on medical matters—one can have *paideia* with respect to medicine—even if one does not have the corresponding craft. That is why Aristotle in this passage countenances the idea of the generally educated person, someone well placed to evaluate arguments on any given subject, even though they do not, and could not, possess specialized expertise in every field.

What specific sort of knowledge counts as being educated when it comes to the human good? There is something puzzling about this idea, since having a good grasp of the human good seems just as comprehensive as the idea of a general education, such that no specific kind of knowledge would seem to suffice. Aristotle introduces the idea of experience to handle this puzzle. There is a general grasp of human life—its limitations and its vicissitudes, what conduces to our benefit and to our detriment—that enables one to follow arguments about the human good but still has a determinate content. Indeed, having experience enables one not only to follow these arguments but also to make use of them. Unlike other subjects, it is not enough to accept the conclusion of an abstract argument about ethics. Since the point of ethical knowledge is action, one needs also to make use of these conclusions.

For all that Aristotle says in T4, however, it remains possible that the ability to make use of ethical arguments is merely an accidental concomitant of having experience. That is because Aristotle makes his point negatively: youth deprives one of experience as well as the ability to regulate one's life by reason. Are these two distinct privations? In the next chapter of the *NE*—in another text I introduced in Chapter 1—Aristotle returns to this topic and links habituation closely to the knowledge needed to appreciate ethical arguments. The capacity to appreciate ethical arguments and the capacity to make use of them will, then, turn out to be closely connected. In fact, experience, as a form of ethical knowledge, is a *product* of habituation—point ii above (HABITUATED KNOWLEDGE).

40 ARISTOTLE'S PRACTICAL EPISTEMOLOGY

These remarks fill out the more indirect mention of experience in *NE* I.3.

2.1.2 Inquiry begins from what is better known to us (*NE* I.4)

In *NE* I.4, Aristotle returns to the idea that we need education as the starting point for inquiry in a passage that I discussed in Chapter One. Here, he lays out an account of the relationship between this starting point and the goal of inquiry, drawing on a comparison to Plato's reflections on the subject:

> [**T3**] We should not overlook the fact that arguments from first principles and arguments toward first principles differ. For Plato also rightly puzzled over and inquired whether the path led from first principles or to them, as from the judges to the turning post in a stadium or the other way round—[rightly], since we must begin from what is knowable to us, and this [sc. knowable] has two senses, some things being knowable to us, and others knowable simply speaking. Perhaps, then, we at least must begin from what is knowable to us. That is why one must be raised with noble habits if one is to be a capable student of the noble and the just and politics in general. For the starting point is what is so (*to hoti*) and if this is sufficiently apparent, there is no need in addition for the reason why (*to dioti*): someone in this position either has or could easily get the starting points. (*NE* I.4, 1095a30–b7)

Logically speaking, there are three possibilities: (1) inquiry does not bring us knowledge, (2) inquiry brings us knowledge but we begin in total ignorance, or (3) inquiry brings us knowledge but we begin with some knowledge. Of these three possibilities, Aristotle opts for the last (as he does elsewhere—cf. *Physics* I.1). We begin with what is knowable to us and proceed, through inquiry into the

ETHICAL EXPERIENCE IN THE *NICOMACHEAN ETHICS*   41

human good, to what is knowable simply speaking. (To be 'more knowable' is to be more *fundamental* in the order of knowledge.) The knowledge that gets inquiry off the ground is the product of good habituation, which is also described here as knowledge of 'what is so.' As we know from *Metaphysics* Alpha 1 and other texts, knowledge of 'what is so' is just what the person with experience has, though such a person falls short of understanding, which requires a grasp of the reason why. These ideas, together, support points ii–v in my overall interpretation above, especially ii and iii— HABITUATED KNOWLEDGE and BASIC FACTS.

Note that Aristotle agrees with Plato that knowledge of first principles is the most desirable state for an inquirer to be in. The passage recalls Socrates' almost despairing remarks in the *Republic* about the shadows that are cast by our ignorance of the Form of the Good, the unhypothetical first principle (VI. 504d ff.); without such knowledge, our inquiry into what is good in human life may seem to be entirely unmoored. Given the stop-start nature of the opening chapters of the *Nicomachean Ethics*, we might at first suspect that Aristotle shares the worry articulated in *Republic* VI, at least in broad outlines.

On closer inspection, the distinction drawn in this passage between the two senses of what is knowable is meant to put us at ease with respect to precisely this concern. For Aristotle's point is this: we do not *already* need a grasp of first principles, that is, a grasp of the reason why, in order to get going. In other words, we do not begin in total ignorance. In this respect, Aristotle's procedure calls to mind another idea from Platonic epistemology, which Socrates articulates in a number of dialogues, most notably in the *Meno* (82b9–85b7) and the *Phaedo* (72e3–73b2). We do seem to have knowledge within us that inquiry can bring to the surface, even if we are not immediately aware of it.

One of the reasons that Aristotle's emphasis on knowledge in these passages on method in *NE* I.3–4 has remained underappreciated is the sheer array of formulations he uses,

42 ARISTOTLE'S PRACTICAL EPISTEMOLOGY

including education (*paideia*), what is knowable to us (*ta gnorima hēmin*), grasping the starting points (*tas arkhas*), and knowledge of 'the that' (*to hoti*). I hold that all these formulations are united in a single notion: experience in the actions we must undertake in life.[3] My claim may well be surprising, since experience is referenced here once and only in the negative, as what young people lack.

Recall that, on my view, experience (*empeiria*) is, at once, a product of habituation, the knowledge we need to begin to inquire about ethics and politics, and the starting point from which we develop practical wisdom (claims ii–v above). In *NE* I these different roles are run together and not always clearly differentiated. The reason that experience plays these different roles stems ultimately from the most fundamental of my claims— claim i, PRACTICAL KNOWLEDGE—the claim that experience is a type of practical knowledge of how to act in accordance with virtue.

I defend my view further in the next two sections by turning to the most detailed discussions of experience in the *NE*: first, a passage in *NE* VI where experience is shown to be ordinary practical knowledge of the human good; and second, a passage at the end of the treatise, *NE* X.9, where Aristotle describes its essential role in political inquiry, the topic that unites the *NE* and the *Politics* as two halves of a single investigation into human life. The idea that experience is practical knowledge is prominent in both texts. These passages, which analyze experience more explicitly, provide support for the interpretation I have offered of *NE* I.3–4.

---

[3] Compare the very different account of what Aristotle's well-habituated audience knows in Dominic Scott, *Listening to Reason in Plato and Aristotle* (Oxford University Press, 2020), esp. "Introduction to Part II: The Target Audience of the *NE*," 119–130. Scott argues that the audience has, as a result of their upbringing and experience, a set of moral intuitions rather than practical knowledge.

2.2 The practical contribution of experience

2.2.1 Experience as a product of habituation

So far, I have been primarily concerned with the *epistemic* contribution of experience: experience of actions is a type of knowledge, generated by habituation, that enables its possessor to scrutinize and respond appropriately to reasoned claims about the human good. Experience, however, is not itself a body of claims about the good to which further propositions can be brought, e.g., to be tested for coherence. Rather, it is essentially a form of practical knowledge, something that is especially evident from its origin in the process of habituation.

Habituation is the process by which one's desires, emotions, pleasures, and pains are organized in order to conform to what is in fact noble and shameful for a human being to do and feel. Interpreters of Aristotle's ethics have tended to focus on what we might call, in an Aristotelian mood, the *matter* of habituation (i.e., what habituation works on), which are states of the non-rational soul (*NE* II.3, 1104b11–16). Aristotle does in fact hold that we need to be habituated because our natural tendencies are insufficient to ensure obedience to rational prescriptions, which include instructions from our parents and other authorities, the law itself, and of course the reasoned decisions we ourselves reach through well-formed courses of deliberation. It is easy, therefore, to think of habituation as a purely *external* process of training.

As Nancy Sherman and others have convincingly argued, however, such a view of habituation is untenable, given the intertwining of desiderative, perceptual, and ratiocinative processes that is characteristic of ethical maturity.[4] For the virtuous person, in particular,

---

[4] See Sherman, *The Fabric of Character: Aristotle's Theory of Virtue* (Oxford University Press, 1991), esp. Chapter 5, "The Habituation of Character."

44 ARISTOTLE'S PRACTICAL EPISTEMOLOGY

these processes operate harmoniously, ensuring that we notice what we must and think, act, and feel accordingly. Habituation is responsible not only for bringing about the mere *compliance* of potentially recalcitrant desires but also an active *readiness* for virtuous action. Much of habituation into virtue requires the person being educated to orient themselves, albeit with guidance.

Some readers of Aristotle have acknowledged this important fact but taken note of its significance solely for the fully virtuous person, whom Aristotle says must also be practically wise. For my present purpose, what is most important is that practical knowledge will be relevant even for the learner, as what enables crucial aspects of further habituation. For example, to internalize the principle that a particular sort of fact tends to be salient in certain types of situations is not merely to outwardly manifest behavior that corresponds to this principle. After all, any given behavioral regularity underdetermines the principle to which it corresponds.[5] I will return to this topic with a concrete example inspired by Aristotle's remarks in *NE* VI.7. Let us now turn to that text.

2.2.2 Experience and practical success

Aristotle's treatment of practical wisdom differs from his investigation of the character-virtues through the processes for their development in *NE* II. In fact, he says very little at any point in *NE* VI about how we come to have practical wisdom, except to remark that young people tend to lack it, since it requires experience to develop, which in turn takes time (VI.8, 1142a11–16).

Instead, the dominant mode of Aristotle's inquiry is contrastive. First, he distinguishes practical wisdom from the other intellectual

---

[5] For an interpretation of Aristotle that foregrounds this idea, see John McDowell, "Virtue and Reason," *The Monist* 62 (1979): 331–350.

ETHICAL EXPERIENCE IN THE *NICOMACHEAN ETHICS*   45

virtues, which are states of the soul by which we grasp the truth (VI.2–6). Then, in VI.7, he turns to the distinctive way that the practically wise person grasps the truth of what we should do within the sphere of deliberation (what he earlier called, evocatively, "practical truth").[6] It is in this discussion that he introduces the idea that experience in ethics is knowledge of the particulars, which is necessary but not sufficient for having true practical wisdom:

> [T5] Nor is practical wisdom [knowledge] of universals alone; rather one must also have knowledge (*gnōrizein*) of the particulars, since it [sc. practical wisdom] is exercised in action (*praktikē*) and action concerns the particulars. That is why even some who do not know (*eidōtes*) are more capable of action than others who do, and in other cases it is those with experience [who are more capable]. For if someone knows (*eideiē*) that light meats are easy to digest and healthy, but is ignorant (*agnooi*) of which meats are light, he won't create health; instead the one who knows (*eidōs*) that bird meats are light and thus, healthy, will [be the one to] create health. (*NE* VI.7, 1141b14–21)

Aristotle here distinguishes three kinds of knowledge: knowledge of universals, knowledge of particulars, and the sort of knowledge that combines both. I will argue in Chapters 3 and 4 that, in practical or productive domains like ethics and medicine (the source of the passage's example), understanding—the best state knowledge we can be in—is knowledge of both universals and particulars together. For now, what matters is the way that Aristotle associates knowledge of particulars with experience and practical success.

Notice that there are two ways to have practical success apart from knowledge of universals. One is simply to have the capacity

---

[6] This framing, which is important for understanding practical wisdom, is the topic of Chapter 3.

46 ARISTOTLE'S PRACTICAL EPISTEMOLOGY

to act correctly without having any knowledge at all. This sort of knowledge is what Socrates envisions in the *Gorgias* (462b11–c3) when he speaks of experience (*empeiria*), knowledge that is not only habitual but also mindless, amounting to a mere knack (*tribē*).

Aristotle explicitly distinguishes experience from this kind of mindless capacity for practical success. It may be that it is not possible, in the case of ethical knowledge or in medicine, to have such a mindless capacity at all. If we take this line of interpretation, then "in other cases" (*en allois*) means "in other domains," i.e., in domains where mindless practical success is impossible. Alternately, Aristotle means that in one and the same domain, some people may achieve practical success without knowledge while others succeed on the basis of their experience, which involves knowledge of particulars. Either way, experience is set up as a form of practical knowledge and closely associated with practical success, even as it falls short of practical wisdom.

Aristotle goes on to provide an example of such practical success, which is drawn from the domain of medicine. The example is enormously rich, despite coming in a single sentence. Indeed, in this sentence, we get an account not only of what experience is but also how it differs from knowledge of universals and how these two kinds of knowledge might relate to each other when a single person possesses both. In fact, the compressed character of the example is so confusing that it has led editors to suspect the text.

Instead of turning immediately to such fine-grained exegetical matters, I will begin a little further back with a survey of the different sorts of medical knowledge one might be said to have in Aristotle's world. The reason for this apparent digression is that the same distinctions will return in the next section, where I consider what Aristotle says about political experience in *NE* X.9 and where medicine, again, is his favored example.

ETHICAL EXPERIENCE IN THE *NICOMACHEAN ETHICS*　47

2.2.3　Different ways of knowing how to heal

The ideal of medical knowledge is of course the doctor, the possessor of the craft of medicine (*tekhnē iatrikē*), whom we may also call the medical expert. The medical expert is in a position to systematically bring about bodily health. Note that bodily health belongs to human beings by nature, even as no individual human being could instantiate it perfectly. The complexity of medicine is due to the fact that the power to heal any given individual requires (i) an understanding of the general principles that govern the natural state of health, (ii) discernment of the particular state that a patient is in and what in that state might constitute a deficiency, and (iii) knowledge of skills and techniques that effectively intervene in order to promote health in patients.

In theorizing medical knowledge for ourselves, we may well accept these as components, each on a par with the other, when reflecting on the work of skilled doctors. For Aristotle, it also matters that the art of medicine is essentially a productive art, where the product is (improved) states of bodily health in individuals. (If it sounds awkward to speak of these states as a *product*, then the word "result" may be substituted.) If we accept this claim that the art of medicine is productive knowledge, our attention may be drawn particularly to the third of these aspects, that is, knowledge of skills and techniques. For this aspect seems most closely connected to the actual bringing about of the product. In particular, it is implausible that a person has *any* share of medical knowledge without having any ability to actually intervene in the healing of patients.

The salience of such skills and techniques to the attribution of medical knowledge raises a question: Could one have this sort of skillful knowledge independently of the other two aspects? There is a limited sense in which one can: one can possess knowledge of medical skills and techniques without the other two aspects because applying these skills to patients, in some cases, need not require a full grasp of their condition in light of general principles,

48 ARISTOTLE'S PRACTICAL EPISTEMOLOGY

but only a rough appreciation of what might be wrong in their particular case. This rough appreciation is not the full discernment of the medical expert, backed by expertise, but it can still work in concert with knowledge of skills and techniques. Of course, this grasp is still a kind of discernment, so at least some form of the second aspect of medical knowledge is needed, but a grasp of general principles of medicine is not required to be capable of healing.

To be sure, the different aspects of medical knowledge are highly intertwined in the case of the medical expert. For instance, one's discernment of health and disease in particular patients is transformed by the possession of a general understanding of health. Despite this fact, there is still some extent to which the aspects come apart, both in the ideal case of medical expertise and, as I have just argued, in less ideal cases. The relative independence of knowledge of skills and techniques allows us to identify a second way of knowing how to heal that falls short of medical expertise: medicine as *practical art*.

What I mean by medicine as practical art is best illustrated by example. Medicine in many modern cultural contexts tends to be strongly associated with scientific expertise. In the ancient world, too, we can see efforts to bring about this association, most prominently in the Hippocratic treatise "On Expertise" ("Peri tekhnēs"), which responds to various criticisms of medical practice. Both in Aristotle's context and our own, however, formal training in medicine sits alongside a range of folk practices of healing. These folk practices range from the advice dispensed by wellness gurus for a diet that will make you feel better to the familiar home remedies for common ailments that are recommended by wise elders and passed down from generation to generation. Anyone who has taken a honey-ginger-lemon concoction for a respiratory illness has a familiarity with the kind of knowledge characteristic of medicine as a practical art.

Those who profess to heal on the basis of such nontechnical knowledge are described as empirics (*hoi empeiroi*) by Aristotle, a

ETHICAL EXPERIENCE IN THE *NICOMACHEAN ETHICS* 49

description that accords with the emphasis in the medical writers of his time on the importance of *empeiria*. These healers were the ancestors of the ancient medical school of Empiricism, which emphasized the practical dimensions of medicine and the in-utility and speculative character of the more theoretical forms of medicine represented by the so-called Dogmatists.[7] By Aristotle's lights, however, to count as an empiric one had to be able to at least somewhat reliably heal patients; no formal rejection of theory, which characterized both the Empiricists and the Methodists in later antiquity, was required.[8]

The third type of medical knowledge, which may escape our notice altogether, arises when we consider an even more limited example of healing powers than those possessed by the empiric doctor. The empiric can apply medicine as a practical art by drawing on associations between treatments and symptoms. But to count as a *practitioner* of medicine, even the empiric must be able to treat others on something like a reliable basis. Practical success marks off the social categories associated with craft knowledge, after all. Barring this, the putative empiric is nothing more than a quack. Still, we can imagine a further etiolation of the empiric's knowledge, where the associations between patterns of symptoms and treatments are themselves not perceived. Rather what is grasped is only the peculiar condition of a *single* patient and the apparent appropriateness of a given treatment.

What would it mean to know how to treat just a single person? The example Aristotle offers is knowing how to treat *yourself*

---

[7] For a survey of the various camps of ancient medicine, with critiques of each, see Galen, *Sects for Beginners [de sectis]*. Galen's emphasis on the need for both practical experience and theoretical knowledge in medicine reflects Aristotle's conception of craft as involving both. For the influence of the Empiricist school on Galen, see Inna Kupreeva, "Galen's Empiricist Background: A Study of the Argument in *On Medical Experience*," in *Galen's Epistemology: Experience, Reason, and Method in Ancient Medicine*, ed. Matyáš Havrda (Cambridge University Press, 2022), 32–78.

[8] See the discussion of medical Empiricism in relation to Aristotle in Lorenz and Morison, "Aristotle's Empiricist Theory," esp. 435–437.

50   ARISTOTLE'S PRACTICAL EPISTEMOLOGY

because adults tend to acquire a working knowledge of how particular ailments tend to affect them and what might be of help, especially the sorts of minor ailments that do not require the help of a medical practitioner. We can imagine other cases, however. Caregivers, including parents, often develop a profound understanding of the needs and difficulties of those whom they care for, even apart from any particular general knowledge of medicine. This quasi-perceptual type of medical knowledge also involves analogues of the second and third components of medical expertise—a form of discernment, which is quite narrow in scope, coupled with a sense of what interventions might help, which in turn falls well short of knowing any particular skills or techniques.

Since the two less-than-ideal types of medical knowledge I have discussed involve the second and third components, we may wonder whether it is possible to possess just a grasp of the principles of medicine on their own. In fact, Aristotle countenances just this possibility in the passage I began to analyze above in *NE* VI, but he would deny that someone who has this kind of knowledge knows medicine to any extent. For without powers of discernment or a grasp of skills and techniques needed to heal, the medical knowledge such a person has it entirely cut off from the end this knowledge has, healing. Even the highly individualized knowledge I described just above meets this condition, though no one with it would be recognized as a doctor.

In this section, I have discussed, from a philosophical point of view, the kinds of medical knowledge there are. I began with the ideal case, the medical expert who most of all merits the name of doctor, who possesses a range of cognitive states and abilities that might be termed knowledge: a grasp of principles, powers of discernment, and knowledge of skills and techniques of intervention. When we consider various ways of falling away from this ideal, while still being able to heal, we get two further kinds of medical knowledge: the empiric's grasp of medicine as a practical art, and a highly individualized power to heal. Finally, merely knowing the

ETHICAL EXPERIENCE IN THE *NICOMACHEAN ETHICS*   51

principles of medicine entails that one fails to know how to heal at all.

2.2.4 Experience as a knowledge of practical generalities (*NE* VI.7–8)

We are now in a position to appreciate Aristotle's illustration of the difference between practical wisdom and experience by means of a comparison to medical expertise. I quoted the passage T5 in full above in order to introduce the key notions and to discuss the passage generally. Now I will work through T5 in three stages, corresponding to three subsections of the passage, which are increasingly difficult to interpret. These subsections establish (A) the close connection between practical knowledge and success in particular cases, (B) experience as a form of practical knowledge, and (C) the illustration of A and B by means of an example from medicine.

In the first part of the passage, Aristotle argues that attributions of knowledge in practical matters depend on the agent being capable of acting successfully: "(A) Nor is practical wisdom [knowledge] of universals alone; rather one must also have knowledge (*gnōrizein*) of the particulars, since it [sc. practical wisdom] is exercised in action (*praktikē*) and action concerns the particulars." Aristotle has already marked off *phronēsis* from theoretical wisdom (*sophia*) both by their difference in subject matter and their ways of knowing those subjects (*NE* VI.2, 1139a6–17), but he feels compelled to reinforce the idea that *phronēsis* is concerned with action on particular occasions, rather than a sort of wisdom that can regard the particulars of human life at a distance.[9] I will return to this topic

---

[9] The latter sort of knowledge is well within the semantic range of *phronēsis* in ordinary Greek (as we saw in my discussion of Isocrates' *Taking My Turn* in Chapter 1) and in the philosophical Greek of Plato, where *phronēsis* can mean either intelligence generally or a more specific, exalted form of wisdom equivalent to *sophia*.

52 ARISTOTLE'S PRACTICAL EPISTEMOLOGY

in Chapter 5, where I explain what sort of universal knowledge belongs to the person of practical wisdom. For the present purpose, it is enough to note that the claim about particulars contained in (A) is not confined to *phronēsis* but generalizes to all forms of practical knowledge, including experience itself.

Aristotle turns in the second part of the passage to the ways knowledge and practical success are aligned in different domains: "(B) That is why even some who do not know (*eidōtes*) are more capable of action than others who do, and in other cases it is those with experience [who are more capable]." At first blush, the idea that a *lack* of knowledge is consistent with practical success may seem quite bizarre, given that Aristotle has just argued that knowledge of particulars is needed for *any* practical success.

The precise epistemological vocabulary of the passage must, however, be kept in clear view. Aristotle here is using the verb *eidenai* in a narrow sense, to refer to precise or scientific types of knowledge, the very kind of knowledge associated with universals.[10] Hence, the remark is apt, since part of Aristotle's goal is to show that universal knowledge *on its own* is insufficient for success in action. For example, someone with an excellent grasp of universal principles of military strategy may make a poor leader—and thus fail to achieve victory, which is the goal of strategy—if they lack other types of knowledge, while someone without any formal training in strategy of this kind may well be able to succeed. Knowledge of universal principles that is gained in such formal training is especially apt to be described with forms of the verb *eidenai*.

Perhaps acknowledging the oddness of this binary contrast between having universal knowledge and lacking it in a discussion of the way that knowledge promotes practical success, Aristotle shifts to speaking of other cases where *experience* enables successful action. Indeed, in the case where someone succeeds in military

---

[10] On this use of *eidenai*, see David Bronstein, *Aristotle on Knowledge and Learning* (Oxford University Press, 2016), 19–21.

ETHICAL EXPERIENCE IN THE *NICOMACHEAN ETHICS* 53

leadership without formal training, what enables their success is apt to be called experience. Such experience, by Aristotle's lights, should be counted as a kind of knowledge (*gnōsis*, cf. the use of the verb *gnōrizein* in A), even as it falls short of the exalted knowledge picked out in the first half of the sentence by the verb *eidenai*.

In fact, the knowledge possessed by those with experience is precisely knowledge of particulars, which the argument in (A) made indispensable to practical success. Over the course of (A) and (B), then, Aristotle steadily draws his readers away from thinking of knowledge purely in terms of generalities, especially in the case of practical knowledge.

As I suggested above, the most complex part of T5 is its concluding example, which illustrates these two points about practical knowledge, taken generally, and about experience, more specifically. This medical example depends, implicitly, on the picture I sketched in the previous section of an ideal conception of medical expertise and a set of ways of falling short of this ideal while still being forms of medical knowledge. I will now work through the example and its various parts with reference to that implicit picture. Aristotle continues as follows: "(C) For if someone knows (*eideiē*) that light meats are easy to digest and healthy, but is ignorant (*agnooi*) of which meats are light, he won't create health; instead the one who knows (*eidos*) that bird meats are light and thus, healthy, will [be the one to] create health."

The first observation to make is that experience is being contrasted with universal knowledge in both halves of this sentence, which together are meant to provide an example of the way that someone with experience may be practically successful, while someone without experience and who has universal knowledge alone will be unable to act successfully. The primary challenge of understanding the example comes from the fact that *discernment,* the second component of medical expertise that I identified above, is not clearly distinguished from the other components of medical knowledge but is allowed to stand in for them instead. To be sure,

54   ARISTOTLE'S PRACTICAL EPISTEMOLOGY

no one lacking discernment can make use of the knowledge they have, whether of universal principles or of skills and techniques, but neither is discernment the whole of practical or productive knowledge.

As a result of this elision, interpreters have generally read this text—along with an allusive reference to the healthfulness of different sorts of waters in the following chapter—through the lens of the practical syllogism, an idea Aristotle uses both in *NE* VI–VII and in several places in the psychological works (*De Motu Animalium* VII; *De Anima* III.10) to account for how thought and perception together lead to action.[11] While the reasoning implicitly represented here might be reconfigured to fit the model of the practical syllogism, talk of premises or conclusions of reasoning is absent, which is the hallmark of the practical syllogism and syllogistic talk more generally.[12] Moreover, using the notoriously contested idea of the practical syllogism to make sense of the present passage is a case of using the obscure to explain the obscure. Instead of reading Aristotle's medical example through the theory of the practical syllogism (the operative question being, what explains action?), I propose instead to understand it as a part of his practical epistemology (where the question instead is, how does knowledge enable practical success?).

The second observation to make is that the passage is rife with universals in the sense of general terms, which makes its central point about the need for knowledge of particulars harder to appreciate. The subject matter of both knowledge of universals and knowledge of particulars is described here with general terms. That should make us wary of assimilating knowledge of universals to knowledge of what is general. In fact, these notions are carefully

---

[11] For a sophisticated such account, see R. Kathleen Harbin, "The Practical Syllogism and Practical Cognition in Aristotle," *Archiv für Geschichte der Philosophie* 104 (2022): 633–662, along with further references there. I return to Harbin's account in 109 fn. 12.

[12] See also Lorenz and Morison, "Aristotle's Empiricist Theory," esp. 446–447.

ETHICAL EXPERIENCE IN THE *NICOMACHEAN ETHICS* 55

distinguished in *Posterior Analytics* I.4, where 'universal' (*katholou*) is defined *in terms of* the more basic notion of '*holding in every case*' (*kata pantos*), which corresponds to the intuitive idea of a general term or predicate (73b25–33). The best way to make sense of the present passage is to take knowledge of universals to mean knowledge of principles and causes. For there is just one notion that picks out a principle or cause of health, the notion of the *easily digestible*, which we find associated with a knowledge of universals.[13]

With these observations in hand, we can tackle the concluding portion of **T5** directly: "(C) For if someone knows (*eideiē*) that light meats are easy to digest and healthy, but is ignorant (*agnooi*) of which meats are light, he won't create health; instead the one who knows (*eidos*) that bird meats are light and thus, healthy, will [be the one to] create health." We learn here that the person with universal knowledge who is unable to act successfully still has knowledge that is relevant to bringing about health; specifically, they may have the knowledge that the easily digestible is healthy and that light meats are easily digestible. What they lack, which the person of experience has, is, e.g., a grasp of which meats, specifically, are light, including that bird meats are light. In the terms I laid out in the previous section, the person with universal knowledge has a grasp of principles and causes while lacking discernment.

Nothing Aristotle says here bears directly on whether they possess knowledge of skills and techniques, but it is reasonable to assume that, since being able to exercise such knowledge depends on having some degree of discernment, they lack this knowledge, too. By contrast, the person with experience does have discernment. Moreover, by parity with my reasoning above, we may suppose that, since practical success demands a knowledge of at least some methods of applying one's discernment to cases, the

---

[13] Two supporting reasons for taking easily digestible this way: this notion cannot be perceived directly, and it adverts to a mechanism of action, namely, processes of digestion.

56   ARISTOTLE'S PRACTICAL EPISTEMOLOGY

person with experience also has some knowledge of relevant skills and techniques. The knowledge of the person with experience is not confined to discernment, then, though discernment is really what marks them off from the person who merely has universal knowledge.

Because both the empiric and the person with universal knowledge grasp something about what promotes the end of health, they each count as having a form of medical knowledge, even though only the former can bring about health and could be described, in the context of social practices, as a healer or doctor. After all, the empiric, as much as the medical expert, has a form of practical knowledge.

Interpreters have generally failed to see the importance of the connection between discernment and the other practical abilities needed to bring about health, which must be brought in to make sense of experience as a form of practical knowledge. Indeed, some editors have suspected the text and omitted the words I translated "and thus, healthy" at the end of part C of T5. These words are essential to the force of the passage, when it is understood as an analysis of different kinds of practical knowledge. For they establish that the empiric, too, has a grasp of what promotes health.

As a result, the empiric must know that light meats are healthy, just as the person with universal knowledge does; what differs is the way that these two types of knowers grasp this fact. The person with universal knowledge can explain this claim as a matter of a principle or cause of health: the easily digestible quality of light meats. The person with experience instead grasps this notion as part of their practical knowledge. More precisely, they know that, in some circumstances, what is needed to promote health are light meats. Aristotle simplifies the example by omitting the reference to circumstances or

ETHICAL EXPERIENCE IN THE *NICOMACHEAN ETHICS* 57

other qualities of the patient. As a result, it may seem confusing that the empiric and the person with universal knowledge know the same fact. Only the empiric, however, will understand, as part of their powers of discernment, which circumstances call for the use of this fact in promoting health. The reference to circumstances will be made explicit when Aristotle describes political experience and the art of legislation in *NE* X.9, which I discuss in the next section.

To sum up my lengthy analysis of T5, Aristotle establishes experience as a form of practical knowledge that enables someone to act successfully even if they lack knowledge of causes and principles. That is just what we should expect given the kinds of knowledge that go together in the ideal case of the medical expert and the different ways one might be in a position to heal despite falling short of this ideal. The most significant claim to emerge from this inquiry for Aristotle's overarching account of experience in the *Nicomachean Ethics* is what I labeled PRACTICAL KNOWLEDGE in the first part of this chapter (claim i): the claim that experience enables one to act successfully, which in the case of ethical experience means being able to act in accordance with virtue. We also get a deeper analysis of claim v, ORDINARY KNOWLEDGE: the claim that the person with experience falls short of practical wisdom because they lack understanding, specifically, a grasp of causes and principles.

In *NE* VI.8 itself, immediately after part C of my focal passage T5, Aristotle turns to discussing the equivalence between practical and political wisdom. I will return to this important topic in Chapter 6 of the book. For now, this equivalence plays an important role in grounding the relevance to the present argument of Aristotle's longest and most detailed analysis of experience in the *NE*, in its final chapter, which serves as an introduction to the inquiry into legislation carried out the *Politics*.

58 ARISTOTLE'S PRACTICAL EPISTEMOLOGY

2.3 Political experience in *NE* X.9

2.3.1 Reason and moral education

Aristotle concludes the *NE* with a summary of what he has shown about the cultivation of virtues needed for happiness and a return to the overarching topic of the treatise: how to bring about the highest good for human beings. The summary is straightforward and is grounded in a familiar idea about the plurality of sources for virtue; nature, habit, and reason all make a contribution but in different ways (*NE* X.9, 1179b20–34).

From the point of view of someone setting out to cultivate virtue in themselves or in another, nature can be set aside, because the contribution of nature is up to chance and, hence, is not subject to deliberation (X.9, 1179b21–23). We are simply fortunate if those who are to be educated are well prepared by nature for the task. Moreover, as Aristotle argued in *NE* II, our natural capacities are perfected by virtue, such that the attainment of virtue is, in a way, the most natural of outcomes, even if it is rare and requires considerable effort (II.1, 1103a23–26). Here in *NE* X.9, Aristotle does not wheel in his own metaphysical theory of nature, but we may supply the crucial point on his behalf from *Politics* I.2: nature is an *end* and not only a starting point (1252b31–33). Nature in the sense of a starting point can be set aside, practically speaking, since it cannot be changed. But we do not leave nature behind when we come to acquire the virtues through education; rather, we fulfill what is natural for us.

Habit and reason are treated together by Aristotle. Again, taking the point of view of the educator, he argues that habit is essential and, temporally, precedes the work of reason, since the target of moral education must be attached to what is noble or fine and this result can only be brought about by habit (X.9, 1179b23–26). What is noble must seem intuitively good and what is shameful bad to a person before they can make further progress toward virtue

ETHICAL EXPERIENCE IN THE *NICOMACHEAN ETHICS*   59

(1179b7–10). This point about habit and motivation is apt not to seem controversial, but Aristotle here stakes out a claim with two important implications.

First, the claim entails that even a good nature is insufficient for the passionate attachment to the noble that Aristotle describes. For that reason, habituation is indispensable for those who are well disposed by nature and for others alike. Indeed, even as Aristotle singles out the masses as liable to live by their passions in this passage (X.9, 117911–16), he also rejects the aristocratic contention that nobility can come by birth (1179b21–23).[14] Second, Aristotle follows Socrates in Plato's *Republic* in thinking that our motivations must be oriented properly for reason to get the proper hold on us (*Republic* III.401e1–402a4). The resulting picture of virtue and vice is one where the operations of reason are not independent of our motivations, and, specifically, where reason can be *co-opted* if we have the wrong motivations at the outset.

In fact, Aristotle's point about reason is simply that the various manifestations of reason—one's own reasoning, the instructions of one's parents, and the injunctions of the law—each depend for their efficacy on the proper functioning of one's motivations and desires. The harmony of one's own reasoning and motivations is nothing other than character-virtue, obedience to one's parents depends on love and friendship, and compliance with the law depends on either virtue or, lacking that, fear of punishment.

2.3.2 The need for and superiority of understanding

The point of these remarks about moral education and moral psychology in the first part of *NE* X.9 is not only to summarize

---

[14] For a picture of what such an aristocratic morality might come to, we have the literary evidence of the elegiac poetry of Theognis, a sharp social critic of the mid-sixth century.

60   ARISTOTLE'S PRACTICAL EPISTEMOLOGY

the main conclusions of the *Nicomachean Ethics* but also to pre-
pare the way for a bolder argument that is more directly relevant
to my larger topic, practical epistemology. Aristotle argues in the
next part of *NE* X.9 that anyone who wants to employ reason for
the purpose of moral education, not just in politics but also in their
own household, must aim to achieve some degree of *understanding*
of legislation (1180b20–28). The grounds for this proposal lie in
NE V.1, where Aristotle argued that because the general purpose
of law is to secure happiness for the citizens, laws concern all the
virtues and not only, say, specific virtues needed for social cooperation (1129b17–25).[15] Aristotle here adds the idea that law, in
its ideal form, is nothing other than an impersonal form of practical wisdom (X.9, 1180a21–22). The equivalence between legislative and practical understanding is thereby established in both
directions.

Despite the clear grounds for this equivalence, which resonates
with the earlier claim in *NE* VI.8 that practical and political wisdom
are the same state, the strength of Aristotle's claim about the need
for understanding in moral education is still surprising. After all,
one may quite reasonably think that an understanding of the principles of legislation is essential for those who design constitutions
or hold the highest magistracies. But Aristotle's argument commits
him to thinking that even a parent will be best placed to educate
their children if they have such understanding, something that he
admits flies in the face of the commonplace that the intimate knowledge afforded by parenthood—knowing the individual nature of
one's child—is sufficient for moral education along with the natural affinity and affection that binds parents and children together
(X.9, 1180a29–b11). As we shall see when we turn more closely to
the text below, such intimate knowledge falls short of the kind of

---

[15] A good example of the alternative view comes from the Great Speech of Plato's
Protagoras, where Protagoras singles out justice and reverence (*aidōs*) as the virtues necessary for human social existence, which law and other social institutions demand of
everyone (*Prt.* 320c–328d).

ordinary practical knowledge that has been my main subject in this chapter, though Aristotle invokes both kinds of knowledge.

This topic of parenting and education is not further pursued in *NE* X.9 as Aristotle's real aim is to inaugurate his study of the principles of legislation in the *Politics*. Nevertheless, the contrast between experience as ordinary practical knowledge and political or practical understanding is explored in some depth in this later discussion because Aristotle goes on to criticize earlier inquiries into legislation for not being sufficiently grounded in experience.

In addition to confirmation of several of the claims I laid out at the start of the chapter—e.g., claims iv and v, STARTING POINTS and ORDINARY KNOWLEDGE—two further points of special importance for my argument in this chapter emerge from these two discussions of experience in *NE* X.9. First, in both passages, experience is shown to be more than a set of perceptual or quasi-perceptual abilities. This point is central to appreciating that experience is a form of practical knowledge just as much as practical wisdom is. It also tells firmly against a view that some interpreters have pursued on the basis of Aristotle's limited mentions of experience in the theoretical works, especially in *Metaphysics* Alpha 1, on which experience is reduced to such perceptual abilities.

Second, experience is described as a grasp of how certain kinds of circumstances call for certain kinds of actions. The reference to circumstances expands on a point that was left incomplete in the medical example in *NE* VI.7. There, experience seemed to be a matter simply of recognizing how a goal might be pursued with an action or instrument of a particular type (e.g., light meats lead to health). But in ethics as in medicine, the goal is so complex that grasping such connections could not amount to genuine practical knowledge, at least by Aristotle's lights. Rather, a grasp of such connections, in the absence of a sensitivity to circumstances, would more resemble the skilled guesswork of the deflationist picture I attributed to Isocrates in §1.1. Hence, the reference to circumstances as well as action-types in *NE* X.9 both confirms my

62 ARISTOTLE'S PRACTICAL EPISTEMOLOGY

account of experience as a form of practical knowledge and offers us a way to make sense of how experience contributes to deliberation.

Let us turn now to the first of the two passages about experience in X.9, where Aristotle argues that moral education calls for a grasp of universal principles. Since this passage is quite long, it will help to divide my discussion of it into two parts. The first part runs as follows:

> [T6] Moreover, individual courses of education are even superior to common ones, as in medicine. For rest and fasting on the whole (*katholou*) help someone with fever, but perhaps not a certain person, and the pugilist perhaps does not prescribe the same mode of fighting to everyone. Indeed, it would seem that the individual [course] (*to kath' hekaston*) is more precise when the care is personal (*idias*), since each more likely obtains what suits him. But the best care for each is that of the doctor, likewise the trainer and everyone else who has universal knowledge, [knowledge of] what holds for all cases or for all of a particular type (for knowledge is and is held to be of what is common). (1180a34–b16)

Aristotle begins this passage by acknowledging what the proponents of individualized knowledge get right, which also picks up on the main idea of the *NE* VI.7 passage I treated above. In practical as in medical knowledge, we aim to get things right in the particular case and in a way sensitive to the specific circumstances. For that reason, we may be led to think that individualized care without regard to general principles is the most precise, since it is purely concerned with particulars. Contrary to this, Aristotle argues that expert knowledge is superior. Moreover, expert knowledge is not individualized in the sense of beginning from particulars but rather universal. Still, the expert is the person best positioned to apply that universal to any given case at hand.

Here, implicitly, Aristotle is drawing on the differences between the three components of ideal medical knowledge I discussed in §2.2.3. As I noted there, there may be kinds of highly individualized

ETHICAL EXPERIENCE IN THE *NICOMACHEAN ETHICS* 63

knowledge that enable practical success in specific cases that resemble the cognitive powers of discernment that the expert and the empiric possess, while falling short of both. In remarking that knowledge is "held to be of what is common" at the end of T6, Aristotle notes that even his opponent should grant that such an individualized grasp is not a paradigmatic case of knowledge and cannot serve as a standard relative to which expertise falls short. Because the expert's knowledge is not confined to a grasp of principles but also embraces discernment and a grasp of skills and techniques needed to achieve success in particular cases, it cannot be criticized for standing apart from the specificities on which successful care depends.

This first part of the passage deals in fairly broad terms with the contrast between individual and general kinds of knowledge and echoes aspects of Aristotle's view of practical knowledge that we saw in operation in *NE* VI.7. The remainder of the passage relates these ideas to the difference between expertise and experience:

[T7] Nevertheless, perhaps nothing prevents some one person from being educated well by someone who lacks knowledge (*anepistēmona*) but is aware of what happens to that person on given occasions thanks to experience (*empeiria*), just as some people are thought to be their own best doctors though they are of no help to another. But all the same it would seem that someone who wants to be skilled and knowledgeable, anyway, must advance to the universal and come to know it insofar as it is possible, since it is said that knowledge concerns this [sc. the universal]. Perhaps also someone who wants to make people better through discipline, whether many or few, must try to acquire legislative knowledge, since it is through laws that we become good. For not just anyone can handle well someone put in front of him, but if anyone can, it is the one who knows, as in medicine and the rest of what is governed by any sort of care and practical wisdom (*epimeleia tis kai phronēsis*). (1180b16–28)

64 ARISTOTLE'S PRACTICAL EPISTEMOLOGY

Aristotle begins this part of the passage by clarifying the scope of his claim about individualized care and success. He grants that, in the absence of expert knowledge,[16] success can nevertheless be achieved through experience or even the sort of purely individualized knowledge that falls short of experience. Still, a grasp of principles is required for a person to act in a genuinely skillful way.

How should we understand the difference between acting successfully without skill and acting as the skilled craftsman does? One possibility that may come to mind is the contrast drawn in *NE* II.4 between acting in accordance with skill and acting skillfully (1105a21 ff.). As an example of the former, Aristotle points to the case where someone accidentally hits upon the correct action (a22–23). This example may suggest a picture on which skillful action is reduced to something like intentional success, with only accidental performances—where the agent contributes little or nothing to the outcome—counting as exceptions.

A more gradated picture emerges from *NE* X.9, with the extremes of pure accident and complete skill forming a continuum.[17] For that reason, it makes better sense to think that acting skillfully is a threshold concept on the upper end of the continuum, since it is distinguished here not just from the other pole of accidental performance but also from individualized success and experience, which also involve the agent's contribution to their actions across different cases. The end of the passage offers a way of making good on this suggestion. When Aristotle says that only the expert can achieve success when presented with *any given case*, we are drawn to consider the ways that novel cases can outstrip previous familiarity by presenting features or aspects of a situation that have not

---

[16] Note, as with *eidenai* in *NE* VI.7, the use of a cognate of *epistēmē* in a narrow sense to signify expert knowledge.

[17] The other example given in *NE* II.4—of action under someone else's guidance (*allou hupothemenou*)—also points to a continuum, since even if the other agent is in some sense an initiator of the action, so is the person acting under their guidance (1105a17–26).

ETHICAL EXPERIENCE IN THE *NICOMACHEAN ETHICS*   65

been previously encountered or presenting them in combinations that present practical challenges. Moreover, patterns of experience track generalizations that are themselves defeasible. Only someone with a grasp of the underlying features—in Aristotle's terms, the causes and principles—can know what counts as a defeater to an otherwise valid principle.

As in *Metaphysics* Alpha 1, Aristotle in this passage valorizes universal knowledge because of the greater practical success it enables. In the *Metaphysics*, Aristotle goes on to argue that such knowledge is more valuable in its own right, too, but that consideration does not arise here.[18] Indeed, he goes on, in the next passage I discuss from *NE* X.9, to analyze the way that experience surpasses mere familiarity. In his practical epistemology, Aristotle tends to highlight experience more for its worth than its deficiencies with respect to understanding. In the terms I laid out at the start of this chapter, the stress is on the claims I labeled BASIC FACTS and STARTING POINTS rather than on ORDINARY KNOWLEDGE.

2.3.3 Experience as knowledge of what circumstances warrant

In the intervening lines of *NE* X.9, Aristotle complains about the difficulties that face a person who hopes to acquire an understanding of legislation and constitutions. The main difficulty is that teachers are hard to come by: those who profess to teach politics are the sophists, who lack experience; those who have the experience do not have the understanding needed to teach others (1180b28–81a9).[19] Still, experience is indispensable and, as a form of genuine

---

[18] I discuss *Metaphysics* Alpha 1–2 in some detail in Chapter 4 (§4.1).

[19] Aristotle's despair also echoes what Protagoras says in Plato's *Protagoras* about the inability of politicians to educate their sons (*Prt.* 326e–327c4). The other difficulty that Aristotle goes on to discuss is the inadequate systematicity of previous inquiries into legislation (1181b22 ff.).

66 ARISTOTLE'S PRACTICAL EPISTEMOLOGY

practical knowledge, surpasses a mere familiarity with the topic, a point Aristotle introduces just before the second key passage about experience.

> [T8] But surely experience seems to contribute not a little, since people do not become politically capable [merely] through a familiarity (*sunētheia*) with politics. Hence, those who want to have political knowledge seem to require experience in addition [sc. to such a familiarity]. Those who profess [to teach politics] among the sophists seem to be very far indeed from teaching. For as a whole they do not know what sort of thing it is or what it concerns. (1181a9–14)

We saw above that Aristotle distinguishes genuine understanding from lesser states that can, in some circumstances, enable practical success, labeling the latter with the term 'experience' indiscriminately. Here, however, he introduces more precision and distinguishes experience, which allows one to advance to understanding through reflection and inquiry, from mere familiarity. In the next part of this key passage (skipping a few lines of complaint about the sophists), we get a more precise accounting of how these states differ.

> [T9] In each area, those with experience make discriminations about products correctly, i.e., they comprehend the means and modes of bringing them about and what sorts [of products] harmonize with what sorts [of situations], while those who lack experience must be content with not failing to notice whether a product is well or badly made, as in painting. (1181a19–23)

Aristotle explains that, if someone possesses mere familiarity without experience, the best they can hope for is to make successful judgments after the fact. While such judgments may guide future deliberation in some way, the real task of acquiring

ETHICAL EXPERIENCE IN THE *NICOMACHEAN ETHICS* 67

practical knowledge lies in learning how to intervene on the basis of generalizations that link successful outcomes or actions to features that apply to the situation. These links are described metaphorically as harmony, but the word connotes a form of normativity that we may further unpack in terms of suitability or appropriateness. What the person with experience knows, then, is how to handle classes of *situations*, while the person with familiarity can only judge the outcomes.

It has sometimes been thought that experience, because it is described by expressions such as "knowledge of particulars," is itself only a grasp of particular cases. We have already seen, with respect to *NE* VI.7, how the universal-particular contrast must be understood in terms of the difference between underlying principles and perceptible available features. In this part of X.9, we get important confirmation of this point. While the highly compressed Greek corresponding to the words I translated "what sorts [of products] harmonize with what sorts [of situations] (*poia poiois sunaidei*)" requires supplementation to get its proper sense, that Aristotle is using qualitative relative pronouns to pick out *general* terms is unambiguous.

The rest of this key passage fills out the way that experience is a prerequisite for inquiry in politics, precisely because we need to understand the relationship between situations—the qualities of a particular constitution or political community, by analogy to the symptoms of a medical patient—and the kinds of actions that tend to work in them.

[T10] Laws appear to be the products of political knowledge. How, then, could one acquire legislative understanding from [studying] these, or become able to determine [which are] the best? For people don't seem to become doctors from handbooks. Yet these [handbooks] try not just to specify treatments but also to describe how people might be healed and how one ought to treat each type of case, by distinguishing conditions. These seem to

68 ARISTOTLE'S PRACTICAL EPISTEMOLOGY

> be useful for those with experience (*tois empeirois*), though useless for the ignorant (*tois anepistēmonosin*). Now perhaps, also, collections of laws and constitutions could be useful for those capable of theorizing and making determinations about what is [done] well or the opposite and what sorts of things fit what sorts [of cases]. If those who do not possess the state [of knowledge] go through these sorts of things, it wouldn't belong to them to make determinations well except by accident, though they might gain some comprehension (*eusunetōteroi ... an ginointo*) in these matters. (1181a23–b12)

Aristotle's overall point is that if we fail to see what it was that called for a given action, we can hardly make progress by studying how such actions succeed. In this way, *NE* X.9 refines the picture I began to develop of experience as practical knowledge in *NE* VI.7. There, it seemed that there were different kinds of knowledge that enabled a person of experience to act successfully, which were distinct from a grasp of principles of causes that the person with expertise or understanding has, but which were themselves not clearly related to one another. Here, we see that a grasp of how general or repeatable features of circumstances warrant specific types of action lies at the heart of experience.

2.4 Experience and technical knowledge

2.4.1 Experience and the pseudo-courage of professional soldiers

Throughout this chapter, I have defended the view that ethical experience is a form of practical knowledge, which allows the person with experience to act in accordance with the virtues, even as they fall short of full virtue and practical wisdom. I will conclude my account by taking up an important objection to this view, grounded

ETHICAL EXPERIENCE IN THE *NICOMACHEAN ETHICS* 69

in passages from Aristotle's treatment of courage in the ethical treatises.[20] In both *Nicomachean Ethics* III and *Eudemian Ethics* III, Aristotle describes a series of forms of pseudo-courage, one of which is the ability exercised by professional soldiers in war to resist the dangers they face. Specifically, these soldiers are confident in facing up to dangers that might dissuade others because they know they can succeed in these cases. The professional soldiers are not motivated by what is noble, which is why their confidence fails to be a kind of courage. Moreover, they fall short of practical success because in other cases, when they ought to stand firm, they fail to do so simply because they foresee defeat.

The objection to my account of experience as practical knowledge turns on the fact that Aristotle's describes the ability that professional soldiers have as *empeiria*. Hence, one may infer, experience is not a form of practical knowledge, that is, knowledge of how to act in accordance with virtue. For in the case of professional soldiers, experience is merely pseudo-virtuous, the sort of knowledge whose exercise mistakenly gives the impression of virtue. If this line of thinking is right, then a different account of experience—such as Jimenez's—is required, even if we want to hold on to the thought that experience plays a crucial role in the development of practical wisdom.

Let us turn now to the key section of the passage from *NE* III.8 that grounds the objection.

[T11] Experience in particular domains (*he empeiria hē kath' hekasta*)[21] is also held to be courage. For that reason, in fact,

---

[20] My discussion here is aimed at bringing my view into conversation with the view of *empeiria* in Jimenez's important paper, "*Empeiria* and Good Habits in Aristotle's Ethics," esp. §3 (375–381), on the case of courage. As I noted in note 1 above, Jimenez rejects PRACTICAL KNOWLEDGE and HABITUATED KNOWLEDGE and takes a different view of BASIC FACTS, which does not confine *empeiria* to strictly ethically relevant topics. It is this last feature of Jimenez's view that I want to draw attention to in raising this objection.

[21] An important interpretive question here is how to render *kath' hekasta*, which I have translated as "in particular domains." Jimenez, by contrast, renders the phrase "with regard to particular facts." We have already seen in *NE* VI.7 that experience is

70 ARISTOTLE'S PRACTICAL EPISTEMOLOGY

> Socrates thought courage was expert knowledge (*epistēmē*). It is professional soldiers [who have this knowledge] in battlefield situations, while other such people have this knowledge in other cases. For it seems that there are many empty dangers that feature in war, which they [the professional soldiers] comprehend best. Hence, they appear courageous because others do not know the sorts of things these [dangers] are. (III.8, 1116b3–8)

Does Aristotle here frame experience in a way inconsistent with my claim that ethical experience is practical knowledge?

I hold that he does not. For the overarching point of this passage is that professional soldiers have a share in *craft*-expertise (*tekhnē*). That point in turn implies that the soldier's experience is of a technical kind rather than the ethical *empeiria* I have been discussing, which is a precursor to practical wisdom. More specifically, the professional soldiers have a grasp of skills and techniques that enable them to act competently, the third component of expert knowledge that I identified above (§2.2.3). But these skills and techniques are relative to the specific end that their technical knowledge achieves rather than the ethical ends that are the concern of the virtues of character and practical wisdom.[22]

Independently of the specifics of this text, there are also reasons to think of this example as technical rather than ethical. First, Aristotle uses military knowledge—*stratēgikē*, which is properly the knowledge of a military leader, to which other

closely connected to knowledge of particulars, but Aristotle does not refer to experience as a kind of knowledge except in the following sentence where he mentions Socrates' contrasting view. The closer parallel is instead *NE* X.9, 1181a19, a passage I analyzed above in §2.3.3, where we find a similar phrase, *peri hekasta*, which is best translated "in each case." The flow of that passage moves from general remarks about experience to the specific case of experience in legislation, which suggests the reading of *hekasta* that I prefer, that is, as referring to specific domains rather than knowledge of particulars.

[22] Aristotle distinguishes *tekhnē* and practical wisdom in a number of different respects in *NE* VI.4–5. These differences include (i) the fact that *tekhnē* is exercised in producing, while practical wisdom is exercised in acting (VI.4, 1140a2–6); (ii) the fact

ETHICAL EXPERIENCE IN THE *NICOMACHEAN ETHICS*   71

forms of military knowledge are subordinate—as an example of a *tekhnē* in *NE* I.1, where victory is said to be its proximate end (1094a6–14).[23] What the soldiers know would be some part of this overarching craft. Second, the parallel to the discussion of courage in Plato's *Laches* offers further evidence of this point, a discussion that Aristotle perhaps has in mind in *NE* III.8 when he brings up the Socratic view of virtue as knowledge. In that dialogue, Socrates refutes the view, propounded by Laches, that courage is simply the military skill that enables some to stand firm in battle (*Laches* 190e–191e), on the basis that courage is displayed in more situations, both on and off the battlefield, than this. In Aristotle's terms, what Socrates shows is that courage is not confined to a specific domain of expertise.[24]

2.4.2 Two kinds of knowledge of particulars

The confusion about experience that arises in relation to Aristotle's discussion of the professional soldiers stems from the fact that both technical and ethical knowledge are concerned with particulars.

that the *tekhnai* brings about partial goods (*agatha kata meros*), while practical wisdom is concerned with living well in general (*to eu zēn holōs*) (VI.5, 1140a25–30); and (iii) the fact that there is virtue in the use of *tekhnē*, that is, a commendable way of using it, while there is no virtue in the use of practical wisdom but rather practical wisdom *is* a virtue (VI.5, 1140b21–25), a point Aristotle explores in greater, albeit more confusing, detail in *EE* VIII.1. Note that points (i) and (iii) flow from point (ii). Specifically, (i) and (iii) follow from the fact that living well is the aim of practical wisdom and that living well is our highest end. Here, in distinguishing the knowledge of the professional soldiers from practical knowledge, I am drawing especially on (ii), which lies at the heart of Aristotle's conception of practical (as opposed to productive) knowledge. Both practical and productive knowledge concern what is contingent, by contrast to theoretical knowledge (VI.4, 1140a1–2).

[23] Strictly speaking, military knowledge is described here as belonging among crafts or branches of knowledge (*tekhnai kai epistēmai* at 1094a7), but a remark in *NE* I.6 makes clear that military knowledge is a craft just as medicine or weaving is (1097a8–14).

[24] Again, this is the key feature of the difference between practical wisdom and *tekhnē* in *NE* VI.4–5 (see 70 fn. 22).

72 ARISTOTLE'S PRACTICAL EPISTEMOLOGY

Specifically, both the craftsperson and the virtuous person reason about how to affect things that can be otherwise (*ta endekhomena*, VI.4, 1140a1–2). The idea that experience is knowledge of particulars applies both in craft and in virtue, and given the pervasiveness of the craft analogy in the *NE* and the scattered character of Aristotle's remarks about experience, it is no surprise that interpreters have elided this distinction.

Indeed, the most prominent recent philosophical treatment of the role of experience in Aristotle's ethics—in Rosalind Hursthouse's work on practical wisdom—aims to draw attention to the "mundane" character of both experience and practical wisdom.[25] In this connection, Hursthouse encourages us to take to heart a remark of Philippa Foot's about virtue, namely, that "it is contrary to charity to fail to find out about elementary first aid."[26]

We must notice, however, that Foot's remark is negative. Someone who has not found out about elementary first aid may well be hampered in acting charitably. Still, that point hardly shows that knowing about first aid is itself knowledge of how to act charitably. Indeed, first aid is evidently a part of medical knowledge and properly belongs to professionals like paramedics, even as ordinary members of the public would do well to learn its rudiments. To see why this is, we can make use of Aristotle's thought that there is no excellence in the use of practical wisdom (and, by extension, other forms of ethical knowledge), while there is excellence in the use of craft-knowledge (*NE* VI.5, 1140b21–22). Someone who has learned elementary first aid may use it to act charitably, but they

---

[25] See esp. Hursthouse, "Practical Wisdom." See also Hursthouse, "What Does the Aristotelian *Phronimos* Know?," in *Perfecting Virtue: New Essays on Kantian Ethics and Virtue Ethics*, ed. Lawrence Jost and Julian Wuerth (Cambridge University Press, 2011), pp. 38–57.

[26] Foot, "Virtues and Vices," p. 78, quoted in Hursthouse "Practical Wisdom," 308.

ETHICAL EXPERIENCE IN THE *NICOMACHEAN ETHICS* 73

may also misuse it, for instance, by attempting to help someone who is too badly injured to be moved or by hindering the efforts of medical professionals. We make some allowances for ordinary people in these difficult circumstances, and we are inclined to credit people for trying to help. Still, judgment is needed in the use of such technical knowledge, judgment that belongs properly to practical wisdom.[27]

Could one rebut my view by arguing that it too sharply distinguishes the practical success that technical knowledge enables and practical success in the exercise of virtue? After all, Aristotle does not think that intentions alone matter to virtue. One must be able to *act* as the virtues require, and acting in this way requires the capacity to bring about certain external results. While this view of the intelligence needed for virtue is a serious one, it is not Aristotle's. There is no suggestion in his discussion of virtue and agency that ignorance of anything but ethical principles, or facts readily available to perception, is blameworthy (*NE* III.5, 1113b30–14a10). The external results needed for virtuous action, equally, are described in straightforward ways, e.g., as involving action-types that fall within the reach of most people. Virtue does depend on the social world—Aristotle comments in the *Politics* (II.5, 1263b5–14) that to abolish private property, as Socrates recommends for the guardian class in the *Republic*, would do away with generosity—but not on specialized knowledge of it.

What this helps us see is that the person who has ethical experience is not simply acquainted with bodies of knowledge that help them navigate their social world. Rather, as I have argued throughout this chapter, ethical experience is a form of practical

---

[27] See also Lorenz and Morison, "Aristotle's Empiricist Theory," who argue that the virtuous person may themselves have the relevant sort of technical knowledge but may just as well adopt the right views "by deferring to experts who have the right kind of experience with the subject-matter" (448).

knowledge, knowledge of how to act in accordance with virtue. Indeed, such experience is the analogue of practical wisdom for the learner in virtue and arises from the same good habits that have oriented such a learner toward noble ends and actions and away from shameful ones.

3

THE NATURE OF THE VIRTUES

OF THOUGHT

3.1 Practical wisdom as an exceptional achievement

3.1.1 Practical wisdom and right reasoning

As I laid out in the Introduction, the goal of the remainder of this book is to analyze *phronēsis* as an exceptional achievement that surpasses ethical experience, the body of ethical knowledge out of which *phronēsis* itself develops. Moreover, I hold that *phronēsis* surpasses ethical experience in kind and not only in degree. Key to my investigation is the notion of a virtue of thought or intellectual virtue (*arētē dianoētikē*), one of the four core features or marks of *phronēsis* identified in the Introduction. I argued in Chapter 2 that experience is sufficient for a considerable degree of practical success and, furthermore, that ethical experience should be understood as a form of practical knowledge, namely, knowledge of how to act as virtue requires. But as we learn over the course of *NE* II–VI, being able to act as virtue requires (*hōs dei*) is not the same as acting as the virtuous person does. To act as the virtuous person does, we need deliberative excellence, not merely the deliberative competence that experience supplies.[1]

---

[1] The distinction I deploy here is not the same as the one we find in *NE* II.4, between acting (merely) in accord with virtue and acting virtuously. For one, acting (merely) in accord with virtue appears to involve a lower standard, where perhaps even accidental

Aristotle's Practical Epistemology. Dhananjay Jagannathan, Oxford University Press.
© Oxford University Press 2024. DOI: 10.1093/9780197781517.003.0004

76 ARISTOTLE'S PRACTICAL EPISTEMOLOGY

Nicomachean Ethics Book VI as a whole is devoted to analyzing *phronēsis* as the virtue of thought whereby we might excellently deliberate about and choose the actions that fulfill the ends that the virtues of character supply. While Aristotle clearly provides answers to certain questions about excellence in deliberation that are left open by his preliminary account of deliberation and choice in *NE* III.1–5, he goes further by locating *phronēsis* among the other virtues of thought. No doubt, part of Aristotle's motivation is that, in ordinary language and in Platonic ethics, no clear distinction was made between *phronēsis* and *sophia*. Both words were frequently used as appellations for the intelligence needed to live a successful life.[2] Moreover, the analogies between practical and technical reasoning that pervade not only Plato's dialogues but also Aristotle's own ethical theory necessitate a discussion of how *phronēsis* is related to the crafts (*tekhnai*). Despite this range of

---

performances may count (though the chapter is less than clear about how to apply the initial analysis of skilled action, where the case of accidental performance is raised, to the case of virtue). A useful way of thinking about the higher standard involved in acting as virtue requires (as compared with acting merely in accord with virtue) is to take each of the three conditions placed on acting virtuously as *partially* met when one acts as virtue requires. In other words, in acting as virtue requires (*hōs dei*), one has not merely stumbled on a virtuous action but also chosen it with a degree of knowledge, for its own sake, and with some motivational stability, even if one has not yet met these standards in the most demanding way.

[2] Plato's usage of these terms is complex, and there is considerable variability among the dialogues. On the history of *sophia*, see David Wolfsdorf, "'Sophia' and 'Epistēmē' in the Archaic and Classical Periods," in *Knowledge in Ancient Philosophy: The Philosophy of Knowledge: A History*, vol. 1, ed. Nicholas D. Smith (Bloomsbury, 2019), 11–29, at 24. On Plato's use of *phronēsis*, see Monique Dixsaut, *Platon et la question de la pensée: études platoniciennes* (J. Vrin, 2000), "De quoi les philosophes sont-ils amoureux? Sur la phronèsis dans les dialogues de Platon," 93–119. For a comprehensive linguistic approach to Plato's epistemic vocabulary, see John Lyons, *Structural Semantics: An Analysis of Part of the Vocabulary of Plato* (Blackwell, 1963). Christopher Rowe has recently argued that even the books belonging solely to Aristotle's *Eudemian Ethics* do not show a strong contrast between *phronēsis* and *sophia* ("Sophia in the *Eudemian Ethics*" in *Investigating the Relationship between Aristotle's* Eudemian *and* Nicomachean Ethics, ed. Giulia Di Basilio [Routledge, 2022], 122–136.)

THE NATURE OF THE VIRTUES OF THOUGHT 77

topics, we can nevertheless discern a core line of argument running through the book.

Books II–V lead us to expect both that deliberative excellence is the province of *phronēsis* and that right reason or reasoning (*orthos logos*) belongs to the person of practical wisdom (the *phronimos*). Indeed, *NE* Book VI begins with a proposal to investigate right reasoning in relation to acting (VI.1) and ends with a reminder that we need *phronēsis* to discern the means to virtuous ends, the role that right reasoning plays in relation to acting (VI.12–13). For these reasons, it is tempting to represent Aristotle's overall line of argument as follows:

(1) Acting virtuously requires a grasp of right reasoning.
(2) *Phronēsis* supplies a grasp of right reasoning.
(3) Hence, acting virtuously requires having *phronēsis*.

But Aristotle's own treatment of the topic in the intervening chapters shows that the conclusion 3 does not follow, strictly, from the premises 1 and 2. For nothing in this analysis precludes our relying on someone else's *phronēsis*—or the *phronēsis* embodied in the laws of one's political community—for the right reasoning we need in order to act virtuously.[3] More formally speaking, for the conclusion to follow, we need to be assured that we must ourselves possess *phronēsis* in order to grasp right reasoning about how to achieve virtuous ends:

---

[3] For the idea that law is *phronēsis* embodied, see Chapter 2 §2.3.2. The embodiment of wisdom in the social world around us—and not only in the divine order of the cosmos—is a central difference between the Aristotelian perspective on these questions and the Platonic one, as significant as the distinction between theoretical and practical-political wisdom employed by Aristotle to make this case. The difference should not, however, be overstated. See Julia Annas, *Virtue and Law in Plato and Beyond* (Oxford University Press, 2017), for a study of the relationship between law, social practice, and cosmic reason in Plato's *Laws*.

78 ARISTOTLE'S PRACTICAL EPISTEMOLOGY

(2′) Only the possession of *phronēsis* guarantees a grasp of right reasoning.

The gap between 2 and 2′ should seem especially significant given my account of ethical experience as a form of practical knowledge. Of course, one could not really live a virtuous life in a state of dependency, in which every decision demanded some consultation of those wiser than oneself. But if, as I have argued, good habituation by itself can lead to a form of practical knowledge that is sufficient for a degree of success in choosing virtuous actions, then perhaps consultation with the wise could make up the difference.

3.1.2 Ethical experience and deliberative competence

Consider the following scenario by way of illustration of this point about ethical experience and the deliberative competence it engenders. (I use the modern virtue of charity as a point of contrast to the Aristotelian virtues of giving, namely, generosity and magnificence, but nothing turns on that choice.)

Through his upbringing and ongoing ethical development in adulthood, Lars has faced a range of situations in which being charitable is called for and has learned how he should conduct himself in them. Lars knows, for instance, that he should give generously if he can to those who are in need in his own community, so he regularly contributes to food drives organized by his workplace and to a local homeless shelter. He also looks for similar opportunities to be charitable. Audrey, a friend of Lars, learns that all of Lars's charitable activities involve local organizations, so she asks him whether he's considered contributing to OxFam or to organizations that supply anti-malaria bed nets for those who need them elsewhere in the world. Lars is torn: he feels his contributions to his community are doing tangible good, and,

THE NATURE OF THE VIRTUES OF THOUGHT   79

because he expects to remain relatively comfortable, he wants to expand his charitable giving in the future. Should he increase the amount he gives to charities he already supports in his community or start contributing to the global causes that Audrey is bringing to his attention?

Here, we have a plausible example of someone whose good upbringing has equipped them with ethical experience, relative to the specific virtue of charity. Lars genuinely knows how to be charitable and to give well in a range of circumstances. We do not need to assume, for that reason, that Lars has practical wisdom, since experience is enough for what I called deliberative competence. In other words, in circumstances that are relatively similar to those in which he had success in the past, Lars can successfully identify how to act in a way that comports with the virtue of charity.[4]

Faced with Audrey's challenge to his practices of giving, however, Lars may not be in a good position to address this problem. In particular, Lars may know that he will need to expand his current practices in order to meet the demands of charity, without knowing the best way to do so. One possible response to this problem—which I began to describe above—is to hold that the deliberative scenario that Lars faces is relatively unusual and could be addressed by consulting others. For instance, Audrey herself—or someone else Lars knows and trusts in this area—may have a fuller grasp of the demands of charity and be able to resolve the problem he faces. Lars's practices could then be modified accordingly, and his deliberative competence would expand without necessarily changing.

---

[4] It is a philosophical mistake, driven perhaps by the notion of "right action," that there is exactly one action that is simply the virtuous thing to do, at least for a very broad range of circumstances. Rosalind Hursthouse tries to recover a notion of right action from within a broadly Aristotelian framework in *On Virtue Ethics* (Oxford University Press, 1999), as does Daniel Russell in Part I of *Practical Intelligence and the Virtues* (Oxford University Press, 2009). For the contrasting view that such a synthesis of Aristotelian ethics and modern assumptions about deliberation and action is impossible, see Talbot Brewer, *The Retrieval of Ethics* (Oxford University Press, 2009).

80   ARISTOTLE'S PRACTICAL EPISTEMOLOGY

Let me briefly bring this example back to Aristotle's context. If Lars had lived in the Athens of Aristotle's time and if he had been among its wealthiest citizens, he might have faced the *leitourgia*, the practice of enforced giving or taxation by which such citizens were required to support a range of public activities, from choruses at dramatic festivals to the upkeep of the navy. Aristotle assigns giving of this kind, enforced and otherwise, to the special virtue of magnificence, though his general remarks on generosity also apply. (The special mark of magnificence is to give elegantly and grandly, which opens up an area of discretion even with an enforced expenditure.) For instance, we can imagine someone approaching the *leitourgia* with resentment as well as with pleasure in doing one's civic duty. Only the latter counts as generous or magnificent (*NE* IV.1, 1120a23–31).

The question I want to ask about ethical experience in relation to practical wisdom, then, is this: Why can't the deliberative competence that is supplied by ethical experience, plus consultation of the wise as a supplement, be adequate to the task of living well and acting virtuously? What does practical wisdom *add* that is distinctive?

3.1.3 The Independent Agency Criterion: a leading thread

Aristotle's answer to this question, as I will argue in this subsection, can be found by tracing a leading thread that runs through the argument of *NE* VI, which I will call the "Independent Agency Criterion." At one point in *NE* VI, Aristotle describes *phronēsis* as commanding or prescriptive (*epitaktikē*), a form of the term the Visitor uses in Plato's *Statesman* to describe the political wisdom by which a ruler knows how to give orders to others and structure their activities (VI.10, 1143a4–10 = **T23**, which I analyze further in the Appendix, §A.1). I will return to the specifically political

THE NATURE OF THE VIRTUES OF THOUGHT   81

resonances of Aristotle's view in Chapter 6, but in the context of the *NE* VI—or so I argue below—the word serves to indicate the fact that the person with *phronēsis* is the one we consult for ethical guidance and does not need such guidance themselves.[5] Ethical life is such that we cannot be content with ethical experience if we are to act virtuously, since we cannot simply rely on the guidance of others to make up for what experience does not cover. Only the possession of practical wisdom, which involves genuine deliberative *excellence*, supplies the needed independence from the guidance of others. That is the Independent Agency Criterion.

There are, in fact, three other places in *NE* VI where Aristotle either describes the Independent Agency Criterion explicitly or assumes it indirectly: in the opening inquiry into right reasoning and excellent thinking (VI.1–2), in the course of differentiating craft (*technē*, productive excellence) and *phronēsis* (VI.4–5), and in the concluding remarks of the book explaining how *phronēsis* and theoretical wisdom (*sophia*) are beneficial (VI.12–13). The regular recurrence of this motif or leading thread, which has not generally been noted, suggests an important dimension of unity in Aristotle's thinking about practical wisdom and the virtues of thought generally.

In the rest of this chapter, I follow this leading thread in order to show why Aristotle holds that *phronēsis* is not simply the supreme practical virtue but also at once a virtue of thought or perfection of the intellect alongside theoretical wisdom and craft-excellence. Understanding the superiority of *phronesis* to ethical experience turns on this latter point. Key features of the interpretation I defend in the rest of this book as a whole also begin to emerge when we

---

[5] This aspect of Aristotelian practical reason is taken up in scholastic philosophy in the notion of *imperium* (and its cognate verb *imperare*), which, for Aquinas, characteristically follows upon deliberate choice (*Summa Theologiae* I–II, q. 17), inasmuch as the will moves the powers of the soul. It is characteristic of the difference between the Thomistic metaphysics of action and Aristotle's that what Aristotle simply describes as an *aspect* or feature of the exercise of practical wisdom is assigned to a discrete act in the theory of Aquinas.

82 ARISTOTLE'S PRACTICAL EPISTEMOLOGY

take proper account of this point, as well as my central claim that *phronēsis* is practical understanding.[6]

3.2 Practical wisdom amidst the virtues of thought

3.2.1 Are there two overlapping inquiries in *NE* Book VI?

I will argue in the remainder of this chapter that the Independent Agency Criterion is reflected in the idea that *phronēsis* is a virtue of thought, that is, an excellence or perfection of the human intellect. In reading *NE* VI, however, it can be difficult to make out the relevance of the idea that practical wisdom is a virtue of thought to my initial question about deliberation and exercising the virtues of character.

Indeed, Aryeh Kosman has noted that, on the surface, the opening of *NE* VI presents us with two apparently distinct inquiries, one inquiry that concerns the form of right reasoning that helps us exercise the virtues of character and another inquiry that concerns the excellences that human beings are capable of because we are thinking beings.[7] Practical wisdom, of course, features centrally in each of these inquiries, but, as Kosman points out, the overall point of *NE* VI would certainly differ if we took one of these inquiries to be the primary one, and we might even begin to wonder whether there was a degree of incoherence in the book's

---

[6] We also get further support for the claim, which I discuss in more detail in relation to the problem of the "Grand End" in Chapter 5, that having *phronēsis* means grasping the human good as such and not simply the particular goods we pursue on any given occasion.

[7] Kosman, *Virtues of Thought: Essays on Plato and Aristotle* (Harvard, 2014), "Aristotle on the Virtues of Thought," 280–298.

THE NATURE OF THE VIRTUES OF THOUGHT 83

execution, perhaps due to its complex editorial history.[8] Kosman responds to this worry by arguing that, once we recognize how, in Aristotle's view, thinking itself is a species of human activity, the sharp difference between these inquiries falls away. To think well we need the virtues of thought, and practical wisdom is exercised in acting well in all the ways that human beings act, including in thinking, whether that thinking is itself directed to acting, making, or theorizing.

Kosman's view, however, cannot fully dissipate the problem from which he begins. Practical wisdom, after all, turns up in very different ways in the two inquiries he describes, either as the supreme practical virtue or as simply one of a number of coordinate virtues of thought. Even if we take thinking seriously as a human activity, thinking is neither an action nor a passion; yet, we need the virtues of character only where action and passion are concerned (as courage is needed because we feel fear and confidence and act accordingly). Crucially, there is a difference between the notions of activity (*energeia*) and action (*praxis*): not all activity involves choice, while action always proceeds on the basis of choice (VI.2, 1138b31–33).[9]

---

[8] The main question in this regard is whether the version of the book that has been transmitted to us in the manuscripts was originally part of the *Eudemian Ethics* (as its fifth book) and only later revised for inclusion in the *Nicomachean Ethics* as its sixth book. Even if there are strata of such a developmental process, a further question remains whether the revised version is argumentatively coherent.

[9] We can see the difference between the place of *energeia* and *praxis* in Aristotle's ethical theory most vividly, perhaps, by considering that perception (*aisthēsis*), too, is a fundamental mode of human activity but does not generate its own virtues apart from the virtues of character. This point about perception could be formulated as an objection against a formal thesis defended by Kosman, but I take Kosman to be not so much arguing directly for a claim about how Aristotle conceives of thinking as a human activity and represents its attendant virtues but to be evoking a sort of thought-picture within which Aristotle's various claims can seem to make sense to us and to cohere with one another. So, my worry about perception and the lack of uniquely perceptual virtues should be understood as an attempt to inaugurate a distinct thought-picture with the same aim as Kosman's of reconciling Aristotle's claims with each other (and, perhaps also, reconciling ourselves to them).

84 ARISTOTLE'S PRACTICAL EPISTEMOLOGY

3.2.2 Practical and theoretical wisdom

Interestingly, Aristotle himself takes up a version of the problem Kosman describes in a passage that Kosman does not discuss, which comes in the concluding lines of *NE* VI. This discussion of practical and theoretical wisdom is a fitting place to start, since one of my aims is to consider the structure and purpose of Book VI as a whole:

> [**T12**] With all that said, it [sc. practical wisdom] still is not in charge of theoretical wisdom (*sophia*) nor of the better part [of the intellect], just as medicine is not in charge of health. For the former does not employ the latter but looks to how it may arise. Hence, the former directs for the latter's sake but does not direct it. Further, it is as if someone were to say that political expertise rules the gods because it directs every matter in the city. (*NE* VI.13, 1145a6–11)

This short passage at the end of a long discussion of the relationship between practical wisdom and the virtues of character may seem to be an afterthought. If I am right about the Independent Agency Criterion as a central motif, however, the passage actually connects that long discussion of virtue of character to an important theme of the whole book, which Aristotle also touches on earlier in the same stretch of argument in VI.12 (a text I discuss in detail below). At any rate, this passage focuses on the relationship between *phronēsis* and *sophia*, the two most exalted virtues of thought. Hence, it ought to shed some light on the place of *phronēsis* among the virtues of thought.

As a first observation, let us note that Aristotle's characterization of the relationship between *phronēsis* and *sophia* in this passage is teleological. The central point of the passage is that, while practical wisdom is prescriptive knowledge, it does not give orders *to* theoretical wisdom; rather practical wisdom provides for theoretical

THE NATURE OF THE VIRTUES OF THOUGHT   85

wisdom's being brought about, presumably by bringing about the conditions of leisure that theoretical wisdom's acquisition and exercise require.[10] The passage therefore cautions us against conflating two ways in which something can be superior teleologically. One way of being superior is by giving instructions, as a superior craft gives instructions to a subordinate craft; this relationship always holds between pursuits and other pursuits controlled by the former. Another way of being superior is by being of higher value and thereby conferring value to the corresponding pursuit; this relationship always holds between a good and the pursuit of that good.[11]

Each of these kinds of teleological superiority also features in the opening argument of the *Nicomachean Ethics* (I.1-2), which can in turn help us understand the point Aristotle is making in *NE* VI. In that argument, Aristotle argues that there are chains of teleological dependence connecting higher and lower pursuits (the first kind of superiority I noted above) on the grounds that we often pursue goods for the sake of further goods (the second kind of superiority). Aristotle's examples of such chains in *NE* I.1 can be illuminated counterfactually, as follows. For example, if bridles had no use, making a bridle might be a sort of self-contained activity pursued for its own sake; but as things stand, bridle making is governed by the practice of horse riding, which sets the terms for the activity of bridle making. Goods like bridles are the goals of one kind of activity (the activity of bridle making) and employed

[10] The point about leisure is made in the parallel discussion from the *Magna Moralia* (A.34, 1198b12–20), which offers an analogy between *phronēsis* and the steward in the household, who manages everything so that the master has the requisite leisure. The analogy is imperfect, since *phronēsis* itself is among the things one can exercise in a leisurely way, especially in the political arena.

[11] Gabriel Richardson Lear develops a different distinction in the ways that higher pursuits stand with respect to lower pursuits: by supplying the criteria for their success and by governing the conditions of their exercise. See *Happy Lives and the Highest Good* (Princeton University Press, 2004), 17–19. By "giving instructions" I mean to include both these dimensions of being a higher end. See also Susan Sauvé Meyer, "Living for the Sake of an Ultimate End," in *Aristotle's* Nicomachean Ethics: *A Critical Guide*, ed. Jon Miller (Cambridge University Press, 2011), 47–65, at 50–51.

86 ARISTOTLE'S PRACTICAL EPISTEMOLOGY

instrumentally as part of a distinct activity (the activity of horse riding). Aristotle stresses that such intermediate goods are less valuable than the goods of the higher activity that employs them. Likewise, the expertise or capacity that governs this higher activity gives instructions to the expertise or capacity that governs the lower one. But these two kinds of subordination, though related in this way, are distinct.

Turning back to *NE* VI, we may again illustrate Aristotle's point about the relationship between practical and theoretical wisdom (and their respective exercises) counterfactually. Suppose that the only kinds of rational activity were productive and practical activity (i.e., activities of making and doing, in the narrow sense). We know, from the argument in *NE* I.1–2, that chains of productive activity must be governed, ultimately, by some activity that is valuable for its own sake. If the only candidate activity that is valuable for its own sake is practical activity, then the expertise or capacity that governs practical activity (which Aristotle tells us in *NE* I.2 is political expertise or wisdom, 1094a26–b7) will both bring about that activity when exercised and aim at the manifestations of that activity. But on Aristotle's view, the counterfactual assumption fails to hold good. While human life is a life of practical rationality (*NE* I.7, 1098a3–4), the highest good turns out to be the exercise of theoretical and not practical or political wisdom. Hence, we get the distinction in *NE* VI.13 between prescriptive knowledge itself (*phronēsis*) and the expertise or knowledge whose exercise it aims to bring about (*sophia*).[12]

---

[12] A great deal of confusion over the structure of Aristotle's ethical theory may be resolved by attending to these claims about practical and theoretical activity. In particular, the view of happiness and its different forms in Book X.6–8 can easily be seen as fitting with the picture of activity and excellence being developed in this passage of Book VI and its context.

3.2.3 The choice-worthiness of exercising phronēsis

How does Aristotle's teleological conception of rational activity shed light on the place of *phronēsis* among the virtues of thought? As I will argue in the rest of this chapter, the fulcrum between the two apparently distinct inquiries in *NE* VI is not, as Kosman holds, the notion of thinking as a human activity but rather truth as the goal of the intellectual soul. First, however, we must appreciate the precise way in which *phronēsis* and its exercise in practical reasoning are choice-worthy; that is what I discuss in this subsection.

We have already seen that *phronēsis* is the most authoritative kind of knowledge, even if it is not itself the most valuable. The image of the steward that the author of the *Magna Moralia* uses to illustrate this idea[13] might lead to us to think (wrongly) that the exercise of *phronēsis* is not intrinsically choice-worthy, as would be the case if there were no real difference between practical and productive thought.[14] The exercise of *phronēsis* may not itself be of supreme value compared to theoretical activity, but both *phronēsis* as a state of soul and its exercise in practical reasoning are choice-worthy, as Aristotle argues in a passage that I discuss immediately below. Consideration of this further point about the teleology of the virtues of thought will lead us to the role of truth as the goal of the intellectual soul and each of its parts.

The passage in question, which spans *NE* VI.12–13 and to which **T12** above is a coda, treats the utility of *phronēsis* and clearly illustrates the Independent Agency Criterion. At the outset of *NE* VI.12, Aristotle asks, on behalf of an objector, why we need to have *phronēsis*, given that in other domains it is enough to have a valued state (e.g., health) and not also the knowledge that produces this state (e.g., medicine):

---

[13] See 85, fn. 10.
[14] To borrow a term from an Aristotelian thinker, if there were no such difference, practical activity would always be alienated.

88 ARISTOTLE'S PRACTICAL EPISTEMOLOGY

> [T13] One may raise as a puzzle whether they [theoretical and practical wisdom] are useful. . . . If, in fact, practical wisdom is concerned with what is right and noble and good for a human being, and doing these is characteristic of a good man, we won't be made more capable of action by having knowledge (*tōi eidenai*) of these matters, granted that the virtues are states. In the same way, we are not [made more capable] in the case of [having knowledge of] what is healthy and what [in general] is in a good condition, which are attributed not by doing but on the basis of the state one is in, since we are no more capable of action by possessing medical knowledge and knowledge of physical training. (*NE* VI.12, 1143b18–28)

The answer Aristotle gives to this question comes in two stages. First, he points out that, as the excellence of one part of the intellectual soul, *phronēsis* is worth having, full stop (1144a1–3). In a second stage, Aristotle refers us to his earlier discussion of character virtue and notes that *phronēsis* supplies right reasoning about how we are to act, which is needed to exercise the character virtues (1144a6–22): in other words, just and courageous actions require the guidance of practical wisdom. We are well-prepared for this answer by *NE* II, though Aristotle makes it more explicit here that the special function of *phronēsis* is determining what actions will promote a given virtuous goal (1144a7–9; 20–22). This point, in turn, rests on the argument earlier in *NE* VI.9 that *phronēsis* involves excellence in deliberation, *euboulia* (1142b16–33), and, hence, on his claim, developed in *NE* III.2–4, that deliberation is always of what promotes some goal and not of the goal itself.

The contrast between Aristotle's view of the ethical case and the medical analogy used by the objector in **T13** is instructive. In the case of medicine or training, what is needed for bodily health is, generally speaking, occasional interventions and a regimen. We do need to be prudent and thoughtful in our concern for our physical well-being, and it is even part of the character virtue of moderation

THE NATURE OF THE VIRTUES OF THOUGHT   89

(*sophrosunē*) to have the right regard for health in relation to our appetites (*NE* III.11, 1119a11–20). Still, what is *valuable* in the case of health and medicine is the outcome, and if we could have bodily health without any serious intervention, we would obviously prefer it. Perhaps there are even some people who are naturally healthy in this way.

Because *phronēsis* is devoted to bringing about something distinct from *phronēsis* itself, namely, success in acting (*eupraxia*), it is easy to suppose that we would have the same preference for outcome over means when it came to action, too.[15] But the right analogue to health in the case of ethics is not some kind of internal harmony of the soul that, but for interference from the world, could endure over time.[16] The relevant sort of end or outcome is an *entire life of action and activity*, in whose description *phronēsis* and the virtues of character alike cannot be omitted. We engage in healthy actions, like taking appropriate exercise or pursuing a certain regimen, because they promote and preserve our health. We act well because it is in acting well that our happiness lies.[17] Hence, the fact that we need *phronēsis* in order to choose the relevant means to virtuous goals is not brought up to defend *phronēsis* on separate,

---

[15] For *eupraxia* as the aim of action that *phronēsis* aims to bring about, see VI.5, 1140b7; for such success as the aim of practical (goal-directed) thought as such, see VI.2, 1139a35–b4.

[16] It is interesting to consider whether in these chapters (*NE* VI.12–13), Aristotle is engaging not only with the Socratic-Platonic idea of virtue as knowledge (explicitly mentioned at VI.13, 1144b28–30) but also with the Socratic-Platonic idea of virtue as psychic health (see, e.g., *Chrm.* 157a–b). Perhaps the objector envisioned at the start of *NE* VI.12 is someone who holds—or at least is attracted to—such a conception of virtue.

[17] To forestall an obvious worry about this way of talking, I wish to clarify that I am speaking of the teleological relationships of value, not the motives of any given person. Healthy actions are valuable because they conduce to health. We might instruct someone to perform healthy actions for the sake of health, even though they do not themselves know this fact. (Consider getting a child to eat healthily as a matter of habituation; at an early stage, no explicit mention of the specific end of health may be made.) They would be acting *because* their actions conduce to the end of health without awareness of this end. The value of exercising *phronēsis* depends (in part) on happiness being an end for human beings, even if one's own (or another's) happiness is not the proximate goal aimed at by the deliberator on that occasion. It is a further question whether there is a tension between these ways of looking at one's own action.

90 ARISTOTLE'S PRACTICAL EPISTEMOLOGY

instrumental, grounds from Aristotle's defense of it as choice-worthy all by itself. These defenses are in fact two stages in the unfolding of a single picture of the best human life as one governed by *phronēsis* that goes on to occupy *NE* VI.12–13.

We can now turn back to the first stage in Aristotle's response to the objection in *NE* VI.12, where he establishes that both *phronēsis* and *sophia* are choice-worthy: "First, we should say that these [states, *phronēsis* and *sophia*] are, of necessity, worth choosing just for themselves, since they are excellences (*aretas*), each of one of the two parts [of the reasoning part of the soul], even if neither of them has any results" (VI.12, 1144a1–3). Here, Aristotle is drawing on the view, first introduced in VI.2, that there are two fundamental modes of thinking, each governed by its respective excellence: thinking about contingent things, over which *phronēsis* is supreme, and thinking about things whose principles are eternal, over which *sophia* is supreme (VI.2, 1139a6–17). We should take note that this view implies that *phronēsis* is superior to other excellences that concern contingent things, a superiority that is borne out in Aristotle's remarks about craft (VI.4–5) as well as his reflections on the other excellences of practical thought, such as comprehension (*sunesis*) and judgment (*gnōmē*), in VI.10–11 (1142b34–43a32).[18]

Since all human beings must choose and act thoughtfully, and *phronēsis* is indispensable to thinking well about choice and action, it is evident that we all stand in need of *phronēsis* in our lives. Indeed, even if we were not in a position to act, it would be better for us to have *phronēsis* than to lack it or to be positively foolish. It is admirable to have this quality of soul, just as it is admirable to have the other excellences (and, correlatively, it is blameworthy to lack it). But our reason for admiring the practically wise person depends

---

[18] In a related way, Aristotle is committed to the superiority of *sophia* over scientific knowledge (*epistēmē*) and intellectual intuition (*nous*), which it comprises.

THE NATURE OF THE VIRTUES OF THOUGHT 91

on our seeing *phronēsis* as not simply one excellence among many but as one that is central to living a good human life.

The reason for the centrality of *phronēsis* in our lives is further clarified by Aristotle's remarks on the relationship between *phronēsis* and craft (*tekhnē*) in VI.4–5. Each craft is devoted to a single human good, whether as mundane as horse riding or as apparently all-encompassing as health; *phronēsis*, by contrast, is devoted to bringing about what is good for human beings as such (VI.5, 1140a25–28).[19] The overarching character of the good pursued by *phronēsis* is, of course, due to its being directive of other human activities. We need *phronēsis*, at minimum, to organize our other activities in light of this overarching or highest good. Indeed, one of the key problems to which *phronēsis* addresses itself is the proper pursuit of activities subordinate to the highest good.

We can put the point even more generally. If our basic practical stance in life were limited to considering only the local and temporally limited context in which we find ourselves, the skills and crafts (*tekhnai*) might be enough for pursuing our particular goals in any given context. (Recall the deflationist view of practical reason that I discussed in Chapter 1, which rests on the thought that we cannot reason well about the future, a point that could be reframed in terms of short- and long-term pursuits.) But as soon as our practical gaze, as it were, extends beyond the here and now, we stand in need of some way of organizing our pursuits with respect to one another and to the highest good that these pursuits either constitute or subserve.

Let me now take stock of what I have argued in the last two subsections. In the previous section (§3.2.2), I showed that the teleological relationship between practical and theoretical wisdom can illuminate the precise way in which practical wisdom is central to human life: practical wisdom is authoritative or prescriptive knowledge, which is consistent with its exercise not being the

---

[19] See 70 fn. 22.

92 ARISTOTLE'S PRACTICAL EPISTEMOLOGY

highest good for human beings. Aristotle reserves the latter status for the exercise of theoretical wisdom in contemplating eternal realities whose value surpasses our own and the goods of human life generally (VI.7, 1141a33–b3). In this section (§3.2.3), I have been arguing that we should not take Aristotle's view of the superiority of theoretical wisdom to imply that *phronēsis* might somehow be dispensable. Not only is *phronēsis* choice-worthy all by itself, so are its exercises, which are part of a well-lived human life, a life that must be organized by practical reason.

In the next part of this chapter, I will complete my response to Kosman's puzzle about the two ways that *phronēsis* seems to turn up in Aristotle's theory by showing how the idea of a virtue of thought centers on the notion of truth. It is the fact that *phronēsis* realizes practical truth that sets it apart from other kinds of knowledge of how to act (or knowledge of contingent matters generally) that we might have. Moreover, to grasp practical truth is not to grasp the truth of what we should do piecemeal, one practical belief at a time, but to grasp it in a comprehensive way, on the basis of one's understanding of the human good.

3.3 Virtues of thought and the possession of truth

3.3.1 The catalog of the virtues of thought

In beginning to explore the question of what right reasoning might be in relation to virtuous action, Aristotle identifies practical wisdom (*phronēsis*) and theoretical wisdom (*sophia*), respectively, as the chief virtues of thought, because it is by them that "each [of the two intellective parts of the soul] most of all achieves the truth" (VI.2, 1139b12–13). The relevant sort of truth, however, is different in the two cases. In a fascinating and difficult text leading up to this declaration, we learn that *phronēsis* aims at practical truth, the sort of truth exemplified in a virtuous choice that is the result of

THE NATURE OF THE VIRTUES OF THOUGHT 93

both correct desire and thinking that is in harmony with this desire (VI.2, 1139a21–31). As Aristotle goes on to say, theoretical wisdom, on the other hand, like its elements scientific knowledge (*epistēmē*) and intellectual intuition (*nous*), hits on the truth about what cannot be otherwise, the necessary and eternal verities studied by mathematics and the sciences (VI.3, 1139b18–24; VI.6, 1140b31–41a-8; VI.7, 1141a17–20).

Craft (*tekhnē*), too, is a state that hits on the truth, completing a list of five such states (VI.3, 1139b14–18), but we are not told what sort of truth, even in the later, more detailed discussion of craft (VI.4, 1140a6–23). It cannot be practical truth, since craft-production does not depend on correct desires. Nor can it be the sort of truth that theoretical wisdom concerns, since, like actions, productions concern what is contingent. In light of the basic two-fold division of the intellectual soul, it seems plausible that craft, while it achieves whatever truth there is to be had in the sphere of making, is subordinate to practical wisdom and the truth it achieves. In the same way, scientific knowledge is subordinate to theoretical wisdom because the latter state requires a grasp of first principles that ordinary demonstration-based scientific knowledge cannot achieve (VI.6, 1140b31–35; VI.7, 1141a17–20).[20]

These complications about what kinds of truth there are may, for my present purpose, be set aside. Aristotle's goal in highlighting these five states by which we achieve the truth is to demonstrate the special connection between truth as a goal of the intellectual soul and the virtues of thought. Truth as a goal is different from the truth that particular mental states might embody. In possessing a true belief, we may avoid falsity, but we do not achieve the goal

---

[20] Note that Aristotle is using *epistēme* in *NE* VI.3 to pick out demonstrative scientific knowledge alone rather than more casual uses that might include less precise forms of knowledge and a broader use that includes non-demonstrative scientific knowledge that turns up in the *Posterior Analytics*. See Zeev Perelmuter, "Nous and Two Kinds of *Epistêmê* in Aristotle's *Posterior Analytics*," *Phronesis* 55, no. 3 (2010): 228–254, on the relationship between such non-demonstrative knowledge and the indemonstrable grasp of principles that is *nous*.

94 ARISTOTLE'S PRACTICAL EPISTEMOLOGY

of the intellectual soul, an achievement Aristotle describes using the verbal form *alētheuein*, which I therefore translate "achieve the truth."[21] An important feature of states by which we achieve the truth is that their deliverances are never false. But it seems conceivable that we could have a stable true belief about something unchanging. Hence, Aristotle's point must be taken to have modal force: by these five states, he holds, it is impossible that we fail to achieve the truth, though we may, of course, fail to exercise them and fall short of that achievement.

Practical wisdom, then, earns its place among the virtues of thought because its deliverances exhibit practical truth. I will now argue for the stronger claim that practical truth cannot be achieved without practical wisdom.

3.3.2 Practical truth and virtuous choice

The intricate passage in which Aristotle introduces the notion of practical truth has been the subject of considerable dispute and discussion.[22] Commentators on practical truth have not tended to dwell on the passage's argumentative context, but, as I will show, this context helps narrow down the most plausible interpretation.

The question Aristotle raises just before the passage on practical truth is simple if somewhat opaque: What faculty controls or is the principle of action? Three possibilities are mentioned: thought,

---

[21] It would not make sense to translate "be true," since the subject of the verb is the thinker, not the state they are in.

[22] A useful analysis of the space of possible views is given by Sarah Broadie, "Practical Truth in Aristotle," *American Catholic Philosophical Quarterly* 90 (2016): 281–298. My view belongs to Type C in Broadie's taxonomy. Christiana Olfert in *Aristotle on Practical Truth* (Oxford University Press, 2017) defends a more mundane conception of practical truth than the one I advocate here. A similar view, which also holds that practical truth is the mundane truth of a certain sort of practical judgment, can be found in Michael Pakaluk, "The Great Question of Practical Truth," *Acta Philosophica* 19 (2010): 145–162. My analysis in this section draws on my essay "Right Reason and Practical Truth," in *Practical Reason, Knowledge, and Truth: Essays on Aristotelian Themes*, ed. Christopher Frey and Jennifer Frey (Oxford University Press, forthcoming).

THE NATURE OF THE VIRTUES OF THOUGHT   95

desire, and perception (VI.2, 1139a17–19). Perception is ruled out quickly as a principle of action on the grounds that it is shared by non-rational animals (1139a19–22). Yet, we might naturally think, perception is required for the sort of deliberate action Aristotle has in mind. Consideration of that fact can help us see what Aristotle means to pick out by the notion of a "principle of action" (*arkhē praxeōs*, 1139a19): for a faculty to be such a principle is for the quality of its exercise to determine whether action is successful or not, that is, whether it is good or bad.[23] While we need perception in order to act, we do not act well *in virtue of*, say, keenness of sight or acuity of hearing.

With this framing in mind, we can now appreciate that Aristotle's remarks about practical truth come in the course of his arguing that thought and desire are joint principles of action, with neither having priority over the other. This claim depends on the more fundamental idea that practical thought is, essentially, thought that aims at bringing about a desired goal in action (VI.2, 1139a35–36). We can, of course, entertain possibilities for acting that we cannot ourselves bring about, but in doing so, our thinking is not practical in the strong sense, though it concerns practical matters. In other words, the special teleology of practical intellect means that desire cannot be left out of a proper account of its operation. This characterization is an important advance over the picture in Aristotle's psychological works, where thought and desire feature as apparently independent levers on action.[24] Importantly, desire in this passage of *NE* VI must refer to a desire for *ends*, what Aristotle elsewhere calls wish (*boulēsis*), not the desiderative aspect of choice itself.

Let us now consider the practical truth passage itself:

---

[23] Important confirmation of this interpretation comes from Aristotle's talk of the intellectual faculties achieving their goal or having success (*to eu*, literally "the well," i.e., "the doing well") in the practical truth passage itself (VI.2, 1139a27–31).

[24] See, e.g., *De Anima* III.10 and *De Motu Animalium* 7.

96 ARISTOTLE'S PRACTICAL EPISTEMOLOGY

> [T14] Character-virtue is a state issuing in choice and choice
> (*prohairesis*) is a deliberative desire. Hence, it must follow that
> reason (*logos*) be true and desire be correct for the choice to be
> worthy, and the former affirms the same things that the latter
> pursues. This, then, is truth and desire of a practical sort. In the-
> oretical thinking but not in practical or productive thinking, suc-
> cess and failure are [mere] truth and falsity, since this [hitting on
> the truth] is the task of every intellectual faculty. But of what is
> practical and intellectual, success is truth that stands in agree-
> ment with correct desire. Now, choice is the principle of action—
> as the source of motion not the goal—and the principles of choice
> are desire and goal-directed reason. (VI.2, 1139a22–33)

We learn in **T14** that practical truth is exemplified in virtuous choice.
Choice (*prohairesis*), for Aristotle, has a dual character and can be
understood both as desiderative thought (insofar as it gives the form
to the actions we choose) and thinking desire (insofar as it brings
these actions about). Virtuous choice, specifically, is shaped by a wish
for noble ends and expresses wise deliberative thinking—here ellip-
tically referred to simply as reason (*logos*), as it is in the definition of
character-virtue in *NE* II.6, 1106b36–1107a2—about how to achieve
these ends. The affirmation of practical reason that the text speaks of,
then, would be that a given action is an apt way to fulfill a given virtuous end that is wished for (i.e., what desire "pursues").

Note that desire and thought are not principles of action as independent constituents of choice. Rather, desire in the form of wish
and thought in the form of deliberative thinking converge as principles of a single hybrid state of choice, which in turn controls action.
That is why there is a distinct form of truth that practical intellect
can achieve. We should not think that deliberative thinking could
have correctness independently of virtuous wishes, nor is this correctness inherited from a prior correctness of desire.[25] Indeed, we

---

[25] I return to the topic of correctness in deliberation when I discuss Aristotle's treatment of deliberative excellence (*euboulia*) in Chapter 5 (§5.1.2).

THE NATURE OF THE VIRTUES OF THOUGHT   97

might say that the whole practical orientation of the virtuous and wise person puts them in a position to achieve practical truth.

An important consequence of this reading of T14 is that the achievement of practical truth, since it depends on virtuous wishes and wise deliberation, is the mark of the practically wise person. Someone who falls short of practical wisdom may form similar practical judgments to the practically wise person and thereby act as virtue requires. But just as scientific understanding cannot be reduced to a set of true beliefs but rather consists in the power to demonstrate theorems from first principles, practical wisdom, too, cannot simply be a composite of practical judgments to act as the virtues of character require. Rather, practical wisdom rests on the ability to reason well on the basis of an understanding of the human good to the virtuous choices that display practical truth, in which a harmony of thought and desire is achieved. That ability to reason well is what is denominated by the term "right reason" or "right reasoning" (*orthos logos*), though, plausibly, this phrase is also sometimes used by Aristotle to pick out the exercises of this ability on a given occasion.[26]

3.3.3 Practical wisdom and ethical experience

I have argued, in §3.3.1 and §3.3.2 above, that practical wisdom is marked out, as a virtue of thought, as that state by which we are able to achieve practical truth, which is the goal of the part of our intellectual soul that deals with contingent things. The idea of practical truth as the goal of this part of the soul helps us see why practical wisdom is superior to other states that help us act well, including

---

[26] Cf. Jessica Moss, "Right Reason in Plato and Aristotle: on the Meaning of *Logos*," *Phronesis* 59 (2014): 181–230, who argues that the term instead picks out the explanatory accounts that are grasped on particular occasions in the exercise of practical wisdom.

98 ARISTOTLE'S PRACTICAL EPISTEMOLOGY

ethical experience. It is not enough to be able to act as virtue requires, even in a wide range of situations, as someone with considerable ethical experience might be able to do. The reason is that a well-lived human life is a life of practical reason—not just a life that is *improved* by individual exercises of practical reason (which is trivially true of every adult human life), but a life that is *shaped and guided* by the successful employment of practical reason. Only such a life allows for the achievement of practical truth, which stems from a grasp both of the virtuous goals that are the principles of our actions and of the situations in which we find ourselves.

Moreover, as I argued earlier in this chapter, practical wisdom is prescriptive or authoritative knowledge, the knowledge we need to conduct this life ourselves. Because of the special difficulties of practical reasoning and ethical life, we cannot succeed by relying on others. Even an abundance of ethical experience would leave us in a state of dependence. It is essential to consider the special teleology of both the practical intellect as a whole—with its pursuit of practical truth—and practical wisdom as its chief perfection, by which we aim to bring about the goal of action itself, success in acting (*eupraxia*). Success in acting is not a matter merely of choosing the right action or hitting the mark on a given occasion but doing so in the sustained way that requires us to have practical wisdom and the virtues of character. Indeed, with this analysis, we can see how Aristotle's theory of practical intellect corresponds to his theory of the virtues of character and their exercise, especially the stability condition described in *NE* II.4.

These arguments are, admittedly, schematic. They do not provide a precise analysis of what the practically wise person knows that the person with ethical experience fails to know, which I take to be the same as what Aristotle labels "knowledge of universals" in the passage of *NE* VI.7 that I analyzed in Chapter 2 (**T5**). I will turn to this topic over the next two chapters, first by arguing that we should not identify practical wisdom or ethical knowledge of universals with scientific knowledge (in Chapter 4) and then by

THE NATURE OF THE VIRTUES OF THOUGHT   99

explaining how an understanding of the characteristic goals of the character-virtues and their place in human life (and the *polis*) characterizes the practically wise person (in Chapter 5). For now, let me conclude my analysis by showing how my teleological approach to practical intellect and practical wisdom can resolve Kosman's puzzle.

To recall the core thesis of this book, *phronēsis* is practical understanding, that is, intellectual mastery of the domain of ethical action (described in *NE* I.4 as "the just, the noble, and the political," 1095b4–6). It is only when we have practical wisdom that we can be said to have right reason or reasoning (*orthos logos*) in this sphere. Kosman's worry about the unity of Book VI is that practical wisdom seems to be described not just as right reason relative to ethical action but also as a perfection of the intellect, topics that seem to belong to distinct inquiries. I have bridged these distinct roles for *phronēsis* in the argument of *Nicomachean Ethics* Book VI with the notion of practical truth. As the kinds of creatures we are, we are constituted to reason about contingent things and for that reason we strive for practical truth. But truth as a goal of the practical intellect reflects what practical reasoning is *for*, by contrast to the theoretical intellect. This purpose is nothing other than choosing the actions we ought to do and making these choices well. To choose in this way requires an understanding of the goals that are desired and sought by a virtuous person and not only the means they take to advance those goals.

There is another, perhaps more perspicuous way of putting the same point. It is the special role of choice in human life, with its connection to individual actions (as the reasoned outcome of deliberation) and to our overall goals (as an expression of what we wish for), that explains the apparent duality of *phronēsis* in the argument identified by Kosman. Because choice is always of particular actions (and because *phronēsis* is a state issuing in the reasoning that shapes choice), *phronēsis* itself is right reason in the sphere of actions. Because choice is always in the service of our overall goals in life, equally, choice depends on *phronēsis* as a state of intellectual mastery, that is, as practical understanding.

These dualities can, more generally, be dissolved when we see that a life of practical reason does not consist of a set of unstructured or independent actions. If it did, then ethical experience might accumulate in such a way that we could have a wide-ranging grasp of the extraordinary variety of situations we might find ourselves in and the appropriate actions for them. But we need practical reason to organize our actions in relation to one another and in service of the goals we ought to pursue. When it comes to these goals, Aristotle's conviction is that there is a subject matter there to be known systematically, which is human life itself from a practical point of view. Because such practical understanding organizes our pursuits (as prescriptive knowledge), we should aspire to have it, even as the vast majority of people depend instead on others and on the wisdom embodied in the laws. That is the force of the Independent Agency Criterion. In fact, one might even say that there is a Kantian strain in Aristotle's thought, which emphasizes that learning to employ our own reason is a practical imperative for us as human beings.

4

PRACTICAL UNDERSTANDING AND

ETHICAL SCIENCE

4.1 The superiority of understanding

In this chapter, I show that the idea that *phronēsis* is practical understanding need not—and should not—commit us to thinking that it is scientific in character or partly consists of scientific knowledge (*epistēmē*), a view I label "intellectualism." The argument of this chapter is, therefore, preliminary to my positive argument in Chapter 5, that the practically wise person's grasp of principles is an understanding of the goals characteristic of the virtues of character, on the basis of which they are able to choose and act in line with these virtues. In this section (§4.1), I offer a schematic argument against the intellectualist position and clarify that my dispute with the intellectualist is not merely terminological. I then (in §4.2) explain how Aristotle's conception of practical reasoning provides decisive arguments against the most straightforward version of the intellectualist position before arguing against more moderate intellectualist positions that hold that ethics is an inexact or stochastic science (in §4.3).

Recall that in Chapter 3, I argued that our starting point for appreciating how practical wisdom goes beyond ordinary ethical knowledge must be Aristotle's method, in *Nicomachean Ethics* Book VI, of locating *phronēsis* among the virtues of thought. Since I have emphasized that practical wisdom is a virtue of thought, my view of practical wisdom in Aristotle may seem to have affinities with intellectualism. In particular, my analysis of *phronēsis* as practical understanding means I accept that Aristotle's analogies

Aristotle's Practical Epistemology. Dhananjay Jagannathan, Oxford University Press.
© Oxford University Press 2024. DOI: 10.1093/9780197781517.003.0005

102   ARISTOTLE'S PRACTICAL EPISTEMOLOGY

between *phronēsis* in the domain of practice and theoretical wisdom (*sophia*) and craft (*tekhnē*) in the domains of theory and production are substantive, insofar as all three states turn out to involve knowledge of causes or explanations and, for that reason, count as forms of understanding. All the same, I have claimed that my interpretation does *not* entail that there is a theoretical or scientific aspect to *phronēsis*.

As a result, the intellectualist interpreter might well object that my only dispute with their view is terminological. One line of argument would run as follows.[1] An intellectualist such as Reeve holds, as I do, that the person of practical wisdom is in the best intellectual condition with respect to ethical matters. Moreover, given what Aristotle thinks about the virtues of thought, this knowledge involves a grasp of principles or causes, at least as far as its "universal" or situation-independent aspect is considered.[2] Since Aristotle also says that *epistēmē*, scientific knowledge, is the most precise sort of knowledge there is to have and that it is characterized by its universal and explanatory character, it would be strange—so the intellectualist argues—if he then denied that the practically wise person had any such knowledge.

We can represent this line of argument as follows:

P1. Universal and explanatory knowledge is scientific.

P2. Ethical knowledge is, at least partly, universal and explanatory.

Hence, there exists at least some scientific knowledge in ethics.

---

[1] I base my remarks in this paragraph on the view defended in C. D. C. Reeve's *Practices of Reason* (Clarendon Press, 1992), Chapter 1, "Demonstration and Dialectic," 7–66. The line of reasoning I present reflects the first two of three arguments Reeve presents for there being unconditional scientific knowledge (*epistēmē haplōs*) in ethics (see esp. Reeve, 24–26).

[2] In Chapter 5, I will argue that the "universal" knowledge of the *phronimos* is knowledge of the goals that the virtues are for (e.g., as equality among the citizens of a community is a goal for justice) and that virtuous actions characteristically bring about or promote.

PRACTICAL UNDERSTANDING AND ETHICAL SCIENCE   103

My response to the intellectualist is this: the major premise of this argument P1 is not well-founded and should be rejected. While it is true that, for Aristotle, all fundamental scientific knowledge is universal and explanatory, the converse is not true.

The underlying reason for this disparity among the different kinds of understanding is Aristotle's teleological conception of understanding and its varieties. What makes the scientific knower superior to others is that they not only grasp a given scientific claim but also are able to *demonstrate* it on the basis of fundamental explanatory principles. Indeed, it is really the grasp of these fundamental principles, the axioms and hypotheses of a scientific discipline, that marks the scientific knower. Demonstration exhibits this scientific understanding on particular occasions.[3] In the domain of action, by contrast, excellence is a matter of *acting well*, not of demonstrating.[4] (Whether or not demonstration of ethical claims is possible is beside the present point, though I will return to this question later in this chapter.) While one cannot act well without the intellectual excellence of practical wisdom guiding the deliberation that leads to the action, the excellence is manifested in the actions, not in the underlying knowledge that helped bring it

---

[3] I speak here of demonstrating rather than contemplating since Aristotle has more to say about the former than the latter, but what I say below could equally be said of contemplation as the exercise of theoretical wisdom. See Matthew Walker, *Aristotle on the Uses of Contemplation* (Cambridge University Press, 2018) for a defense of the idea that contemplation is useful in the life of rational animals, which would give it a different teleological role than the one I identify for demonstrating as the exercise of scientific knowledge here.

[4] Arguably, the corresponding claim is also true of craft, i.e., craft-excellence is a matter of *making well*. As I see it, the difference between craft and action (*praxis* in the narrow sense) is that making well is a matter of a *good product being realized*, whereas acting well essentially involves the desiderative state of the agent. The analogies and disanalogies between making and acting well in *NE* II.4 are more complicated than has often been thought. See the recent work by Sukaina Hirji, "Acting Virtuously as an End in Aristotle's *Nicomachean Ethics*," *British Journal for the History of Philosophy* 26 (2018): 1006–1026; and Marta Jiménez, "Aristotle on Becoming Virtuous by Doing Virtuous Actions," *Phronesis* 61 (2016): 3–32, on the teleological and motivational aspects of this problem, respectively.

104 ARISTOTLE'S PRACTICAL EPISTEMOLOGY

about. In this way, practical wisdom, though it is a form of understanding, is *for acting*.[5]

Another way of putting this point is that the universal or situation-independent knowledge of the person of practical wisdom is essentially incomplete. Aristotle explains the character of the knowledge in question in *Nicomachean Ethics* VI.7: "Nor is practical wisdom [knowledge] of universals alone; rather one must also have knowledge of the particulars, since it [practical wisdom] is for acting and action concerns particulars" (1141b14–16). Without particular knowledge, which includes (i) the ethical experience that enables one to connect one's universal knowledge to what is going on in a specific situation and (ii) situational knowledge itself, practical wisdom is incomplete as the kind of understanding that it is.

This difference between action and theory means that we can reject the motivation of the intellectualists that leads them to endorse P1 in the argument above. That motivation was the thought that *epistēmē* is simply how Aristotle denominates the best kind of knowledge, such that depriving the practically wise person of such knowledge would lower the status of their excellence or even remove the grounds for attributing to them a genuine virtue of thought. I have been arguing here, the contrary, that the character of understanding differs based on the domain. Let me turn now, briefly, to address the intellectualist's positive case that Aristotle thinks that the best kind of knowledge in any given domain must be scientific.

On a careful consideration of the texts, we can see that even when Aristotle exalts scientific knowledge, he restricts the domain

---

[5] For this point, we can also draw on Aristotle's reflections on what is inadequate about the life of a virtuous person who is never in a position to exercise their virtue, e.g., someone in a permanent sleep like the mythical Endymion (I.8, 1098b31–99a3). The difference between practical wisdom and theoretical wisdom that I put forward here is closely related to the fact that Aristotle holds that what is ultimate in the domain of practice and in the domain of theory are in opposite positions—the ultimate practical things are actions themselves, while the ultimate theoretical things are the first principles of science (VI.11, 1143a32–b5). I discuss the difficult text in which Aristotle makes this point (T16) in §4.2.

PRACTICAL UNDERSTANDING AND ETHICAL SCIENCE   105

of comparison. In the most general epistemological passage in the corpus *Metaphysics* Alpha 1–2, Aristotle at first speaks quite generally about the superiority of knowledge of causes to other kinds of knowledge, such as experience, ranging over craft and theory alike (A.1, 981a5–30). It may therefore seem that Aristotle is adopting a domain-neutral notion of superiority. As his examples demonstrate, however, the comparisons can only be aptly made within a given domain. Hence, the master craftsman is superior to the merely experienced person with respect to knowledge of that specific craft (A.1, 981a30–b10). By the end of Alpha 1, it becomes clear that Aristotle raises the superiority of the knowledge of causes in these other domains as a preliminary heuristic tool in order to introduce the idea that theoretical wisdom must be knowledge of the first causes and principles (981b25–29).

Aristotle then separately makes the case for the superiority of theoretical wisdom to all other kinds of knowledge (in Alpha 2), but this superiority is attributed to the greater fundamentality of such wisdom. Only such wisdom concerns the causes and principles of everything that there is rather than the causes and principles in a particular domain (A.2, 982a8–10). By contrast to Alpha 1, the kind of superiority at issue does in fact concern knowledge in different domains (theoretical wisdom is, e.g., ranked above craft), but the dimension of superiority is one that is fully appropriate only to theoretical sciences. The reason for making such cross-domain comparisons is that aspects of theoretical knowledge, such as exactness and dealing with causes or principles, are shared with craft-knowledge. But Aristotle's goal is only to argue that craft-knowledge, like the lower theoretical sciences of mathematics and physics, at best imperfectly imitates theoretical wisdom itself *in these respects*.[6] In other words, if we are wondering what

---

[6] If we think about the *objects* of knowledge, Aristotle can be seen to make a parallel point, both in the *Metaphysics* and the *Nicomachean Ethics*. It is no obstacle to there

106 ARISTOTLE'S PRACTICAL EPISTEMOLOGY

sort of knowledge has the best claim to being wisdom, *given* that exactness and comprehensiveness are marks of wisdom, then theoretical wisdom (*sophia*) wins out. But that is not to say that the best kind of knowledge in any given domain must have this character.

To sum up: I've argued that we should reject the direct argument presented by the intellectualist for the claim that the person of practical wisdom must have scientific knowledge. Understanding—the best kind of knowledge in each domain—differs based on the domain. It is only in the case of theory that scientific knowledge is superior with respect to specific dimensions of assessment such as exactness. While Aristotle entertains certain kinds of cross-domain comparisons of kinds of knowledge, as in *Metaphysics* Alpha 2, the point remains that there is no single kind of understanding that is the best in each domain. We can, therefore, safely reject the intellectualist's motivation for thinking that, for Aristotle, *epistēmē* denominates the best kind of knowledge in any domain, including the domain of action.

It should be clear from these considerations that, even though I have claimed that the person of practical wisdom has knowledge that is universal and explanatory, my disagreement with the intellectualist is not merely terminological. There are important interpretive stakes involved in attributing scientific knowledge to the person of practical wisdom.

4.2 The exercise of understanding

So far, I have argued for a sharp division between practical wisdom, on the one hand, and scientific knowledge or theoretical wisdom,

---

being a *highest* practical good for human beings, a domain-relative good, that this good is not supreme among all goods, compared across domains. It is a mistake to confuse the two dimensions of comparison. See *NE* I.6, 1096b32–97a13 for a related point in Aristotle's rebuttal of the Platonists' conception of the Form or Idea of the Good.

PRACTICAL UNDERSTANDING AND ETHICAL SCIENCE   107

on the other hand, on the basis of considerations about the general shape of Aristotle's epistemology. When we turn directly to Aristotle's survey of the virtues of thought in *Nicomachean Ethics* VI, we find further epistemological remarks that directly support this position, including the blunt denial that practical wisdom is the same as scientific knowledge:

> [T15] Hence, if scientific knowledge (*epistēmē*) involves demonstration and there is no demonstration of those things whose starting points can be otherwise . . . and it is impossible to deliberate about what is the case of necessity, practical wisdom could not be scientific knowledge, . . . since a thing to be done (*to prakton*) can be otherwise. (VI.5, 1140a33–b2)

As intellectualist interpreters have argued, of course, a denial of identity is not a denial of overlap.[7] One might think, for all Aristotle says here, that *one component* of practical wisdom must be scientific knowledge. The considerations I have raised provide a philosophical motivation for Aristotle to reject even this weaker overlap thesis. As I hope to show in this section, the grounding of Aristotle's distinction between practical wisdom and scientific knowledge in *metaphysical* considerations about the domains of action and theory provide further confirmation that no part of the knowledge possessed by the person of practical wisdom should be thought scientific. That will help me, in the following section, to address more moderate intellectualists who want to argue that ethics is a special sort of science.

Aristotle goes on to argue in the passage where he distinguishes practical wisdom and scientific knowledge that the starting points for action are goals (VI.5, 1140b16–17), which serve as first principles for deliberation in the sense that deliberation presupposes and

---

[7] See, e.g., Joseph Karbowski, *Aristotle's Method in Ethics* (Cambridge University Press, 2019), 159.

108   ARISTOTLE'S PRACTICAL EPISTEMOLOGY

aims at a specific goal.[8] Despite the talk of first principles, there is no sense in which understanding how an action promotes a goal through deliberation amounts to grasping something that is the case *of necessity*. First principles—starting points for reasoning about which there is no further reasoning—operate entirely differently in the two domains.

Aristotle makes precisely this point in *NE* VI.11, albeit in one of the most challenging and obscure passages of the entire text:

> [T16] All things to be done (*ta prakta*) belong to the class of particulars and ultimate things. For the practically wise person, too, must know these. . . . There is insight (*nous*)[9] also of ultimate things, in both directions [particular and universal]. For concerning both the first and the ultimate terms, there is insight and not argument (*logos*). On the one hand, in the case of demonstrations, there is insight of the unchangeable and first terms. On the other hand, in practical matters, there is insight of what is ultimate [i.e., the action] and capable of being otherwise, and the second [minor] premise [of practical reasoning]. For these are the starting points for the goal, since universals come from particulars. Of these [sc. the particulars], then, one must have perception, and this is insight. (VI.11, 1143a32–b5)

While there is probably no complete interpretation of this passage that does not rely on a host of background assumptions, a few

---

[8] See Heda Segvic, "Deliberation and Choice in Aristotle," in *From Protagoras to Aristotle: Essays in Ancient Moral Philosophy*, ed. Myles Burnyeat (Princeton University Press, 2009), 144–171, on how this idea underlies the infamous Aristotelian slogan that there is no deliberation of goals.

[9] I have translated *nous* as "insight" in this passage on the grounds that Aristotle is using the term more loosely to pick out an immediate sort of intellectual access, which can even be provided by perception, as he says at the end of the passage. This sense of *nous* can be contrasted with *nous* as an excellence, which is understanding of the first principles of science and a component of theoretical wisdom. I have used "intellectual intuition" to capture the sense of *nous* as an excellence, e.g., in discussing the five states by which Aristotle says we achieve the truth in *NE* VI.3 in Chapter 3 (§3.3).

PRACTICAL UNDERSTANDING AND ETHICAL SCIENCE 109

relatively uncontroversial points can be drawn from it.[10] The notion of an ultimate or last term is simply that of a stopping point for reasoning, something on which reason relies without there being further reasoning (or an account, to supply a different sense of *logos*). In the case of scientific knowledge, the ultimate terms are in fact *first* or primary, meaning that they are explanatorily basic. By contrast, in the practical case, the ultimate terms are not subject to reasoning because deliberation requires a grasp of a situation, though there is no explanatory priority between the particulars that characterize a situation and anything else. As a result, these particulars are ultimate in the sense of lying beyond further deliberation or analysis.[11]

Perhaps the most puzzling line in the passage is the claim that the particulars "are the starting points for the goal, since universals come from particulars." We need not ask of an interpretation of this difficult passage that it can show what this cryptic sentence must mean; rather, it would suffice to adequately account for this remark in Aristotle's train of thought in the passage. On my reading of the passage (which concurs with that of Wiggins), Aristotle has just described the way that descriptions of a situation feature in deliberation. That this is so is strongly confirmed by his reference to the second or minor premise of practical reasoning, which concerns the facts that confront the deliberating agent in a particular circumstance.[12] The idea that such particulars could be a starting point for the goal might reflect the thought that we form general conceptions

---

[10] David Wiggins—in his essay "Deliberation and Practical Reasoning," reprinted in Amélie Oksenberg Rorty, ed., *Essays on Aristotle's Ethics* (University of California Press, 1974), 221–240—so despairs of providing a thorough and satisfying interpretation from an uncontroversial basis that he offers a paraphrase of it with supplementary commentary instead.

[11] For perception of particulars as a stopping point of deliberation, see *NE* III.3, 1112b33–13a2.

[12] Most commentary on Aristotle's account of the premises of practical reasoning focuses on *NE* VII.3, where he uses this conceptual machinery to provide an analysis of how weakness of will involves a failure to know something, spanning both psychological and ethical considerations, rather than the distinctly ethical concerns in *NE* VI.

110 ARISTOTLE'S PRACTICAL EPISTEMOLOGY

of valuable goals through first identifying individual instances of those goals as good or worthwhile.[13] For instance, we form a generalized conception of honor as good by first judging individual cases of being honored to be good, perhaps in light of perceiving or experiencing them this way. On this reading, we can take Aristotle as bolstering his argument that particulars serve as a stopping point for reasoning by pointing to a case where we must have a grasp of these particulars before we have a clear conception of a relevant goal, understood in universal terms.

In **T16** as a whole, Aristotle sharply distinguishes starting points for theoretical reasoning, which support necessary inferences but which cannot themselves be established by argument, and starting points for practical reasoning, which support individual courses of deliberation that connect an agent's picture of goals to be promoted to their picture of the situation in which they must act.[14] The reason that there is no argument for the two kinds of starting points is, correspondingly, different. Demonstration needs a foundation to avoid circularity, since in demonstration we are always moving

---

R. Kathleen Harbin has recently argued against taking the psychological and the ethical accounts of the practical syllogism to form a unity ("The Practical Syllogism and Practical Cognition in Aristotle," *Archiv für Geschichte der Philosophie* 104 [2022]: 633–662). Harbin also holds, as I do, that the person of practical wisdom acts on the basis of a grasp of underlying values or goals as well as the particular situations in which they find themselves. What is distinctive in my view is that I take the universal principles understood by the person of practical wisdom to go beyond the narrowly specific (but still general) principles that the person of experience knows. I lay out my view of the content of these universal principles more fully in Chapter 5, using as my main example the character virtue of justice.

[13] This process goes under the name "practical induction" in the secondary literature. See Terence Irwin, commentary ad loc., *Aristotle: Nicomachean Ethics*, 2nd ed. (Hackett, 2000), 250, who touches on this point briefly; and Jessica Moss, *Aristotle on the Apparent Good: Perception, Phantasia, Thought, & Desire* (Oxford University Press, 2012), Chapter 8, for a thorough analysis of practical induction as a parallel to theoretical or scientific induction. *Pace* Moss, I do not take pleasure and pain to be central to the process of practical induction.

[14] See Wiggins, "Deliberation and Practical Reasoning," 48–49, for a helpful account of the *reciprocal* way that an agent's goals and what he calls situational appreciation—equivalent to Aristotle's "perception" (*aisthēsis*) and the practical use of insight (*nous*) described in the VI.11 passage—bear on one another.

PRACTICAL UNDERSTANDING AND ETHICAL SCIENCE   111

from better known principles to lesser known conclusions.[15] By contrast, practical reasoning needs what we might call *input*. There is no practical reasoning in a vacuum, even if no situation of exigency presses its demands upon us.

With this analysis of the different starting points of theoretical and practical reasoning in mind, we can turn to Aristotle's views of the metaphysics of the sphere of action. Much has been made by both intellectualist and anti-intellectualist interpreters of Aristotle's methodological remark that in ethics the truth about how things are holds good only for the most part (*hōs epi to polu*).[16] In fact, without a better understanding of the underlying metaphysics that support this assertion, Aristotle's point cannot be fully appreciated. I will try, therefore, to show a way past this impasse after discussing the intellectualist and anti-intellectualist alternatives.

Intellectualist interpreters have fastened on to the fact that in the context of natural science, Aristotle holds that what is natural happens either always or for the most part.[17] The echo of this language in the opening of the *Nicomachean Ethics* has therefore suggested to these interpreters that the type of regularity in the two domains is the same or at least highly similar, even allowing for the greater imprecision of ethical matters. Such a similarity would in turn seem to support the inference that these regularities can be known in the same way, i.e., scientifically.

The intellectualist line of interpretation depends on seeing the contingency of the practical as simply a special case of the

[15] See Marko Malink, "Aristotle on Circular Proof," *Phronesis* 58 (2013): 215–248, for an analysis of Aristotle's arguments against this possibility in *Posterior Analytics* I.3 and *Prior Analytics* II.5.

[16] See esp. *NE* I.3, 1094b11–22. I analyzed this passage (**T2**) in my explication of ethical experience as a robust kind of practical knowledge in Chapter 1, where I contrasted Aristotle's position with the Isocratean view that practical wisdom is simply intelligent guesswork.

[17] Reeve, *Practices of Reason*, 7–22; Michael Winter, "Aristotle, *hōs epi to polu* Relations, and a Demonstrative Science of Ethics," *Phronesis* 42 (1997): 163–189; Devin Henry, "Holding for the Most Part: The Demonstrability of Moral Facts," in *Bridging the Gap between Aristotle's Science and Ethics*, ed. Devin Henry and Karen Margrethe Nielsen (Cambridge University Press, 2015), 169–190.

112 ARISTOTLE'S PRACTICAL EPISTEMOLOGY

contingencies of the sublunary, natural world. As Reeve puts it, the case of the natural sciences, such as biology, shows that the scientist can study *enmattered* forms, that is, forms like the natures of plants and animals that manifest themselves only in hylomorphic composites.[18] Despite the variability among individual biological organisms of the same kind, the scientist can still formulate claims with the necessity needed to support demonstration, e.g., that any creature with a heart must also have lungs. Indeed, many of the typical examples of demonstration in the *Posterior Analytics*, Aristotle's general treatise on scientific reasoning, are cases of this sort, rather than being restricted to domains like mathematics where stricter necessities are operative.

I have already argued above, drawing on **T16**, that we have good reason to reject the idea that the contingency of the practical is a special instance of the general contingency of the sublunary natural world. I will argue below that what Aristotle says about the metaphysics of the sphere of action in *NE* VI confirms my view.[19]

Anti-intellectualists, meanwhile, have argued that Aristotle's emphasis on inexactness or imprecision in these contexts shows that he gives up on the prospect of systematic inquiry into ethical universals, the results of which would have a direct bearing on how we should act.[20] A passage the anti-intellectualists tend to draw on to support this line of reasoning comes from *NE* II:

> [**T17**] Matters of action and advantage admit of no stability, just as matters of health do not. When the universal account is like this, still more does the account concerning the particulars lack precision. For it falls under no craft or precept at all, and those

[18] Reeve, *Practices of Reason*, 16–22.

[19] For a similar line of thought about the metaphysics of the ethical domain, which also takes up Aristotle's remarks about nature and convention in *NE* V, see Charlotte Witt, "'As If by Convention Alone': The Unstable Ontology of Aristotle's Ethics," in Henry and Nielsen, *Bridging the Gap*, 276–292.

[20] See Sarah Broadie, *Ethics with Aristotle* (Oxford University Press, 1991), esp. Chapter 4, "Practical Wisdom."

PRACTICAL UNDERSTANDING AND ETHICAL SCIENCE   113

who act must on each occasion look to what is appropriate, as in medicine and navigation. (II.2, 1104a3–10)

It is true that, in this passage, Aristotle connects the imprecision of practical knowledge directly to the need to act in particular circumstances without simply applying universal prescriptions that are decided on in advance. But his denial of stability is simply a denial that a precept could hold once and for all without regard to the circumstances. It is, therefore, not a rejection of the project of ethical inquiry but an explication of how it differs from theoretical inquiry. Moreover, as has too-seldom been noted in commentary on and analysis of this passage, Aristotle explicitly distinguishes between the particular knowledge needed to handle any given situation that confronts the deliberator and the universal account (*ho katholou logos*) he is himself trying to provide. The universal account is not claimed to be pointless or nonexistent. Rather, Aristotle says that it is imprecise, albeit to a lesser degree than an account of the particulars.

In any case, Aristotle's point is not that the fruits of ethical inquiry are to be adopted as a blueprint to be implemented top down on the situations we face.[21] Rather, his aim is to analyze the situation-independent or universal aspect of ethical knowledge in order to prompt reflection on and bring greater clarity to the (partial) understanding that he takes his audience to have. The reflection prompted by ethical inquiry is meant to have direct practical consequences, even though what is described, roughly and in outline, by the inquiry is not itself a component or module of the knowledge possessed by the person of practical wisdom. I will

---

[21] See Richard Kraut's reply to Broadie, "In Defense of the Grand End," *Ethics* 103 (1993): 361–374; and Kristen Inglis, "Philosophical Virtue: In Defense of the Grand End," in *The Cambridge Companion to Aristotle's* Nicomachean Ethics, ed. Ronald Polansky (Cambridge University Press, 2014), 263–287. Such a blueprint view would, indeed, be absurd, but that does not detract from the practical benefits of Aristotle's inquiry into ethical universals.

114 ARISTOTLE'S PRACTICAL EPISTEMOLOGY

return to this point in the last section of this chapter (§4.3), where I introduce an important distinction between teaching-knowledge and user-knowledge, inspired by Albert the Great's commentary on the *Nicomachean Ethics*.

For now, we should turn back to *NE* VI, which begins with one of Aristotle's fullest descriptions of the metaphysics of the sphere of action:

> [T18] Let us posit two [parts of the soul] that have reason, one by which we judge the sorts of realities whose principles cannot be otherwise, and one by which [we judge] those that can [be otherwise]. For in relation to what is different in kind, the parts of the soul oriented to each sort differ in kind, given that they obtain knowledge by a certain similarity and affinity. Let it be stated that one of these is scientific (*to epistēmonikon*), the other calculative (*to logistikon*), since deliberating and calculating are the same and no one deliberates about what cannot be otherwise. (VI.1, 1139a6–14)

Aristotle here follows a principle that he articulates in *De Anima* II.4, 415a14–22, namely, that to understand vital capacities we must turn to the corresponding activities, and to understand these activities in turn we must turn to their respective objects. In the case of cognitive capacities, the objects are what is known by the mode of knowledge in question, distinguished by the sort of reality they have. Aristotle, therefore, ends up endorsing the view of the middle books of Plato's *Republic*, e.g., in the image of the Divided Line, that cognition varies according to the ontological status of its objects but on the basis of his own psychological and epistemological commitments.[22]

The objects of practical and theoretical knowledge are distinguished in a rather curious way in this passage. Of the realities

---

[22] For the importance of this object-based view and its alienness in the light of much modern epistemology, see Jessica Moss, *Plato's Epistemology: Being and Seeming* (Oxford University Press, 2021), especially Chapter 2, "Objects-Based Epistemology," 50–84.

PRACTICAL UNDERSTANDING AND ETHICAL SCIENCE 115

that scientific understanding is concerned with, Aristotle says that their *principles* cannot be otherwise. Here, it is most plausible to read him as concerned to take account of both entirely precise sciences and the sublunary natural sciences. Not everything in the domain of the latter, less precise sciences, will hold entirely of necessity. Nevertheless, the principles of such sciences will have every bit the character of necessary and explanatory starting points for demonstration.

By contrast, Aristotle describes the realities in the case of calculation as themselves being contingent or capable of being otherwise. Here, he means to include both productive and practical modes of reasoning under the general rubric of the "calculative part" (*to logistikon*). This characterization seems to leave open the possibility that while the realities known by such modes of knowledge themselves are contingent, their principles are necessary. But were this Aristotle's point in T18—that there could be practical sciences that considered the necessary principles of contingent matters, alongside the natural sciences—he would have made the division in exactly the wrong way. It would be the fact that the whole subject matter of scientific knowledge concerned what is necessary that would distinguish it from practical and productive knowledge, and not the fact that the principles that govern the objects of scientific knowledge are necessary. The very way that Aristotle carves up the objects of the two kinds of knowledge, then, provides support for the idea that the contingency of the objects of practical knowledge is characteristic of the entire domain, including its principles or starting points and the relationship between these principles and what they explain.

That this is Aristotle's view is explicitly confirmed when he returns to the topic of what differentiates *phronēsis* and scientific knowledge in *NE* VI.5 on the grounds that there cannot be scientific knowledge of things whose principles can be otherwise (1140a33–b2 = T15, discussed above). This explanation of the difference between the states entails that the contingent realities

116 ARISTOTLE'S PRACTICAL EPISTEMOLOGY

known by *phronēsis* do not flow from principles that would admit of scientific knowledge.[23]

4.3 Ethics as a special science

We are now in a position to address a more subtle form of intellectualism, which concedes that the objects of practical understanding cannot be appreciated in just the way that even natural sciences grasp their objects. These more moderate intellectualists, such as Terence Irwin and Karen Margrethe Nielsen, argue that the imprecision and inexactness of ethical understanding set it apart from other forms of scientific understanding.[24] Of course, if all that is meant by such formulations is that there is universal and explanatory knowledge in ethics, I am content to accept these claims as merely terminologically different from my own. Both Irwin and Nielsen, however, defend stronger analogies between sciences in the strict sense and ethics than I do.

Nielsen, for example, characterizes ethics as a *stochastic* science but draws on the identity of political and practical wisdom to establish the scientific credentials of ethical understanding. I will show in Chapter 6 how the political character of practical wisdom is no barrier to its essential practicality, that is, to its complete concern with acting in particular circumstances and, correspondingly, to the need for particular knowledge for its exercise. There is no room for theory apart from practice in the case of political wisdom, though Aristotle tries to carve out room for the philosophical investigation of political matters as a form of reflection that

---

[23] Thanks to Hendrik Lorenz for suggesting that I relate these texts more explicitly to make my case.

[24] Irwin, "Ethics as an Inexact Science: Aristotle's Ambitions for Moral Theory," in *Moral Particularism*, ed. Brad Hooker and Margaret Little (Oxford University Press, 2000), 100–129; Nielsen, "Aristotle on Principles in Ethics: Political Science as the Science of the Human Good," in Henry and Nielsen, *Bridging the Gap*, 29–48.

PRACTICAL UNDERSTANDING AND ETHICAL SCIENCE 117

is immediately relevant to practice. It is misleading, therefore, to identify ethics as a stochastic *science*.

The distinctions that these more moderate intellectualists are pursuing can be helpfully elucidated by turning to the introduction to the (second) commentary on the *Nicomachean Ethics* of Albert the Great (*Ethica* I, tr. 1, c.).[25] Albert argues that teaching knowledge of virtue (*scientia docens de virtute*), which is what he calls the product of Aristotelian ethical inquiry, does not simply prescribe to but can all the same inform and guide (*informans et dirigens*) the operative knowledge of virtue in the virtuous person (*scientia utens de virtute*). Following Albert, we may distinguish between teaching-knowledge and user-knowledge, a distinction that will apply to both practical and productive knowledge.

Albert, of course, speaks of *scientia* (which often translates the Greek *epistēmē*) here, and he goes on to analyze teaching knowledge in much the way that Nielsen and Irwin treat ethics as a whole, by conforming it closely to the model of the theoretical sciences discussed in the *Posterior Analytics*, and, indeed, by emphasizing the possibility of demonstrations (*Ethics* I, tr. 1, c. 4).[26] Despite Albert's theoretical analysis of teaching-knowledge, the idea that the relationship between teaching-knowledge and user-knowledge could be understood as itself practically ordered is important. Indeed, reflection and inquiry of the kind Aristotle pursues in the *Nicomachean Ethics* and the *Politics* can offer a guide to practice, even if the discussion remains at some distance from particular actions.

The very practical ordering of reflective inquiry in ethics— emphasized by Aristotle throughout the *Nicomachean*

---

[25] See the critical edition of Tract 1 in Jorn Müller, *Natürliche Moral und philosophische Ethik bei Albertus Magnus* (Aschendorff, 2001), 325–358.

[26] See Jörn Müller, "Ethics as a Practical Science in Albert the Great's Commentaries on the *Nicomachean Ethics*," in *Albertus Magnus. Zum Gedenken nach 800 Jahren: Neue Zugänge, Aspekte und Perspektiven*, ed. Walter Senner OP, et al. (Akademie Verlag, 2001), 275–285.

118   ARISTOTLE'S PRACTICAL EPISTEMOLOGY

Ethics—provides a stumbling block to even the moderate intellectualist approach to teaching-knowledge, that is, the knowledge that would be the successful fruit of ethical inquiry. For instance, Aristotle speaks of happiness as a first principle or starting point in *NE* I.7, but rather than going on to *demonstrate* conclusions on this basis, he shows how such a starting point coheres with our ethical commitments (in the following chapter, I.8), which can help us identify which of these commitments we should retain (e.g., that the best life is a life lived according to the virtues), which we may need to refine (e.g., in what sense pleasure is good), and which we may even need to jettison (e.g., that goods apart from activity *constitute* our highest good).

Despite this fact about the form of the text, a doggedly intellectualist approach to the *NE* can be found in a recent monograph by Joseph Karbowski, where Karbowski tries to square the circle by arguing that Aristotle is merely aiming to uncover the first principles of legislative science in the *Nicomachean Ethics*, not to use these first principles to show other facts.[27] But given that Aristotle reaches his definition of happiness in I.7, we would expect him, on the scientific reading, either to use it to prove other claims or otherwise to end his scientific inquiry if he was interested only in the 'upward' direction of argument toward first principles. My point here is that he does neither of these things, but he aims instead to show the *practical* consequences of his definition or account of what happiness is.

To be sure, Karbowski rightly rebukes a widely held interpretation of an earlier generation of scholars that characterized ethical inquiry as merely dialectical, that is, as not capable of supplying us with new understanding of a domain.[28] After all, Aristotle promises us in *NE* I.4 that, while we must begin with the grasp of

---

[27] Karbowski, *Aristotle's Method in Ethics*. See esp. Chapter 6, "Facts, Principles, and Aristotle's Demonstrative Ethical Science," 163–187.

[28] Karbowski identifies John Burnet as the originator of this dialectical conception of Aristotle's works, on which Aristotle did not really endorse the views put forward in

PRACTICAL UNDERSTANDING AND ETHICAL SCIENCE 119

ethical matters that we already possess, the purpose of the inquiry is to move us toward a grasp of what is knowable about the subject matter considered in itself (see T3 and the discussion in Chapter 2, §2.1.2). But in rejecting the dialectical interpretation of this passage (and others like it), we need not adopt a scientific one, as Karbowski and other recent interpreters would have us do.[29]

This point holds even if we grant that Aristotle has borrowed, at the start of the *NE*, the distinction between two kinds of things that are knowable from his treatment of scientific inquiry in the *Posterior Analytics*. What matters is what Aristotle in fact goes on to do in the remainder of the *Nicomachean Ethics* to fulfill his promise to uncover principles and explanations in ethics. Tellingly, he does not deduce the list of virtues of character from his account of happiness. Rather, he relies on the knowledge we already have of what kinds of qualities are good and shows that they conform to the model of rational states with regard to passion and action that he uses to unify the domain of the virtues of character. Such a procedure nicely fits the idea that ethics aims at informing and guiding user-knowledge while leaving ample room for reflection that is not devoted to addressing any particular situation.

---

his treatises, and G. E. L. Owen and John Cooper as chiefly responsible for a modified version of the view that came to be more widely endorsed, on which we do not gain *new* knowledge through inquiry, something that is instead reserved for empirical investigation (Karbowski, *Aristotle's Method in Ethics*, 3–4). See John Burnet, *The Ethics of Aristotle* (Methuen, 1900); G. E. L. Owen, "*Tithenai ta phainomena*" in *Aristote et les problems de méthode*, ed. S. Mansion (Publications Universitaires de Louvain, 1961), 83–103; and John Cooper, *Reason and Human Good in Aristotle* (Harvard University Press, 1975).

[29] As Karbowski notes, a relatively recent collection of essays with contributions from a number of prominent Aristotelian scholars largely endorses this line of interpretation: Henry and Nielsen, *Bridging the Gap*. See, e.g., Henry, "Holding for the Most Part," 169–190; and the essay by Karbowski himself, "*Endoxa*, Facts, and the Starting Points of the *Nicomachean Ethics*," 113–129. Some contributors to the volume do sound skeptical notes about this consensus, e.g., Daniel Devereux, "Scientific and Ethical Methods in Aristotle's *Eudemian* and *Nicomachean Ethics*," 130–147; Witt, "'As If by Convention Alone,'" 276–292; and James Allen, "Practical and Theoretical Knowledge in Aristotle," 49–70; although Allen ends up endorsing a middle-ground position. I discuss Allen's views immediately below.

120 ARISTOTLE'S PRACTICAL EPISTEMOLOGY

It may yet be true that one could, as Albert suggests we should, rearrange some of Aristotle's claims about virtue, happiness, and the human good into a syllogistic form. As I have tried to suggest here, the result would not be a *stochastic* or an *inexact* science but a strange theoretical shadow of teaching-knowledge, whose very point is to serve as a guide to our user-knowledge about what to do.[30] Whether or not such a theoretical shadow science is possible, Aristotle seems to have thought it useless. We may recall how he regards ordinary people who listen to lofty discourses on ethics: "realizing their own state of ignorance, they marvel at others who make grand claims that are beyond them" (*NE* I.4, 1095a25–26). Evidently, we can be taken in by the temptation to theorize idly—and Aristotle stops his own inquiry short on several occasions to steer clear of this temptation e.g., in bringing up distinctions among the parts of the soul at *NE* I.13, 1102a23–26—but in doing so, we are not really engaging in ethical inquiry, but rather a peculiar philosophical game.

---

[30] James Allen ("Practical and Theoretical Knowledge in Aristotle") remarks that "a fragment of what the practically wise person knows, the discipline of ethics, will resemble what the theoretical scientist knows or an important part of it. But as in the case of the doctor, the practically wise person's grasp of principles is embedded in a context of cognitive abilities and accomplishments that differ in important ways from those of the scientist" (p. 69). I concur entirely with this framing of the issue but reject Allen's further claim that there is a "theoretical fragment of the ethical discipline that is occupied with fundamental principles" (p. 69).

In fact, we should resist the view that any part of the discipline of ethics has a syllogistic or demonstrative character at all. As Hendrik Lorenz and Benjamin Morison rightly put it, "the domain of contingent truths is not structured by syllogistic connections, and so the task of understanding those truths and appreciating their connections to one another is not a matter of discerning syllogistic connections" ("Aristotle's Empiricist Theory of Doxastic Knowledge," *Phronesis* 64, no. 4 [2019]: 431–464, at 442).

5

KNOWLEDGE OF PRACTICAL

UNIVERSALS

5.1 Knowledge of principles in ethics

In Chapter 3, I explained why Aristotle holds that we need practical wisdom in order to achieve full practical success. I showed there that practical wisdom surpasses ethical experience because only the wise achieve practical truth through the harmony of desire and practical thought. I argued on that basis that what the wise have is a form of *understanding* that enables them to act well in the indefinitely varied circumstances of ethical and political life. In Chapter 4, I considered—and argued against—the view that we should take this understanding to be or even to include scientific knowledge. This is so, even though some of what the practically wise know has a universal and explanatory character, since even craft-knowledge has this character without thereby being scientific.

What is left is for practical wisdom to be a distinctly practical form of understanding, which is the main claim of this book. But if it is not scientific knowledge, what exactly is this understanding? That is the question I take up in this chapter. My claim that practical wisdom is practical understanding will remain obscure without a satisfactory answer to it. I have already indicated that the answer to this question lies in the grasp of the characteristic ends or goals of virtuous actions that belongs to the practically wise. I began making a schematic case for this idea in Chapter 3, but this claim is difficult to evaluate unless we undertake a further analysis of the relationship between virtuous goals and virtuous choices. Through this analysis, I will show why practical universals are essential to

---

Aristotle's Practical Epistemology. Dhananjay Jagannathan, Oxford University Press.
© Oxford University Press 2024. DOI: 10.1093/9780197781517.003.0006

122 ARISTOTLE'S PRACTICAL EPISTEMOLOGY

good deliberation and, hence, why we should attribute a grasp of such universals—which amounts to practical understanding—to those with *phronēsis*.[1]

5.1.1 The very possibility of practical understanding

Before I turn to offering such an analysis in the bulk of this chapter through a discussion of a specific character-virtue (particular justice), I will first introduce some important alternative views of the relationship between principles and the goals pursued by the person of practical wisdom in order to clarify my own position. One such view, which denies any role for what I have called practical understanding, is represented by Sarah Broadie in her book *Ethics with Aristotle*. Broadie argues that the goals grasped by the practically wise person are the *particular* goals to be pursued in any given virtuous action, while any more abstract goals are the concern of either the statesman or the ethical philosopher.[2] I will discuss the relationship between practical and political wisdom in Chapter 6. For now, what matters is Broadie's claim that practical wisdom can be exercised without regard to anything like a determinate grasp of organizing and overarching goals.

---

[1] There has been remarkably little discussion in the secondary literature of the implications of Aristotle's claim that the person with practical wisdom has a knowledge of universals in T5. My view that this has essentially to do with the need to understand the ends for which the virtuous person acts may be compared to that of Moira Walsh, "The Role of Universal Knowledge in Aristotelian Moral Virtue," *Ancient Philosophy* 19 (1999): 73–88, who, like me, emphasizes the practical need for knowledge of the human *telos*. See also Howard Curzer, "Rules Lurking at the Heart of Aristotle's Virtue Ethics," *Apeiron* 49 (2016): 57–92, who emphasizes the place of moral rules in Aristotle's ethics, which I take to be more relevant to characterizing ethical experience than practical wisdom. R. Kathleen Harbin has also defended a similar position, pointing to the narrowly specific principles invoked in Aristotle's discussions of practical reasoning ("The Practical Syllogism and Practical Cognition in Aristotle," *Archiv für Geschichte der Philosophie* 104 [2022: 633–662); see 109, fn. 12.

[2] Sarah Broadie, *Ethics with Aristotle* (Oxford University Press, 1991), 179–198.

KNOWLEDGE OF PRACTICAL UNIVERSALS 123

Much of Broadie's argument in favor of this claim turns on the thought that a reflective grasp of goals is otiose for practice. This thought seems directly opposed to Aristotle's insistence that the purpose of the inquiry in the *Nicomachean Ethics*—which is an investigation of the supreme practical goal that is the human good—is itself practical. Broadie, accordingly, reinterprets Aristotle's claim about the practicality of his inquiry by positing a secondary audience that does not consist of ordinary people seeking ethical improvement; this audience consists instead of those who could put the philosophical claims of the *Nicomachean Ethics* to practical use in their communities: educators and politicians.[3]

There does not seem to be any important distinction among the audience members envisioned in *NE* I.3–4, texts which I have already analyzed extensively in Chapters 1 and 2 of this book. In any case, Aristotle says, in addition to his remarks about goals or ends, that what he means to provide in the *Nicomachean Ethics* is clarity about principles (*arkhai*), knowledge of which would guide our action like having a target (*skopos*) to aim at which helps us "hit the mark that we ought" (I.2, 1094a23–24). While they stand above individual goals, these principles are not, to be sure, like the universal good posited by Plato and others, which Aristotle argues fail to be action-guiding in this way (I.6, 1096b32–35).

What, then, are these principles?[4] Throughout *NE* I, Aristotle refers to happiness (*eudaimonia*) as the chief practical principle,

---

[3] Broadie, *Ethics with Aristotle*, 204–205.

[4] To head off any confusion, let me emphasize here that these principles are not principles in the sense of modern ethics, that is, ethical rules or generalizations that have a universal form. Aristotle's paradigmatic example of an ethical principle is happiness, which is evidently not a rule or a generalization, although it is, plausibly, something that can be instantiated by contrast to a concrete particular (happiness as a principle is not *your* happiness or *my* happiness, in other words, but happiness taken in itself as the highest good for every human being). Moreover, as I have already argued, the person with experience has a grasp of ethical generalizations but does *not* thereby have understanding of ethical principles. Confusion over these matters—and Aristotle's use of the language of particulars and universals to describe them—has led to a great deal of generally unfruitful debate over whether Aristotle is a particularist or a generalist in the terms of contemporary metaethics. See Daniel Devereux, "Particular and Universal in Aristotle's Conception of Practical Knowledge," *Review of Metaphysics* 39 (1986): 483–504, for

124 ARISTOTLE'S PRACTICAL EPISTEMOLOGY

since it just is the highest goal for which we act. But Aristotle also speaks of more than one such principle, as in the passage of *NE* I.4 that I analyzed in Chapters 1 and 2 (T3—see §1.1.4 and §2.1.2). As it turns out, since happiness is activity of the soul, the specific kinds of activity that constitute happiness will also be principles— whether the contemplative exercise of theoretical wisdom or the exercise of the virtues of character together with practical wisdom.[5] Furthermore, since such activities are all exercises of human excellences, these excellences, too, belong to the category of principles.[6] For it is only by acquiring these excellences that we can be in a position to exercise them. We find that just these topics—happiness and the two types of human excellence, character-virtues and the virtues of thought—form the core agenda of Aristotle's treatment of the human good in the *Nicomachean Ethics*, alongside pleasure and friendship, which are accompaniments of the happy life, and weakness of will, which is a sort of practical failure that disrupts it.

some of the complexities involved in mapping Aristotle's language to the contemporary debate.

[5] Note: I do not mean to enter the well-worn debate over whether happiness is, for Aristotle, a monistic or composite good, and either view is consistent with what I say here. Some decades after the classic paper of John Ackrill's that defended a composite view and turned the tide in favor of such a view ("Aristotle on *Eudaimonia*," in *Essays on Aristotle's Ethics*, ed. Amélie Oksenberg Rorty [University of California Press, 1980]), 7–33), scholarship has more recently tended toward monism. See esp. Richard Kraut, *Aristotle on the Human Good* (Princeton University Press, 1989), and Gabriel Richardson Lear, *Happy Lives and the Highest Good* (Princeton University Press, 2004), for a compelling defense of monism (sometimes referred to as intellectualism) as the best reading of Aristotle. Other scholars have refined and maintained the composite view, such as Terence Irwin, *The Development of Ethics*, vol. 1 (Oxford University Press, 2007).

[6] To see why the excellences themselves should be understood as principles, we can contrast them with the conditions for their exercise. Even if analyzing such conditions is illuminating for understanding virtuous activities, we want to know how to bring these activities about, and it is acquiring the excellences that is in our control. Hence, from the point of view of a practical inquiry, the excellences are principles. When it comes to legislation, analyzing the conditions for the exercise of the human excellences will be more prominent, since the character of a political community will depend to some extent on whether these conditions are available to its members. This consideration explains the different approaches to the human good in the *Nicomachean Ethics* and the *Politics*.

KNOWLEDGE OF PRACTICAL UNIVERSALS   125

Even if we grant that virtue and happiness are the principles knowledge of which can help us to act well, we are left with the question of the *way* that this knowledge is relevant to ethical action.

If no such direct connection can be found, Broadie's view will turn out to be more plausible than the one I have outlined: Aristotle must not mean to address the ordinary person seeking ethical improvement when he says that understanding the principles of the just, the noble, and the political will help us to act as we should. My goal in the bulk of this chapter is to show that knowledge of the goals appropriate to each of the character-virtues meets this standard of connecting a grasp of ethical principles to action. I will do so by analyzing the virtue of justice, not least since its ends clearly relate to the most encompassing community of which we are part, the political community.

First, however, let us consider the evidence in *NE* VI that practical wisdom involves a grasp of the ends for which we should act, drawing in part on passages I have discussed above in other contexts. That will also help me relate my position to another set of views in the scholarship, on which a grasp of these ends must be relatively situation specific in order to be action-guiding, representing a more moderate version of the anti-intellectualist position of Broadie's discussed in this section.

5.1.2 Practical wisdom as a true grasp of the end

One especially telling piece of evidence comes at the end of Aristotle's distillation of *phronēsis* as characteristically displaying a type of deliberative excellence. The last line, where Aristotle seems plainly to state that practical wisdom involves a grasp of the end for which we should act, has been the subject of dispute, so the passage is worth quoting in full.

126 ARISTOTLE'S PRACTICAL EPISTEMOLOGY

[T19] Since correctness means many things, clearly it [sc. deliberative excellence, *euboulia*] is not just any correctness. For [if that were true] the weak-willed person and the bad one will achieve what they propose on the basis of calculation, and hence will have deliberated correctly, though they have obtained a great evil [viz. by acting badly]. But to have deliberated well seems to be something good, since this is the sort of correctness in deliberation that deliberative excellence is: that which is such as to achieve the good. But it is possible also to achieve this [sc. the good] by means of false reckoning, i.e., to achieve what one ought to do, but not by means one should employ, instead the middle term being false. Hence, this would not yet be deliberative excellence, by which one achieves what one ought but not by means one should employ. Further, it is possible for someone to achieve [what they should] but only by deliberating for too long, while another does so quickly. And so deliberative excellence would not yet be this, but correctness about what is advantageous [simply], that is, for the sake of the right end and in the right way and when one should. If, then, it is characteristic of those who are practically wise to have deliberated well, deliberative excellence would be correctness concerned with what contributes to the end, of which practical wisdom is a true grasp (*alēthēs hupolēpsis*). (*NE* VI.10, 1142b17–33)

The line of thought here, on a surface reading of the whole of T19, is that *phronēsis* enables us to deliberate excellently because it helps us achieve correctness in every dimension, judging not only the right end for which we should act but also the correct means to take toward it and the appropriate time and manner of action.

As I noted, some interpreters, in order to advance an anti-intellectualist view of how we are acquainted with the ends pursued by deliberation, have disputed the meaning of the last line by pointing to a possible syntactic ambiguity in the object of the true grasp that practical wisdom is said to be: "the end" (as the passage

KNOWLEDGE OF PRACTICAL UNIVERSALS   127

seems to say) or "what contributes to the end" (as they construe it).[7] The latter reading, while strained in this context, seems to fit with passages where Aristotle identifies a certain division of labor between *phronēsis*, which helps us discern the appropriate means, and the virtues of character, which supply us with the correct goals.

The problem with this interpretation is that it conflates what we deliberate *about* (means) and what we must know to deliberate well. I argued in Chapter 2 that the latter includes universal as well as particular knowledge, including situation-dependent features, accessible through perception, and knowledge of generalization that connects these features to ends, which belongs to experience. Looking to the overall line of thought in T19 can help us resist the anti-intellectualist view of our grasp of the ends for which we act.

The very first category of apparent correctness in the context of deliberation is being able to work out how to pursue one's goals, no matter what they are. In the next chapter (VI.12), Aristotle will call this capacity cleverness (*deinotēs*) and distinguish it from the ability to pursue the correct goals that belongs to the person of practical wisdom (1144a23–29). Here, he simply points out that achieving bad things cannot amount to deliberative excellence (*euboulia*). In addition to pursuing the correct goals, however, we must pursue them in the right way—using the right means, in the right manner, and at the right time—all of which further refine the conception of deliberative excellence Aristotle is developing in T19. All *four* kinds of correctness (right goal, right means, right

---

[7] The case has been most forcefully made by Jessica Moss, *Aristotle on the Apparent Good: Perception, Phantasia, Thought, Desire* (Oxford University Press, 2012), Chapter 7 (esp. 7.5 and 7.6, 179–198). To lend support to her reading of T19, Moss points to an apparent parallel locution in *Eudemian Ethics* II.10, 1226b20–30, where Aristotle says that adults (in normal states) are able to form a grasp (*hupolēpsis*) of an end unlike children and other animals. But the discussion there is *psychological*, whereas T19 is ethical, distinguishing between a *true* and a *false* grasp of the end. He cannot mean, then, in T19 only that deliberation presupposes an end, since that is equally true of those with a true and a false grasp. That is the point of the first part of the passage, one reason I quote it in full here. Thanks to Jessica Moss for helping me clarify my line of argument in this section.

128   ARISTOTLE'S PRACTICAL EPISTEMOLOGY

manner, right time) belong to the person of practical wisdom and help constitute their deliberative excellence. It would be strange if Aristotle meant to conclude the passage with the idea that the first of these four kinds of correctness (a grasp of the right goals) does not really belong to the person of practical wisdom *qua* practically wise. In fact, he seems to be emphasizing the way that the other kinds of correctness *flow from* the grasp of the goal that belongs to those who are practically wise.

The anti-intellectualist is right to point out that practical wisdom is exercised in working out what means we should take to our end, but they are wrong to infer from the "division of labor" passages that practical wisdom is, for that reason, *not* a capacity that grasps the end. As intellectualist interpreters have argued, the texts leave open a plausible alternative: that practical wisdom works out the appropriate means *as well as grasping the correct end* that the virtues of character supply.[8] My argument has been that we can appreciate this point especially clearly by reflecting on the difference between the person of practical wisdom and the person with experience alone. The person of practical wisdom *understands* the end, while the person with experience, though they can act as the virtues of character require on the basis of knowledge of how certain situation-dependent features reliably promote a given end, does not. If practical wisdom were the only kind of practical knowledge, Aristotle would not be in a position to draw this distinction.

This contrast between practical wisdom and ethical experience also shows the limits of a more moderate version of the anti-intellectualist position, on which the person of practical wisdom has a relatively situation-specific grasp of the goals for which they act. One such view is due to A. W. Price, who draws primarily on Aristotle's characterization of practical *reasoning*, both in the *NE*

---

[8] E.g., David Wiggins, "Deliberation and Practical Reasoning," and Terence Irwin, "Aristotle on Reason, Desire and Virtue," *Journal of Philosophy* 73 (1975): 567–578, both cited by Moss, *Aristotle on the Apparent Good*, at 196–197.

KNOWLEDGE OF PRACTICAL UNIVERSALS 129

and in the psychological works.[9] I have suggested, by contrast, that we need to look to his broader view of ethical knowledge to draw some of the relevant distinctions. Price accepts Broadie's view that the alternative to a "Grand End" conception of practical reasoning must necessarily involve a practical orientation to "a limited and accessible target" that displays "a sensitivity to whatever considerations the circumstances may bring into play."[10] But without adopting any implausible version of the "Grand End" view, one can still attribute to the person of practical wisdom a *determinable* and not situation specific and yet still practical grasp of the goals for which a virtuous person ought to act. Price, furthermore, grants the practical relevance of negative prohibitions in Aristotelian ethics, such as the prohibitions against adultery, theft, and murder that Aristotle endorses explicitly at *NE* II.6, 1107a8–17.[11] Price rightly sees these prohibitions as non-tautological and hence action-guiding but fails to see that a grasp of ethical goals or values might play a positive role in ethical deliberation.

Deborah Achtenberg argues for just such a positive role but identifies the primary universal that is relevant for the virtuous and practically wise person's reasoning as simply 'good.'[12] But such an analogous principle, which applies in widely different contexts, is not plausibly seen as an object of understanding that enables wise choice across those contexts. Achtenberg also identifies an important role for ethical generalizations that hold good for the most part.[13] I have attributed a grasp of such generalizations to the person with ethical experience and so locate the understanding of ethical goals that is characteristic of the practically wise person

---

[9] A. W. Price, *Virtue and Reason in Plato and Aristotle* (Oxford University Press, 2011), esp. Part C2, "Aristotle on Practical Reasoning," 188–250.

[10] Price, *Virtue and Reason in Plato and Aristotle*, 205.

[11] Price, *Virtue and Reason in Plato and Aristotle*, 206–209.

[12] Deborah Achtenberg, *Cognition of Value in Aristotle's Ethics: Promise of Enrichment, Threat of Destruction* (State University of New York Press, 2002).

[13] In this regard, Achtenberg distinguishes her view from John McDowell's, which I go on to discuss below (§5.3).

130   ARISTOTLE'S PRACTICAL EPISTEMOLOGY

at a higher level of generality, albeit one that is more concrete and action-guiding than simply 'good' would be.[14]

Let me turn now to defending my own view. I have, in this first part of the chapter, connected Aristotle's remarks about our need to grasp ethical principles in order to act well with his claim that it belongs to practically wise people to understand the virtuous goals or ends toward which they deliberate. To substantiate this claim—and to highlight its ethical and, indeed, political weight— I propose now to turn to a specific virtue of character, justice, to see why deliberative excellence might demand such an understanding in a specific domain of action. By considering justice as a virtue for Aristotle and, more specifically, the idea that the truly just person as such must have an articulate understanding of the goals justice seeks to achieve, we will be able to appreciate better the central claim of this book about *phronēsis*: that it is practical understanding.

5.2 Justice as a virtue of character

5.2.1 The special domain of particular justice

Justice—and here and throughout this chapter, I mean only what Aristotle calls "particular justice"—is frequently neglected by scholars of Aristotle's ethics, by contrast to virtues like courage and moderation, which more obviously involve the regulation of passions and desires (fear and confidence in the case of courage, bodily pleasure and our desires for such pleasure in the case of moderation). Indeed, justice, as readers of *NE* V soon find, does not appear to be a *paradigm* virtue of character. For instance, the famed doctrine of the mean, which features in the definition of the virtues

---

[14] Achtenberg's view may also be fruitfully compared, on this basis, to those of Howard Curzer and R Kathleen Harbin, which I discussed above (see 122, fn. 1).

KNOWLEDGE OF PRACTICAL UNIVERSALS 131

of character in *NE* II.6, seems either not to apply to it in the way that it does the other virtues.[15] Still, justice is among the most frequently mentioned virtues in Aristotle's general discussions of the virtues of character, alongside courage and moderation. Moreover, the place of justice as a virtue that sustains the political community will also help us understand the nature of political wisdom, the topic of the next chapter.[16]

Any treatment of justice in Aristotle must take into account the initial complexity of the analysis in *NE* V, which is embedded within both a discussion of the virtues of character that runs from *NE* II–V and a longer discussion of the distinctly human excellences (and their opposite states) that runs from *NE* I.13 to VII.10.[17] Still, I wish to begin by narrowing my topic somewhat. As I said above, I mean to treat only what is usually called "particular" justice, that is, the kind of justice that Aristotle identifies as a *specific* virtue of character, parallel to virtues like courage and moderation. My treatment of particular justice below is also meant to be relatively uncontroversial, since my primary aim is not to defend a specific

---

[15] Aristotle discusses how particular justice steers away from both excess and deficiency and therefore is a mean or intermediate state (*NE* V.5, 1134a7–13). The key difference is that excess and deficiency both constitute injustice, which Aristotle seems to represent as a single vice.

[16] My lengthy treatment of particular justice is also meant to head off a frequent difficulty that faces accounts of practical wisdom that take their bearings from his account of courage and moderation, virtues where intermediacy in *passions* is more prominent than intermediacy in *actions*. This difficulty arises from a temptation to reduce the aim of deliberation to achieving an intuitive *balance*, which might be plausible if we focus on passion to the exclusion of action, as in the view of Sarah Broadie, who argues as follows: "If practical wisdom is like the ability to keep one's balance, then the wise man does not have to be guided by a precise picture of what he aims at in order to succeed in achieving it" (*Ethics with Aristotle*, 197). Judging the appropriateness of an action along the many dimensions of correctness identified above in T19 more clearly requires a discernment—indeed, an understanding—of the ends of action.

[17] *NE* V is also the first of the three common books shared by the *Eudemian* and the *Nicomachean Ethics*. The scholarly consensus takes these books to differ in some respects, especially linguistically, from the uniquely *Nicomachean* books, while the arguments are generally taken to fit the context of the *NE* well enough. This fact is perhaps due to the Common Books being in a state of incomplete redaction.

132 ARISTOTLE'S PRACTICAL EPISTEMOLOGY

interpretation of *NE* V but rather to use what Aristotle says to defend my interpretation of *phronēsis* as practical understanding.

Aristotle begins his account by contrasting the particular sense of justice with the meaning of the word *dikaiosunē* that is nearer "righteousness" or "uprightness" and that refers, in a way, to the whole of character-virtue and includes the particular virtue with the same name. This broader sense of justice is typically called "general" justice, though we should remember that this phrase is shorthand for the complex referent of this second sense of *dikaiosunē*. Aristotle describes the person with general justice as *lawful* (*nomimos*), while the person with particular justice is *fair* or *equitable* (*isos*). We can then frame the question of my investigation in this part of the chapter in the following way: What are the characteristic goals pursued by the person who is equitable, and how do their actions relate to their apprehension of these goals?

While the idea that particular justice is closely related to equality or equitability is a helpful start for understanding its distinctive subject matter, this idea cannot exhaust Aristotle's analysis of the virtue. After all, Aristotle also notes that friendship depends on equality in important ways (*NE* VIII.5, 1157b34–58a1). What *sort* of equality, then, does Aristotle have in mind when he characterizes the person with particular justice as equitable?

We are especially helped in addressing this question by the way that Aristotle differentiates two kinds or species of particular justice: distributive justice, which concerns giving and taking an appropriate measure of benefits and burdens when these are shared out among the members of the community, and justice in transactions, which concerns the rectification of social relations when the balance of benefits and burdens is skewed by individual actions (V.2, 1130b30–31a3). These are different sorts of equality with distinct processes of equalization that bring them about.[18] We

---

[18] Aristotle's analysis of the types of equality involved in distributive and corrective justice is one of the less successful parts of his theory of particular justice. He associates

KNOWLEDGE OF PRACTICAL UNIVERSALS 133

may be left to wonder, then, what the connection is between these two types of particular justice. I have argued elsewhere that we should understand both subtypes as concerned with the relationship between the citizens of an existing political community, who are bound by a network of reciprocity that makes that community possible in the first place.[19]

Let me briefly illustrate this claim about the essentially political character of particular justice with reference to each of its sub-kinds. Problems of distribution can arise at any level of social organization, but they are particularly pressing at the level of the political community. The reason is that persistent failures in distribution—where some people receive too many of the burdens and too few of the benefits of shared political life (while others fare the opposite way)—undermine the essential reciprocity that makes each citizen count as part of the community. When that reciprocity is intact, no citizen is able to dominate or exploit another and all of the citizens share in political authority and the benefits that come from it. That said, Aristotle does not reduce political community to an instrumental good for the citizens. But a central enabling condition of such community, nevertheless, is that all the citizens share not only in political life but also in what Aristotle calls "the parts of happiness," that is, the goods that make it possible to live well (V.1, 1129b17–25). To fall short of this standard is to be exploited, indeed, to be treated not like a fellow citizen but as a slave, i.e., a

distributive justice with proportional equality, since what is equalized is not just people but also the goods that are to be distributed. Corrective justice, meanwhile, involves arithmetic equality, since the parties to a given social interaction are meant to be equalized. But this distinction cannot be more than illustrative, since distributive justice depends on equal standing—an arithmetic notion and corrective justice, at least in the case of punishment, also contains a proportional element.

[19] See Jagannathan, "Reciprocity and Political Justice in Aristotle's *Nicomachean Ethics* Book V," *Archiv für Geschichte der Philosophie* 104 (2022): 53–73. For philosophical considerations about Aristotelian justice, I also draw, in this section, on arguments in my essay "A Defense of Aristotelian Justice" (forthcoming in *Ergo*).

134 ARISTOTLE'S PRACTICAL EPISTEMOLOGY

person whose good really can be overridden, or rather, subsumed into the good of others (V.5, 1132b31–33a2).[20]

We can appreciate the political character of distributive justice not only from failures with respect to its norms but also from the positive and prospective criteria the just person would employ to achieve it. The person who embodies particular justice will not seek to gain an advantage over others in the sharing of burdens and benefits but rather to treat them fairly, both when they are in a position to make distributions and when they are simply a party to them. Such treatment, Aristotle explains, will involve accepting and according to others these burdens and benefits according to the relevant standard of merit. While there are clear aristocratic overtones to this conception of fairness or equality (*isotēs*) as depending on merit, Aristotle has in mind not only distributions of material resources but also, and perhaps more importantly, the distribution of political power and honor.[21] Those who are better able to use such power ought to serve in higher office and deserve to receive higher status in the community, at least where such status is relevant.

In other matters, however, the citizens must be treated just the same for relations of equality to obtain among them. One such domain is that of private transactions, especially commercial ones. No difference in status can justify one person defrauding

---

[20] There is an interesting analog of John Rawls' (Kantian) notion of "the separateness of persons" in Aristotle's idea that all the citizens count. Martha Nussbaum argues that a social democratic theory can be built on this Aristotelian notion. See Nussbaum, "Aristotelian Social Democracy," in *Liberalism and the Good*, ed. R. Bruce Douglass, Gerald M. Mara, and Henry S. Richardson (Routledge, 1990), 203–252; and "Nature, Function, and Capability: Aristotle on Political Distribution," *Oxford Studies in Ancient Philosophy* suppl. vol. (1988): 145–184.

[21] Aristotle makes these points most clearly in his discussion of political justice in *Politics* Book III.9–11. There, he criticizes both oligarchs and democrats for their partial vision of justice, while allowing that each side also grasps part of the truth about political justice (III.9, 1280a7–11). Oligarchs intuit that those who contribute more to a community also (in some ways) deserve more, but they mistake the standard and focus wrongly on wealth. Democrats intuit that all free citizens count in the eyes of the political community but fail to see that this is consistent with differences in status. Merit or virtue as a standard reconciles these intuitions while avoiding the problems of both oligarchic and democratic norms of justice.

KNOWLEDGE OF PRACTICAL UNIVERSALS 135

another. Likewise, no citizen is held to be above another in cases of injury, such as adultery or theft. These types of wrong—injury and fraud—together point to the subject matter of the other kind of particular justice, namely, justice in transactions or corrective justice.

Because of the latter label and some of Aristotle's examples, it can seem that he means to describe a relation that holds between the entire political community (or its appointed representatives, judges, or magistrates) and individual wrongdoers. But, in fact, corrective justice is not most clearly exemplified in the process of rectification, even though rectification (described by Aristotle as a process of "equalization") is called for whenever there are transgressions. The judge, as Aristotle says, must be a kind of embodiment of equality to do his work (V.4, 1132a6–10), but the true exemplar of corrective justice, as with distributive justice, is the just citizen, who may serve as a judge at one time or another but must abide by the principles of corrective justice throughout their lives.

Again, we are helped by considering how corrective justice can be understood in terms of positive and prospective criteria, that is, from the perspective of the just person themself. The basic fact that makes corrective justice necessary is this: in our dealings with our fellow citizens, it is possible to deprive them of what is theirs. A just person is sensitive to this possibility and values the mutual benefit that comes from respecting what is another's, since it is only by each having and maintaining what is our own that we can meet on terms of equality in both economic and political interactions, the very interactions that make possible and sustain our common life.

The two kinds of particular justice, therefore, share a subject matter: the good and bad things that contribute to or detract from our living well and that can belong to one person or another. Included in this category are social as well as material goods; hence, Aristotle lists status (*timē*) alongside property or wealth (*khrēmata*)

136 ARISTOTLE'S PRACTICAL EPISTEMOLOGY

and security (*sōtēria*) (*NE* V.2, 1130b1–5).[22] A characteristic of the person with particular justice is having the proper attitude toward these goods (and their corresponding lacks) such that, in their relations with fellow citizens, they strive to maintain equal standing with others. There is, then, a single subject matter and kind of attitude that characterizes particular justice.

We find this point confirmed in Aristotle's explanation of the vice (or vices) of injustice opposed to this virtue. The excessive or overreaching person (*pleonektēs*), who is also a paradigm of injustice in Plato's *Republic*, is someone who wishes for what is not due to them, either in the form of a greater share of benefits or a lesser share of burdens. This person is therefore not simply greedy, as translations sometimes suggest, but also a shirker, that is, someone who flees from the difficulties that political community sometimes demands of us. Likewise, there is a nameless figure we might call the servile person, who fails to pursue the relevant benefits in social life or allows too many burdens to accrue to them. Aristotle focuses far more on the excessive person, just as he focuses on the licentious person in his analysis of moderation, since one of the two vices is in each case by far the rarer. Indeed, it is more psychologically likely that someone would be servile only in certain domains, e.g., by neglecting honor while maintaining a healthy interest in material goods such as wealth. In this way, we can see that the doctrine of the mean applies to particular justice, even though it is not the focus of Aristotle's analysis.

5.2.2 The goals pursued by the just person

Now that I have outlined the outlook of the just person and the subject matter of particular justice, we can consider what the

---

[22] In a closely related context in the *NE*, Aristotle refers to a similar list of goods as competitive goods (*perimakhēta*). The expression "competitive goods" appears in the treatment of self-love and excessiveness (*pleonexia*) in *NE* IX.8, 1169a15–19, where distributive justice is at stake.

KNOWLEDGE OF PRACTICAL UNIVERSALS 137

characteristic goals of such a person are. A helpful example that has some relevance for our own lives in modern societies is that of involvement in politics or access to political power, which for Aristotle is a subject of distributive justice. While the Athens of Aristotle's time was far from a genuinely democratic society—with the mass exclusion of women, enslaved peoples, and a substantial class of foreign residents (known as metics), including Aristotle himself, from political life—political participation was still reasonably widespread by comparison to other forms of political organization, such as monarchies and oligarchies. Since Aristotle himself includes service on juries and in the Assembly as forms of political participation in addition to the traditional magistracies, a large portion of the adult, free male population would count as engaging directly in politics.[23]

What is the ethical significance of one's attitudes toward political participation? We can turn to a literary example for some insight. In Aristophanes' *Wasps*—performed around 422 BCE—we meet Philocleon, whose slave Xanthias tells the audience at the start of the play that his master is addicted to jury duty and so must be kept indoors at all costs (*Wasps* 85–135). The joke, in part, turns on the historical fact that Cleon—the demagogue to whom Philocleon (whose name, roughly, means "fan of Cleon") is devoted—increased the pay for jurors from two to three obols, allegedly in a bid to influence them.[24] But at any rate, the comedy gives us a portrait of a character-type familiar from other Greek texts of the fifth and fourth centuries, the political busybody (*polupragmōn*, literally "doer of (too) much"). Even jury service, then, falls subject to principles of fair participation that one may exceed. In our own time, it is perhaps more common for people to want to avoid jury service, with its relatively meager pay and disruption to ordinary

---

[23] See *Politics* III.1 for the role of this point in Aristotle's definition of citizenship (1275a26–31).

[24] See Arnold Wycombe Gomme, Theodore John Cadoux, and P. J. Rhodes, "Cleon," *Oxford Classical Dictionary*, 4th ed. (Oxford University Press, 2012).

138 ARISTOTLE'S PRACTICAL EPISTEMOLOGY

life. The opposing character-type from the busybody, the political idler (*apragmōn*), is therefore perhaps more relevant to us.

I stressed in the previous section that social goods—like political office and, more broadly, honor in a community—are part of the subject matter of justice, alongside material goods. How, then, should we characterize the just person's outlook on political participation? What goals do they pursue in this domain?

As a first observation, notice that an abstract goal can be formulated just from my delineation of the opposed character-types of the political busybody and the political idler. The just person will seek political involvement not just for the right reasons on given occasions but also from the proper judgment of the *value* of political involvement itself, both for themselves and for the political community as a whole. Otherwise, there would be little hope of determining what level of political engagement is appropriate for oneself. In other words, the just person appreciates not just how to make good use of individual opportunities for political involvement but also recognizes what such involvement is *for*, namely, sustaining the political community of which they are a part. To see oneself as a citizen is to recognize the incumbency of the appropriate degree of political involvement. Of course, an excessive pursuit of status—or whatever else happens to motivate the busybody—represents a deformation of one's role as a citizen just as much as does its deficient pursuit by the idler. Understanding the goal of political involvement, then, is a necessary part of the self-regulation of these desires, including both the desire for honor or esteem that can come of political office and the desire to advance one's private ends, especially material ends, where these might be compromised through political engagement. It is by referring our involvement to that goal that we are able to see it as conducing to the values that are important to any just citizen.

To elucidate this goal further, we can consider an example from a modern context: the venal politician. In liberal democracies, we are familiar with the idea that politicians often pursue public office

KNOWLEDGE OF PRACTICAL UNIVERSALS   139

for private ends. In some countries, going into national politics can be an effective way to amass considerable wealth, while in others, politicians can readily gain influence in other aspects of social life, such as in industries they are meant to regulate or in the political media. Against this background, it can seem naïve to simply assert that these are inappropriate goals of political involvement. But still we sense that something has gone wrong. How can we square these two thoughts?

The Aristotelian framework helps us understand what to say about the venal politician. Political office is indeed appropriately rewarded by social status or esteem (*tīmē*), but this status should not be reduced to personal influence or material gain. These latter benefits are unduly sought by some, which is a failure with regard to distributive justice. Such politicians exploit the citizens whose interests they are meant to represent, especially those who accord them honor for public service when in fact they are pursuing private benefit. The goal of pursuing and exercising political authority should instead be the common good. But the reward of social status need not be effaced from the motivation of the politician altogether. After all, Aristotle sees an appropriate relationship to honor as part of a flourishing life, designating the virtues of magnificence and sincerity to this domain. Politics does not demand self-effacing altruism, in other words; that is how we can avoid the charge of naïveté I raised above.

In pursuing the common good and not private benefit through the exercise of their office and in welcoming, while not unduly pursuing honor, the just politician displays their grasp of the goal of political office. This goal operates not only as a norm for their conduct but also as a standard (*skopos*) to which they can refer their actions and deliberations.[25] Consider a politician who is offered a

---

[25] The idea of a standard or target (*skopos*) features in *NE* I.2, 1094a23–24. The metaphor recurs in *NE* VI.1, where Aristotle argues that the practically wise person must have such a target in view that guides right reasoning (1138b20–25).

140 ARISTOTLE'S PRACTICAL EPISTEMOLOGY

hefty speaking fee to address a group of wealthy citizens. Will this fee warp their future actions in office? Will addressing such a group distort the political process in other ways? These are real questions that people face when they achieve high office. Conceiving of the common good as achieved through an appropriate share for all in the benefits and burdens of society, regulated by the appropriate value and purpose of holding political office, can help them answer it.

5.2.3 Practical understanding and insight into goals of action

There will be some people who fall short of the ideal of the just and wise person whom I have described, who are nevertheless well-disposed in the domain of justice. Such people lack the motive to exploit others that might lead them toward injustice, but they rely primarily on experience to meet the demands of justice. The wise, I have argued, are distinguished by their understanding, since they know how to apply their grasp of the goals of justice to their circumstances. Let us consider another concrete example of deliberation to illustrate this point, this time turning from distributive justice to justice in transactions (i.e., corrective justice).

It is easy to see that fraud, typified by the intentional deprivation of material goods that rightfully belong to someone else, is opposed to justice. But what does justice in commercial transactions demand as a positive matter? Aristotle's political framing of particular justice helps us see what is at stake here. Commercial transactions can be considered on their own as purely economic matters, but in a well-ordered polity, they will be regulated to sustain the collective life of the citizens. These regulations do not simply aim at fairness in a procedural sense but at securing the *good* of the parties involved and indeed the whole community, which seldom has a significant

KNOWLEDGE OF PRACTICAL UNIVERSALS 141

stake in how any given transaction goes but which maintains an interest in the web of economic life that animates it.

Some examples of fraud—especially those that involve deception—are straightforward. The tax cheat or the wage thief do not require much scrutiny. Avoiding such criminal activity is unlikely to be a direct concern of even somewhat decent people, though these examples may still be useful in moral education. But there are in fact cases where subtler kinds of fraud might be a genuine temptation.

Imagine a seller of essential goods in a time of crisis, say a grocer in the wake of a major natural disaster that leaves people vulnerable. In these circumstances, we often see that it is easy for sellers to charge exorbitant prices that their goods would not command in other times. Frequently, the legal barriers to raising prices are ineffectual, even where so-called price gouging is a crime. One may argue, of course, that a fair price is simply whatever the market can sustain. But crises such as natural disasters remind us that the laws of supply and demand cannot be our sole moral guide. Increasing prices dramatically during a crisis counts as exploitation because the seller treats the unexpected need of others purely as an opportunity for profit. Yet the joint activity of buying and selling presupposes that the parties' needs can be equalized without either party being deprived of something due to them. In a crisis, the need of some is artificially and unduly enlarged, making some transactions unjust, despite the possibility that all parties are willing to engage in exchange on those terms.

Intuitively, a scrupulous shopkeeper or business owner may realize that an opportunity to engage in price gouging is no reason to exploit others. But emergencies frequently raise prices for businesses, whether passed on from wholesalers or because of supply disruptions. We can imagine, then, a relatively decent person, brought up to respect the law and principles of just dealing, faced with a circumstance in which a substantial price increase on

142   ARISTOTLE'S PRACTICAL EPISTEMOLOGY

their goods can seem reasonable and not simply ruled out. Such a person must weigh the burden on their business against the burdens on their potential and actual customers.

I have identified the intuitive notion of a relatively decent person with Aristotle's notion of the person who has experience with respect to the virtues of character. The person with experience will, we can imagine, recognize the general principle that a small increase in prices is generally appropriate to cover the prospect of increased costs but that large increases may turn out to be unjust and exploitative. Hence, in a crisis, we can expect such a person to act accordingly, raising their prices only a little but staying well shy of what others (and the law, if a relevant law exists) would consider price gouging. But the truly just person not only recognizes which actions tend to be just but also understands why. The reason that price gouging ought to be avoided is that in raising pricing dramatically, we exploit our fellow citizens by turning commercial transactions, which ought to be entered upon without coercion, into a venue to exert an adventitious power over them. This grasp of *why* price gouging is to be avoided can evidently be a help to the just seller in setting prices appropriately. Our experience of extraordinary circumstances is likely to be limited, after all.

Note that the just seller sees selling not as a morally neutral activity but one that is invested with the fraught possibility of exploitation as well as the happier prospect of mutual agreeableness. Commercial transactions are and ought to be a forum for cooperation, in other words. It is precisely because we *all* depend on one another in a political community that any given economic interaction is invested with this significance. With these or similar thoughts in mind, the just seller acts on the basis of a standard to determine what sorts of price increases might be tolerable—namely, those alone that depend on increased costs to them—and

KNOWLEDGE OF PRACTICAL UNIVERSALS   143

what sorts of increases, while consistent with demand, will amount to exploitation.[26]

There is no precise formula on which to rely, of course. But it is a mark of practical wisdom to see the range of considerations that might bear on such a circumstance, e.g., the length and urgency of the crisis, the degree to which the goods in question are essential, the availability of other sellers in the market, and so on. Yet this very sensitivity is not simply an attunement to all these indefinitely many factors but rather a product of an understanding of the characteristic goal of particular justice: the maintenance of an equality among one's fellow citizens in a political community that makes shared life possible in the first place.

One could, of course, dispute the substantive conception of justice, including the core distinction of distributive and corrective justice, in Aristotle's virtue theory.[27] Or one could accept the broad outlines of his account of justice and reject the characterization of the *goals* of justice that I have provided. Still, I hold that some account of goals such as these and the way that understanding them would shape just action will be part of any broadly Aristotelian account of virtue. Similar accounts must be provided for the other virtues of character, but because justice involves a concern for others as fellow citizens and as sharers in a single political life, it clearly demonstrates the place of an understanding of these goals in the practical reasoning of the virtuous person.

[26] One might object that higher prices are neutral since there needs to be an inducement to bring goods to market when demand rises. But the very *need* of others should provide that inducement. In the absence of individual sellers who can meet this need at non-exploitative prices, the government ought to step in to ensure provision of resources to all, thereby spreading the burden across the community as distributive justice demands. Thanks to Joel David Hamkins for discussion of this point.

[27] For a recent example of a theorist who takes Aristotle's virtue ethics seriously but finds his account of justice wanting, see Mark LeBar, "After Aristotle's Justice," in *Oxford Studies in Normative Ethics*, vol. 10, ed. Mark Timmons (Oxford University Press, 2020), 32–55. For my reply to LeBar, see Jagannathan, "A Defense of Aristotelian Justice."

144 ARISTOTLE'S PRACTICAL EPISTEMOLOGY

5.3 The unity of practical wisdom

5.3.1 An objection to my account of understanding of goals

In the previous section, I defended my core claim that *phronēsis* is practical understanding by arguing that practical wisdom requires a grasp of the characteristic goals of virtuous action, which serve as a standard by which individual actions may be measured. One may object to this account as follows: If acting justly, for example, requires a grasp of the characteristic goals of justice, will there not be a type of practical wisdom associated with each virtue rather than a single excellence that is practical wisdom? In fact, Aristotle frequently contrasts the plurality of character virtues, differentiated by their domains and the actions and reactions appropriate to those domains, with the unitary virtue of thought he terms *phronēsis*. Addressing this objection will also help me introduce the idea of a practical universal, which is a key concept in my analysis of *phronēsis* as practical understanding.

To address this objection, we may turn to a passage in which Aristotle explains the difference between the single goal of *phronēsis* as such and the many goals we achieve by acting virtuously. The context for the passage is Aristotle's differentiation of practical wisdom from craft-understanding, which he argues for in a variety of ways in *NE* VI.4–5, one of which is presented here:

> [T20] Hence, what is left is for it [practical wisdom] to be a true intellectual state for acting in relation to what is good and bad for a human being, since production's goal is distinct [from production itself], while action's goal cannot be. Hence, the very fact of acting well (*eupraxia*) is the goal [of action]. That's why we consider Pericles and others like him practically wise, because they can judge what is good for them and what is good for human beings. We regard such people as capable of

KNOWLEDGE OF PRACTICAL UNIVERSALS 145

managing households and cities. It is also why we give moderation (*sōphrosunē*) its name, on the grounds that it preserves practical wisdom (*sōzousan phronēsis*). For pleasure and pain do not spoil or twist every belief, e.g., the belief that a triangle has or does not have [angles equal to] two right angles, but beliefs that pertain to what is to be done. For the principles of the things to be done are that for the sake of which these things are to be done. A person spoiled by pleasure or pain does not immediately recognize the principle [for which they should act], that is, that they should choose and do all things for its sake or because of it. For vice is destructive of the principle. (*NE* VI.5, 1140b4–20)

Aristotle begins the passage from the observation that each craft has its own proper goal that is distinct from the craft-activities that bring it about, a claim that we find already in *NE* I.1, but which is further developed in VI.4–5. While an artisan deliberates about a partial good (*kata meros*), the person of practical wisdom deliberates about the entirety of the good life (VI.5, 1140a25–28). In the present passage, Aristotle adds the point, also familiar from *NE* I.1, that an action in the narrow sense is its own goal. Since practical wisdom concerns actions, the perfection that it brings will also be contained within these actions, a perfection that deserves the name *eupraxia*, a nearly untranslatable nominalization of the expression *eu prattein*, "acting well," which I have rendered elsewhere as "success in action" or "acting successfully."

In the second half of the passage, Aristotle makes some supporting observations about this claim. The second of these observations is the key for my purpose here. Aristotle notes that vice distorts our grasp of what we should act *for*, here described as the "principle" for action (*arkhē*) or, equivalently, the starting point for deliberation. While we can speak of this principle as the goal for whose sake we act (*to hou heneka*), there is not a single such principle. Rather our actions have many principles (*arkhai*), as the text makes clear. In relation to the beginning of the passage, these

146   ARISTOTLE'S PRACTICAL EPISTEMOLOGY

goals must be understood as different ways of achieving *eupraxia*, the single goal of action that practical wisdom aims to facilitate.

The existence of a plurality of practical principles and goals that are characteristic of the person who has the character-virtues, then, is consistent with the unity of practical wisdom, since the latter has our living well on the whole as its goal. To bring about this single goal, we must, in given circumstances, advance particular goals. But these goals, in turn, should not be understood as *particulars*, in the way that individual actions are. Rather, just because they can serve as the goal of a variety of different kinds of actions, they should be seen as *practical universals*. These include political equality as a goal of justice, safety as a goal of courage, health as a goal of moderation, and so on.

The unity of practical wisdom, then, depends on the unity of what it seeks to bring about: *eupraxia*, or success in action, which in the *Nicomachean Ethics* denotes the aspect of happiness that is up to us. But the person of practical wisdom achieves this aim by acting according to and from the character-virtues given their characteristic goals, which are grasped as practical universals. Other interpreters of Aristotle have observed that a crucial function of *phronēsis* is to rectify the demands of the various virtues, which, even if they cannot come into genuine conflict, nevertheless both place us under a range of constraints and offer us a range of opportunities for action.[28] This aspect of *phronēsis* is accounted for by the unity of *eupraxia* as its overall goal, but a picture of *phronēsis* that too narrowly focuses on rectifying the demands of the virtues will elide the function of the practical universals themselves. We can only deliberate on the basis of a determinate goal. One function of good practical thought in a given circumstance will be to see what goals can in fact be advanced in it.

---

[28] Daniel Russell, *Practical Intelligence and the Virtues* (Oxford University Press, 2009), highlights this feature and offers a philosophical defense of it; see esp. Chapter 11, "Phronesis and the Unity of the Virtues," 335–373.

KNOWLEDGE OF PRACTICAL UNIVERSALS   147

In fact, deliberation as a process of practical thought can begin not only from an abstract consideration of a possible goal to be achieved but also from an awareness or recognition of the resources a person has at their disposal, which can typically be used in pursuit of many different sorts of goals. David Wiggins emphasizes this aspect of wise Aristotelian deliberation, though he wrongly attributes the work of moving back and forth between particulars and universals purely to perception (*aisthēsis*) or what he calls "situational appreciation."[29] We should say that the wise person not only *notices* the relationship between particular actions and goals they can advance but also *understands* the characteristic goals of the virtues of character, which grounds and orients their deliberative thought. While perception is needed for such thought to make contact with the world in the right way, it cannot exhaust the understanding of the wise person.

5.3.2   Is happiness itself a practical universal?

My view bears an interesting resemblance to the view of practical reasoning defended by John McDowell in his writings on Aristotle's ethics. In this section, I aim to further elucidate my conception of practical universals by comparison to McDowell's view. McDowell,

[29] See Wiggins, "Deliberation and Practical Reasoning." The expansion of practical perception to cover virtually the whole of practical wisdom is also a feature of John McDowell's interpretation of Aristotle in "Virtue and Reason," *The Monist* 62 (1979): 331–350, and "Deliberation and Moral Development in Aristotle's Ethics," in *Aristotle, Kant, and the Stoics: Rethinking Happiness and Duty*, ed. Stephen Engstrom and Jennifer Whiting (Cambridge University Press, 1998), 19–35. I engage with McDowell's view in detail below (§5.3.2).
Martha Nussbaum's view is not subject to this criticism, since she argues only for the *primacy* of the particular, but she tends to reduce practical principles to rules or generalizations, which in the practical domain can only be rules of thumb. Aristotle does indeed rule out any such canon by which choice can be governed, but his conception of practical universals is considerably richer, both in the ethical case and in the case of craft-understanding. See Nussbaum, *Love's Knowledge: Essays on Philosophy and Literature* (Oxford University Press, 1990), "The Discernment of Perception: An Aristotelian Conception of Private and Public Rationality," 54–105.

148 ARISTOTLE'S PRACTICAL EPISTEMOLOGY

like Wiggins, emphasizes the importance of perception to the exercise of *phronēsis*. To a greater extent than Wiggins, McDowell emphasizes that Aristotle holds that there is a universal component to the knowledge of the person of practical wisdom, which is a form of understanding. Where my view diverges from that of McDowell is in the shape of this understanding. McDowell takes happiness itself (or, to make a friendly amendment to his view, *eupraxia*, the dimension of happiness that is up to us) to be the universal that the wise person grasps and is able to bring about in acting virtuously on a given occasion. Can we then say that McDowell grants the centrality of practical universals—or at least one of them—to the exercise of *phronēsis*?

McDowell's remarks about hard cases, however, show that he does not recognize the importance of practical universals to the excellent deliberation of the wise person.[30] Hard cases are where practical explanation cannot rationally compel another person—even a relatively well-disposed person—to see things just as you do. In such cases, McDowell argues that explanations can simply run out, a fact that has the tendency to induce a sense of vertigo, given our instinct to seek firm foundations for justification and explanation of all sorts. This move seems to do away with Aristotle's commitment to practical truth by contrast to other concepts, such as practical justification, that would allow for such gaps to open up between well-situated agents. Justification is evidently McDowell's own focus in theorizing rationality, which suggests that his conceptual framework and Aristotle's diverge at precisely this point.

In fact, in "Virtue and Reason," McDowell draws on Stanley Cavell's interpretation of Wittgenstein to argue that rationality quite generally depends on underlying and typically unnoticed concurrences of perspective.[31] In the ethical cases, this shared

---

[30] McDowell, "Virtue and Reason," 340–341.
[31] McDowell, "Virtue and Reason," 338–340.

KNOWLEDGE OF PRACTICAL UNIVERSALS 149

"whirl of organism"—the evocative phrase McDowell draws from Cavell—allows us to share a practical world, to see one another as going on rationally in action and decision. McDowell's explicit target is a rule-based conception of reason, where the rules themselves are the principles that ground the rationality of an agent proceeding in accordance with the rule. Happiness or *eupraxia* is evidently not such a principle, but McDowell seems to regard any intermediate practical principles—those that stand between *eupraxia* and a particular action—as equivalent to rules or rule-like generalizations.

I have been arguing in this chapter that the characteristic goals pursued by the virtuous person are grasped as practical universals and that these are not reducible to rules or generalizations. Rules and other generalizations are in fact a great help in practical reasoning, but reliance on them is properly a feature of the person with ethical experience.

5.3.3 Practical universals and grasping 'the why'

As I have argued throughout this book, Aristotle takes a grasp of 'the why' to be central to each form of understanding, including *phronēsis*. We saw in Chapter 2 that ordinary practical knowledge is characterized in the *Nicomachean Ethics* as a matter of grasping 'the that' or what is so in ethics, by contrast to understanding 'the why.' I have laid out in this chapter my view of what the superior knowledge of the practically wise depends on: a grasp of the characteristic goals of the character-virtues that serve as a measure or standard against which particular actions may be assessed in deliberation (as well as in other modes of evaluation, such as the hermeneutic activity of comprehension, *sunesis*).

In the passages where Aristotle speaks of 'the why,' especially *NE* I.4, it becomes clear that he recognizes that there is some knowledge that is both universal and explanatory in the domain of ethics.

150   ARISTOTLE'S PRACTICAL EPISTEMOLOGY

In Chapter 4, I showed that the existence of universal and explanatory ethical knowledge is insufficient to establish the existence of ethical science. Now, I can characterize my positive view: universal and explanatory knowledge in ethics is a grasp of ethical goals as they are salient for deliberation.

I defended this highly abstract claim by drawing attention to the need for such a grasp of ethical goals to act justly. As I noted above (131, fn. 16), I chose justice because it is harder to argue that a grasp of the value of the burdens and benefits of social life could be merely intuitive as compared to the characteristic goals of the moderate or courageous person. But my choice was dialectical. All of the character-virtues, on Aristotle's demanding conception of them, will require an understanding of their characteristic goals. To be moderate, for instance, demands not only restraint in experiencing bodily passions but also an appreciation of the value of health, propriety, and other relevant goals around which a moderate person orients themselves. To conform our actions and passions to the standard of right reason we need an articulate grasp of our practical landscape. The wise person, in other words, will have something to say not only to justify their actions but also to ground the value of their actions in other values, namely, the ones whose pursuit is characteristic of the several virtues of character.

6

POLITICAL WISDOM

6.1 The political character of Aristotelian practical wisdom

I have argued in the preceding chapters that *phronēsis*, as that concept is articulated in the *Nicomachean Ethics*, is practical understanding. In this final chapter of the book, my aim is to show that my interpretation of Aristotle's views about *phronēsis* is well supported by what he says about *political* wisdom. In a crucial passage of *NE* VI, Aristotle identifies *phronēsis* and *politikē* as the same state. I take this claim seriously and will argue that it reveals an important dimension of Aristotle's ethical-political thinking.

In a way, my arguments already point to a political interpretation of what *phronēsis* is. The grasp of practical universals that I attributed to the person of practical wisdom prominently includes an understanding of the common good. As I argued in the previous chapter, in order for someone to have the virtue of particular justice, they must be in a position to promote the equitable possession of the burdens and benefits of shared life among the citizens of their community. But to be able to act in this way, one must grasp the place of those burdens and benefits in that shared life and in the life of individuals, as well as their relative value and the overarching goal under which they are subsumed, which is nothing other than the common good.

While even ordinary citizens must acquire such an understanding of the common good, there is nothing else that is needed for wise political deliberation than this understanding. That is the force of Aristotle's claim that political wisdom and *phronēsis* are the same state of soul, which I will refer to as the "Identity Thesis."

Aristotle's Practical Epistemology. Dhananjay Jagannathan, Oxford University Press.
© Oxford University Press 2024. DOI: 10.1093/9780197781517.003.0007

152   ARISTOTLE'S PRACTICAL EPISTEMOLOGY

The plan of the rest of this chapter is as follows. I first (in §6.2) discuss the textual basis for the Identity Thesis in the *NE* before considering and arguing against an alternative interpretation on which political wisdom is simply analogous to practical wisdom while having its own proper subject matter. In §6.3 I then turn my attention to the *Politics* where Aristotle identifies practical wisdom as the distinct excellence of rulers, by contrast to what is needed to be a good subject, which he calls "true belief" and associates with the virtues of character rather than with practical wisdom. I argue that this claim must be read together with Aristotle's commitment to the idea that citizens need knowledge of rule from both sides, since citizenship involves both subjection to the kind of rule that is appropriate to free people and participation in such rule. The division of labor being posited here, then, corresponds to the idea that the virtues of character give us the right goals, which citizens must appreciate in accepting the commands of the magistrates and legislators and thereby forming true beliefs. I then show in §6.4 the connection between wise legislation and the grasp of practical universals I discussed in the previous chapter by contrasting legislation with decrees enacted on particular occasions. I conclude by responding, in §6.5, to the objection that the practical universals relevant to legislative and political wisdom are distinct from those understood by the practically wise person.

6.2 The identity of political and practical wisdom

Aristotle declares, bluntly, at the start of *NE* VI.8 that "political and practical wisdom are the same state, though they do not have the same being" (1141b23–24). Yet interpreters have struggled to take him at face value. I will try to show that the surface meaning of this text—the Identity Thesis—makes good sense.

This remark follows immediately on the important passage of *NE* VI.7 relating experience (*empeiria*) to the universal and particular

POLITICAL WISDOM 153

knowledge of the person of practical wisdom that I discussed at length in Chapter 2 (T5). I argued that Aristotle represents practical wisdom as *surpassing* experience because it requires a grasp of universals while nevertheless remaining committed to its practicality, that is, the fact that its exercise is always in acting in particular circumstances. I will defend the surface meaning of the Identity Thesis by showing how it follows from these commitments about particular and universal practical knowledge.

One immediate source of confusion is Aristotle's remark that these states, while being the same, "do not have the same being."[1] What sort of sameness does Aristotle then have in mind? When we turn to Aristotle's logic and metaphysics, we find that Aristotle uses this locution to help pick out the difference between *numerical* identity (constituting one and the same individual entity) and *strict* identity (being specified by the same definition). Two things that are the same but do not have the same being are numerically but not strictly identical. Aristotle's examples of this kind of sameness helps illustrate his point: the road from Athens to Thebes and the road from Thebes to Athens are the same road specified differently (*Physics* III.3, 202b12–14); likewise, the convex and the concave are the same curve specified differently. Hence, the claim Aristotle is making in *NE* VI.8 is just that political and practical wisdom are the same understanding specified differently.

But this clarification of the different senses of the sameness leaves us with a new question. How can two states constitute the same understanding while differing in specification? Knowledge, after all, seems to be picked out intensionally. The gap between numeric and strict identity thereby seems not to open up in this case, as it does for a road or a curved object, which are susceptible of being specified differently. For now, I will simply propose a solution to

---

[1] In this and the following paragraphs, I present some of the ideas from my article "'Every Man a Legislator': Aristotle on Political Wisdom," *Apeiron* 52, no. 4 (2019): 1–20, esp. 10–15.

154   ARISTOTLE'S PRACTICAL EPISTEMOLOGY

this problem while aiming to vindicate it in the rest of this section: the aspect of difference that Aristotle means to indicate is not a difference in *what is known* but a difference in *the context of exercise*. In other words, it is true that practical and political wisdom are an understanding of the same thing, the human good. What makes a given exercise of this single understanding specifiable as political or not is whether the deliberator is occupying a certain social position, e.g., as an officeholder or a magistrate. In reality, however, every exercise of practical wisdom is political in the sense that the common good serves as an overarching goal for the practically wise person.

As a preliminary defense of this idea, we can turn to the opening of the *Nicomachean Ethics*, where Aristotle describes his inquiry into the highest human good as political. He nevertheless proposes to consider the good for an individual on the grounds that this good is the *same* as the good for a political community (I.2, 1094a22–b7). Here, we see a clear articulation of the same structure I am attributing to political and practical wisdom. The human good—happiness—is the same for both an individual and a *polis*. Equally, the wisdom that brings about this good is the same, no matter the scope of practical influence of the one who exercises it.[2]

A great deal of confusion about the nature of the Identity Thesis, however, comes not from the single line I have quoted but from the larger context of the first part of VI.8, which appears to offer simply a taxonomy of different kinds of practical and political wisdom. I will argue that Aristotle's goal is in fact to *undermine* the intuitive idea that political or legislative wisdom is a specialized form of expertise distinct from what individuals need to conduct their own affairs.[3] The key to appreciating this passage is the implicit contrast

---

[2] For the idea that practical wisdom brings about happiness, see *NE* VI.12, 1144a3–9 and cf. VI.13, 1145a6–11, where political wisdom is used to illuminate the point.

[3] Pavlos Kontos has recently defended the view that legislative wisdom is specialized at some length in his book *Aristotle on the Scope of Practical Reason: Spectators, Legislators, Hopes, and Evils* (Routledge, 2021); see especially Chapter 2 on the legislator. See my review "*Aristotle on the Scope of Practical Reason: Spectators, Legislators,*

POLITICAL WISDOM   155

between Aristotle's own view and the view defended by the Visitor in Plato's *Statesman*, which I discuss at length in the Appendix (§A.1).

Here is the Identity Thesis in its broader context:

[T21] [1] Indeed, political and practical wisdom are the same state, though they do not have the same being. [2] In knowledge pertaining to the city, one part, which is architectonic, is legislative wisdom; and another, which concerns the particulars, has the generic name political wisdom. [3] The latter is for acting and deliberation, since a vote is enacted as what is last [in deliberation]. [4] Hence these people alone are said to practice politics, since they alone act in the way manual workers do. [5] But what is thought to be practical wisdom most of all concerns oneself and one person, and this has the generic name practical wisdom. [6] And of these [sc. forms of practical wisdom] there is household management, legislation, and political wisdom, which is divided into the deliberative and the judicial. (*NE* VI.8, 1141b24–33)

In framing a contrast between architectonic political wisdom in [2] and particular political wisdom in [3–4], Aristotle draws on the divisions introduced by the Visitor in the *Statesman*. In the Appendix (§A.1), I discuss how Aristotle's view of practical knowledge in the *NE* rejects the view articulated in the *Statesman*. Here, Aristotle's attention is on the Visitor's conception of architectonic knowledge as removed from practice. In particular, Aristotle is targeting the idea that legislative political wisdom is not involved directly in action in the way that deliberative and judicial decision-making are. That is how the Visitor describes the ruling or royal art,

Hopes, and Evils, by Pavlos Kontos," *Mind* 133, no. 530 (2024), 526–534, for a response to this view.

156 ARISTOTLE'S PRACTICAL EPISTEMOLOGY

as a matter of coordinating the activities of others, just as a master builder or architect directs the manual laborers in building.

As I argued in Chapter 3, Aristotle's goal throughout *NE* VI is to show that practical wisdom *is* architectonic or prescriptive, not insofar as it necessarily directs others, but insofar as it needs no such direction. In this passage, we find a further articulation of this thought. One difficulty for modern readers is that the (post-classical) chapter division between *NE* VI.7 and VI.8 artificially divides a single stretch of argument. At the end of VI.7, Aristotle argues that the universal dimension of knowledge in practical wisdom entails that there is something architectonic about it, by contrast to the knowledge of particulars possessed by people with experience alone (VI.7, 1141b21–23). He should therefore be seen to reject the idea that he mentions in [4], that those who practice politics—those serving in the assembly and the jury—are the ones who really act, while those responsible for framing the laws are inactive. Just as practical wisdom is by itself architectonic and active, so too in the case of politics, all wisdom is devoted to action, though we can (by convention) distinguish household management, deliberative and judicial wisdom, and legislative wisdom as exercised in increasingly broad contexts.

If we take Aristotle to reject the *endoxon* or common opinion mooted in [4], he can be seen to be making a simple linguistic observation in [5], that *phronēsis* is typically used of the exercise of wisdom that concerns a single person. But this word also gets used for the *generic* notion of practical-political wisdom. I am arguing here that this is not a true genus, divided into distinct species or sub-kinds. Rather, we have a case where we employ many terms for a single thing—one state that is numerically identical across its contexts of exercise. Since we can read the rest of T21 as an elaboration of the Identity Thesis, and reading it in a way that distinguishes legislative wisdom from other kinds of practical wisdom would make a hash of the Identity Thesis, we should attribute the more

POLITICAL WISDOM   157

coherent line of thought to Aristotle, despite his highly compressed method of exposition.

Moreover, the Identity Thesis—and the broader version of it that embraces all these different forms or manifestations of *phronēsis*—makes good philosophical sense in relation to Aristotle's other commitments in his value theory. As I have noted, Aristotle holds that there is a single human good, whether for an individual or a community. This highest human good, unlike the goods brought about by the crafts, is comprehensive, spanning the whole of living well for human beings (*NE* VI.5, 1140a25–28). The goods of the crafts, by contrast, are particular—even important goods belonging to highly valued crafts like health (the aim of medicine) and peace (the ultimate aim of the military arts). It would be strange if there were multiple deliberative excellences that aimed at this single good.

As I have argued elsewhere, there tends to be implicit in rejections of the Identity Thesis a modern conception of politics as a distinct sphere of human life, e.g. as a forum for contestation among those whose lives are taken to be fully separate from others, whether the contestation takes place between individuals or between households.[4] The political community, for Aristotle, supersedes these more-individual goods because it affords their fulfillment. Human life just is political; so too, political activity just is human activity.

Of course, in communities of a sufficiently large size, there will be a need for what we might call a political apparatus. As I will show in the next section, Aristotle's conception of such a political apparatus, as well as its attendant division of labor, confirms my robust reading of the Identity Thesis.

---

[4] See my " 'Every Man a Legislator': Aristotle on Political Wisdom."

158   ARISTOTLE'S PRACTICAL EPISTEMOLOGY

6.3 Practical wisdom as the ruler's excellence

What I have called the political apparatus of a sufficiently large and complex community includes what Aristotle describes as the constitution (*politeia*), with its division of political offices, and the governing body (*politeuma*), which carries out the work of exercising rule in the community. In modern political philosophy, the relationship between a state and its citizen is typically framed around the idea of coercive state power and its legitimacy. Political authority for Aristotle, by contrast, is not a matter of coercion (though he recognizes the supremacy of the political community over individual citizens as well as the legitimacy of constraining them to follow the law) but rather the origination of the practical thinking by which the community is governed.[5]

While the fruit of such practical thinking may be a decision to adopt, on behalf of the community, a certain course of action in response to a set of exigent circumstances (a decree or *psēphisma*), the most characteristic result is the adoption or recognition of *laws*, which are general norms or practical principles for the community. The connection between rule and legislation is therefore a close one. But the exercise of political authority is also present in judicial action. Indeed, in one passage of the *Politics*, Aristotle even describes officeholders, in a broad sense, as judges (*kritai*)—judges of the necessary and the advantageous (*Politics* VII.8, 1328b22–3). The common idea in these varied political functions is of deliberation issuing in decision or judgment. The key venues for political authority, then, include magistracies, the assembly, and the courts.

In participating in such bodies or offices, citizens can be said to share in rule by directly taking part in the deliberation and decision-making that is characteristic of rule (*Politics* III.1, 1275a22–23).

---

[5] See Andres Rosler, *Political Authority and Obligation in Aristotle* (Oxford University Press, 2005) for an ambitious attempt to relate Aristotle's thinking about legitimate political authority to this modern framework.

POLITICAL WISDOM   159

But citizens also share in the constitution by sharing in the deliberation and decision-making of others, which is how they are ruled as free and equal members of the community (1275a26–31).[6] This duality—of ruling and being ruled in turn—is the characteristic of political rule, the rule of the free by the free (III.4, 1277a33–b7).[7]

Despite this ideal of alternation, in some constitutions, only very few people will be directly involved in exercising rule as officeholders, while in more participatory forms of government assemblies and juries take on, corporately, executive functions that are reserved for magistrates in oligarchies and aristocracies. Still, in every constitution, Aristotle holds that the *excellences* demanded of a ruler and of a subject are different. In particular, *phronēsis* is the excellence proper to a good ruler, while the virtues of character are the excellences proper to citizen-subjects (III.4, 1277a14–29).

These claims of Aristotle, however, have been widely misunderstood, in part because of a pernicious mistaken correction of the text of the *Politics* that has crept into the most widely used editions and translations. Before turning to this point about the text, we should note that the passage in which Aristotle introduces these claims is framed by a slightly different question: What is the relation between the good man and the good citizen, that is, between citizen excellence and human excellence as such? Aristotle's answer is fairly straightforward; only in the best constitution will these qualities coincide, since citizen excellence is relative to a given constitution:

[T22] Likewise for citizens, too, even though they are dissimilar, the safety of the community is their [common] task, but their

---

[6] I elaborate on this point about indirect participation in relation to the "true belief" that citizens must have below.

[7] On this duality in citizenship, see Malcolm Schofield, "Sharing in the Constitution," *The Review of Metaphysics* 49, no. 4 (1996): 831–858; and David Riesbeck, *Aristotle on Political Community* (Cambridge University Press, 2016), esp. Chapter 5, "Citizenship, Constitutions, and Political Justice," 179–235.

160 ARISTOTLE'S PRACTICAL EPISTEMOLOGY

community is the constitution. That is why the citizen's virtue must be relative to the constitution. If, then, there are many types of constitution, it's evidently not possible for there to be a single virtue of a good citizen that is complete. It is rather the good man whom we say is marked by one virtue that is complete. (*Politics* III.4, 1276b27–34)

Here, Aristotle picks out a single task for citizens, the safety or preservation of the community. But in fact, this common task is something of an abstraction from the citizens' dual work of ruling and being ruled in turn. That is why the topic of the ruler's distinctive excellence is first broached, which Aristotle says *does* coincide with the complete virtue proper to a good man.

The manuscript text should be translated as follows: "Will there be someone to whom the same virtue belongs both as a good citizen and as a good man? Well, we do say that a good ruler is virtuous and wise, and that the statesman must be wise (*ton de politikon anagkaion einai phronimon*)" (1277a13–16). In many editions—going back to the mid-nineteenth-century edition of Richard Congreve—the final clause is emended to read "and that the citizen need not be wise" (*ton de politēn ouk anagkaion einai phronimon*).[8] The emendation is unnecessary, as the slight pleonasm or repetition allows Aristotle to reframe his point in terms of the *knowledge* that, both in his theory and in that of Plato's later dialogues, only the true statesman (*politikos*) possesses. In other words, he is reminding his readers that political and practical wisdom are the same state, despite the different language we are inclined to use about them.

Congreve and editors who follow his lead, such as Sir David Ross in the Oxford Classical Text, as well as recent translators into English, connect this passage to one that appears later in the same chapter, where Aristotle again contrasts the good ruler's excellence

---

[8] Richard Congreve, *The* Politics *of Aristotle* (J. W. Parker, 1855).

with that of the good citizen.[9] Here, Aristotle adds the further thought that the citizen-subject has an excellence proper to their mode of sharing in rule: "Practical wisdom is the only virtue peculiar to a ruler, since the others, it seems, must be common to both rulers and subjects. But the subject's excellence, at any rate, is not practical wisdom but true belief" (*Politics* III.4, 1277b25–28). Nothing in this passage, however, demands that we alter the earlier text. In fact, they fit together neatly, the first passage reminding us of the Identity Thesis, with the second passage elaborating this thought in relation to the excellence proper to citizen-subjects.

In between these two passages, Aristotle argues that a citizen must learn how to rule and be ruled in turn, since that is the special character of political rule. Ruling, then, is *part* of the work of the citizen, which is preserving the constitution. As he puts it, summarizing his thought: "the good citizen must know and be able both to be ruled and to rule, and this is the excellence of the citizen, to know the rule of the free from both sides" (*Politics* III.4, 1277b13–16). In speaking of the ruler by contrast to the subject, then, Aristotle is not identifying distinct categories of people but rather distinct roles that citizens will take up at different times.

Aristotle offers a concrete example of such alternation in Book VII, where he describes the constitution of an idealized city that "we would pray for" (*kat' eukhēn*).[10] There, younger men are envisioned to undertake a period of military service before they become eligible for magistracies. The direct exercise of rule, then, is for later in life, once one's character has reached sufficient maturity and enough time has passed for the virtuous to acquire genuine

---

[9] W. D. Ross, *Aristotelis Politica* (Clarendon Press, 1957). See also C. D. C. Reeve, *Aristotle. Politics. A New Translation* (Hackett, 2017). A notable exception among translators is Peter L. P. Simpson, *The Politics of Aristotle* (University of North Carolina Press, 1997).

[10] See Kontos, *Aristotle on the Scope of Practical Reason*, Chapter 3, esp. 119–147, for an analysis of this notion in terms of the material conditions for political life.

162 ARISTOTLE'S PRACTICAL EPISTEMOLOGY

practical understanding.[11] Yet even in the earlier stage of life, citizens share in rule.

That is precisely why Aristotle identifies two ways of describing the excellences needed by citizens when they are subject to rule. The first is that all citizens need the excellences that human beings need in order to live well, namely, the virtues of character. The second description is that the excellence of citizens is, more specifically, "true belief." While this description is somewhat cryptic, the contrast between practical wisdom and true belief suggests that Aristotle is making reference to the deliberative cooperation that rule over free people demands, by contrast to despotic rule.

In despotic rule, commands may legitimately be given to a subordinate without any direct involvement of the subordinate beyond their recognition of the content of that command. Political rule, by contrast, is characterized by joint deliberation, and one of the tasks that falls to ordinary citizens who do not hold a magistracy and may not even be actively participating in another sort of deliberative body, is an affirmation of the suitability of a proposed course of action in light of the proper goals of the political community, which functions as an after-the-fact endorsement of the completed deliberation of the ruling body. This sort of affirmation can be thought of as a political analog of the practical virtue of *sunesis*, or comprehension, which Aristotle describes in *NE* VI.10 and which I discuss in the Appendix (§A.1). This ongoing affirmation of political decision-making by ordinary citizens lies at the heart of Aristotle's account of political rule and authority, what nowadays is called political legitimacy.

That is why Aristotle describes the excellence of citizen-subjects as "true belief." In the best case, the citizens will not only accept a decree or a law that is handed down to them but also genuinely endorse it in light of a correct account of the human good and the purpose of the political community, which is to bring about or

---

[11] *Politics* VII.9, 1329a6 ff.

POLITICAL WISDOM   163

make possible what is needed for the excellence and happiness of the citizens. The true belief in question is not simply an affirmation of the *authority* of the ruling body, then, but an affirmation that a given decision is itself *authoritative*, well-proportioned to its end, even if the citizens did not themselves participate directly in the decision-making process.

I have argued that the true belief that citizen-subjects who play their part in political life excellently flows from their possession of the virtues of character. Hence, the invocation of "belief" (*doxa*) in this context should not be seen to dismiss the excellence displayed by citizen-subjects. Two passages from the *NE* confirm this link between virtue and belief about goals. In *NE* VI.5, Aristotle speaks of how a lack of moderation allows pleasures and pains to distort one's grasp of the goals of action, which are the starting point for deliberation (1140b13–17, part of **T15**, discussed in Chapter 5). Likewise, in *NE* VII.8, we learn that virtue, natural or habituated, furnishes correct belief about the starting point (*orthodoxein peri tēn arkhēn*, 1151a18–19).

My aim in this section has been to show that the Identity Thesis, on its surface meaning, is supported by Aristotle's analysis of practical wisdom as the distinctive excellence of the wise ruler or statesman. It is what makes the true *politikos* a true *politikos*, since *politikē* is nothing other than *phronēsis* given a new name when exercised on behalf of the political community. Aristotle further clarifies his meaning when he identifies true belief as the excellence needed by good citizens who are not presently exercising rule, which I characterized in terms of grasping the suitability of decisions made by the ruling body. Such a grasp will itself require the virtues of character, since the goals of the political community are just whatever is needed for the citizens to achieve virtue and happiness, not something distinct from what is needed to lead a good individual human life.

164 ARISTOTLE'S PRACTICAL EPISTEMOLOGY

6.4 Practical universals in political life

The epistemic division of labor that Aristotle posits between rulers and citizen-subjects is described at best schematically in the *Politics*. We are helped, however, by another discussion of the political dimension of practical wisdom in *NE* X.9, which provides an introduction to the overarching project of the *Politics*, namely, to discover the principles of legislation in light of which laws and constitutions may be evaluated. Moreover, this text, taken together with the Identity Thesis, gives further evidence for my view that a grasp of practical universals is what sets *phronēsis* apart. For Aristotle characterizes political wisdom—in its legislative form— as a matter precisely of grasping something universal, in light of which the best laws may be chosen or framed.

I discussed *NE* X.9 in detail in Chapter 2 (§2.3), since this text also provides some of the best evidence for how Aristotle thinks of experience. I will now briefly return to the parts of the text that discuss legislative wisdom. In **T6** and **T7** (X.9, 1180a34–b28), Aristotle explores the question of whether individualized or common courses of education are better. In the end (the last part of **T7**), he lands on the idea that someone who wants to educate ought to advance to universal principles, since only then will they be able to act in a skillful or systematic way:

> But all the same it would seem that someone who wants to be skilled and knowledgeable, anyway, must advance to the universal and come to know it insofar as it is possible, since it is said that knowledge concerns this [sc. the universal]. Perhaps also someone who wants to make people better through discipline, whether many or few, must try to acquire legislative knowledge, since it is through laws that we become good. For not just anyone can handle well someone put in front of him, but if anyone can, it is the one who knows, as in medicine and the rest of what is governed by any sort of care and practical wisdom. (1180b20–28)

POLITICAL WISDOM   165

In effect, Aristotle identifies an amphiboly in the notion of educating individuals. If we mean by this *educating some individual person*, selected in advance, then providing specific attention to them may allow for good results. But if we mean *educating any individual whatever*, then only the expert, with universal and systematic knowledge, will be able to succeed.

I have argued that this crucial point can be explained in terms of the wise person's grasp of practical universals, which are articulated conceptions of the goals in service of which they deliberate. In the course of making that argument, I acknowledged the reasons one might have to be doubtful of the practical utility of such universals, at least in relation to exercising the virtues of character, and argued that the virtue of particular justice provides us a clear Aristotelian example of a virtue that demands such an understanding.

In the case of wise legislation, the utility of practical universals is perhaps more straightforward. The difference between decrees and laws, which I mentioned above, gives us some insight into this point. A decree is a practical decision for a particular occasion, while a law, however specific in its content, is meant to apply to a range of situations.[12] Rule solely by decree, as opposed to rule by law, is undesirable for many reasons, both pragmatic and normative. But to frame laws that are both applicable to a sufficiently wide range of cases to be useful and flexible enough to actually cover those cases is no easy task.[13] That is why, in the *Statesman*, Plato has the Eleatic Visitor rank the quasi-divine rule of a perfectly wise statesman over even rule by laws, acknowledging the need for revision and correction (*Statesman* 293a6 ff.). In order to frame a decree that is apt to its situation, one needs a grasp of a relevant practical goal that may be furthered by that decree and the situation in question. But

---

[12] For the significance of this distinction in Athenian political and constitutional practice in Aristotle's time, see Mogens Herman Hansen, "*Nomos* and *Psephisma* in Fourth-Century Athens," *Greek, Roman, and Byzantine Studies* 19, no. 4 (1978): 315–350.

[13] See Aristotle's well-known discussion of equity (*epieikeia*) as a corrective to over-rigid application of the law to particular cases (*NE* V.10).

166   ARISTOTLE'S PRACTICAL EPISTEMOLOGY

to frame a law that is apt to a range of *possible* situations requires, in addition, an understanding of how a range of goals may be balanced across those situations.

The interaction between laws and decrees—over which laws were taken to have normative priority regardless of the temporal priority of the various enactments—can help us see why Aristotle associates legislation with practical universals.

An example is provided by a law proposed by Leptines, against which Demosthenes argued in an extent speech (*Against Leptines*).[14] Grants of exemption (*ateleia*) from public service, such as military service or property taxation, are a paradigm case of a decree, a decision by the *dēmos* to make a specific award, frequently as a commendation for service to the state, to a particular person.[15] The law Leptines proposed would have abolished all grants of exemption, past and future (*Against Leptines* §§1–2), apparently to improve the city's financial situation during wartime. Even though this proposed law was responsive to the ongoing context, it would have curtailed the ability of the Assembly to act in other circumstances, one of the reasons Demosthenes argues against it (*Against Leptines* §§3–4). In fact, Leptines appears to have argued that many of the prior grants of exemption were made because the recipients acted deceitfully. Demosthenes seems right, therefore, to hold that the law has the effect of restricting the Assembly quite generally, placing the city's finances ahead of the propriety of rewarding service duly given.

On Aristotle's conception of legislation, wisely deciding for or against a law like this one—and indeed, making judgments about tax policy in our own time—requires a grasp of the practical

[14] I owe the example to Hansen, "*Nomos* and *Psephisma*," 324–325.

[15] See Léopold Migeotte, "*Ateleia*," *The Encyclopedia of Ancient History*, ed. Roger S. Bagnall, Kai Brodersen, Craige B. Champion, Andrew Erskine, and Sabine R. Huebner (Wiley-Blackwell, 2013) for a broad survey of the Greek institution; and D. M. MacDowell, "Epikerdes of Kyrene and the Athenian Privilege of Ateleia," *Zeitschrift für Papyrologie und Epigraphik* 150 (2004): 127–133 for the Athenian context specifically.

universals that make our conception of the common good articulate, in much the same way as the decisions of the wise shopkeeper I discussed in Chapter 5. Demosthenes argued that the *dēmos* should not let go of its prerogative to award exemptions, while Leptines argued that this prerogative was ultimately detrimental. This debate is unlike a debate over whether to award a specific exemption, where a more intuitive approach might well be sufficient. In particular, awarding an exemption in one case does not bind the Assembly to do so in every relevantly similar case. Part of the Assembly's prerogative is precisely a sort of arbitrariness that legislation abhors, an arbitrariness that exempts the members of the Assembly from having to consider the larger scale goals that the wise legislator understands.

6.5 Political deliberation as ethical deliberation

In the preceding sections of this chapter, I have tried to show that my interpretation of the Identity Thesis—the idea that political and practical wisdom are the same state because they are the same understanding described differently—makes good sense when we attend to what Aristotle says about the excellence of rulers in the *Politics* and wise legislation in *NE* X.9. In sum, it is practical wisdom that is needed to rule wisely because political decision-making, and law-making in particular, requires an articulate understanding of the goals proper to human flourishing. My discussion of the relationship between this deliberative excellence and the excellence of citizen-subjects, who are able to endorse such decisions and thereby play an active role in political life despite not belonging to the ruling body, helps us see that political wisdom will not be confined to a small group of people occupying high office. Not only will rule be broadly distributed in some constitutions—especially in democracy and its uncorrupted counterpart *politeia* (for the

168   ARISTOTLE'S PRACTICAL EPISTEMOLOGY

latter, see *Politics* IV.11)—but also the excellence of citizens quite generally depends on their learning to rule and be ruled in turn.

Still, one may object that the subject matter of politics is still distinct from that of ethics, which entails that there must be some real difference between political and practical wisdom. Positing such a real difference is an essential part of a conception of politics as a special sphere for action, but such a conception is distinctly modern by comparison to the Aristotelian view.

The first step to resisting this objection as a reading of Aristotle is to recognize that the very idea of ethics as a distinct sphere from politics is alien to the *Nicomachean Ethics* and the *Politics*. To be sure, Aristotle distinguishes the aims of these treatises: they are concerned, respectively, with the human good for a single person, understood as a member of family and *polis* (the *NE*), and with the human good for a whole community, as it is organized by a constitution and by laws (the *Politics*). But their subject matter is nevertheless a single thing, the human good, which is the concern of a single discipline or branch of knowledge, politics. (In *NE* X.9, Aristotle offers another name for their shared subject matter: "the philosophy of things human," 1181b15.) That is why central topics in the *NE* return for analysis in the *Politics*, most notably the two kinds of happy human lives, which Aristotle discusses in *Politics* VII.1–3 as a necessary preamble to his study of the organization of the city that we would pray for.

The topic that explicitly links the two treatises in *NE* X.9 is education, and reflection on the way Aristotle thinks of education in this text can help us see our way definitively past the objection. Recall that Aristotle takes up the question in the second half of X.9 of whether individual or common education is superior. Common education is a matter for legislative understanding. Individual education, envisioned as taking place within the household, depends on what Aristotle calls "paternal instruction" (1180a19). The word 'instruction' (*prostaxis*) frequently has a military or political significance, as in a closely related passage of Plato's *Laws* where the

Athenian Stranger is discussing the need for citizens to rank virtue above other human goods (I.631d3). Certainly, Aristotle thinks of common education and individual education as having the same end, which is a political one. That is why he concludes that someone who wants to educate well—whether they are educating one person or many—must "advance to the universal" (1180b21). Just as household justice is a sort of image of political justice (*NE* V.11, 1138b5–8), then, individual education is an image of common education, and the knowledge needed for the one is no different from the knowledge needed for the other.

From the vantage of our highly technocratic societies, it may seem incredible that Aristotle maintains the Identity Thesis, but he has good reasons to do so. Just as practical wisdom unites an understanding of all the considerations relevant to the human good, so too does political wisdom, insofar as the political community is the complete community for human flourishing.

APPENDIX

Further Alternatives
to the Practical Epistemology of the
Nicomachean Ethics

In this Appendix, I return to the inquiry of Chapter 1, where I showed how Aristotle grounds the inquiry of the *Nicomachean Ethics* by securing the possibility of ethical knowledge against the deflationism of Isocrates and the conventionalism of Protagoras. But Aristotle's conception of ethical experience (*empeiria*), which I analyzed in Chapter 2, can also be fruitfully contrasted with two further possibilities that also form part of the intellectual context of the *Nicomachean Ethics*.

One of these is the view we find articulated by the Eleatic Visitor in the opening pages of Plato's *Statesman*, which represents ordinary practical knowledge as intuitive know-how. While Aristotle does not relate ethical experience to this view in the *Statesman*, he does use the analytic terms of this Platonic passage in his analysis of practical wisdom as an authoritative or prescriptive state in *NE* VI, as I noted in Chapter 3, a clear intertext that invites this further comparison. The other view I take up is found in a difficult passage at the end of Aristotle's own *Eudemian Ethics* (VIII.3), where ordinary ethical knowledge is represented as a sort of prudence about what is advantageous or beneficial to human beings. Aristotle's *Eudemian* position depends on a contrast between semi-virtuous or decent people and those who have complete goodness or nobility (*kalokagathia*) that has no clear counterpart in the *NE*, which emphasizes habituation into virtuous motives as the basis for ethical knowledge.[1]

My consideration of these further alternatives in this Appendix not only clarifies the place of the *Nicomachean* view of ethical experience in its own intellectual context, but it also helps us discern the philosophical motivations behind this view.

---

[1] For a consideration of how differences between the treatises in Aristotle's views about character and the origins of ethical beliefs lead to differences in method, see Daniel Devereux, "Scientific and Ethical Methods in Aristotle's *Eudemian* and *Nicomachean Ethics*," in *Bridging the Gap between Aristotle's Science and Ethics*, ed. Devin Henry and Karen Margrethe Nielsen (Cambridge University Press, 2015), 130–147.

172 APPENDIX

A.1 Ordinary practical knowledge as intuitive know-how

Talk of ethical experience can put us in mind of a picture of ordinary ethical knowledge as mere know-how.[2] On such a view, the person with ordinary knowledge acts according to an intuitive sense of what is good and just without any particular reflective grasp of what they are doing. There are two key differences between the know-how view and the deflationism I described in Chapter 1: (i) the know-how view recognizes that know-how is itself a kind of knowledge, despite being unreflective, and not merely a matter of opinion; (ii) the know-how view allows that there may be superior kinds of knowledge of the same subject matter (i.e., how to act), which *are* reflective.

The know-how view is worth taking up because Aristotle sometimes seems to describe practical experience in the crafts in just these terms, and his analysis of practical knowledge in ethics owes much to what he says about craft. In *Metaphysics* A.1, for instance, ordinary craftsmen are said to act mindlessly in the way that fire burns, a paradigmatic case of action without thought or reason (981a24–b6). This analogy to fire burning must be imprecise simply because human action is never fully thoughtless in this way and skilled human action all the less so. Still, Aristotle's picture of ethical experience can seem to emphasize *getting things done* in an intuitive way as opposed to having anything that resembles reflective knowledge.

It's true, of course, that exercising habitual knowledge need not involve the explicit recall and subsequent application of things one knows. But that is because explicit recall is needed primarily by the learner and in special, difficult cases where habitual knowledge does not suffice. A tempting picture of mind associates the exercise of knowledge quite generally with accessing something inward, but knowing *what* one is doing in the sense that entails having reflective awareness of it is not the first step in a causal chain that leads to action but rather a description of the *way* that such knowledge guides one's intentional actions.[3] All the same, we should not be led, in denying this tempting but ultimately strange picture of mind, to reduce all practical knowledge to intuitive know-how or (to use Hubert Dreyfus' expression) skillful coping.[4]

---

[2] I take the tendency to dismiss the sophistication of what Aristotle's experienced people (*empeiroi*) know to be, in part, a product of this assumption.

[3] My remarks here are influenced by the work of Elizabeth Anscombe and the analysis of intentional action and practical knowledge found in *Intention*, 2nd ed. (Blackwell, 1963).

[4] For a clear instance of this temptation, see Dreyfus' essay "Overcoming the Myth of the Mental: How Philosophers Can Profit from the Phenomenology of Everyday Expertise," *Proceedings and Addresses of the American Philosophical Association* 79 (2005): 47–65.

APPENDIX   173

I will show in this section that Aristotle resists this temptation, and that, in doing so, he rejects the picture of practical knowledge developed by the Eleatic Visitor in the opening pages of Plato's *Statesman* (258b3–260c5). Only by seeing how ordinary ethical knowledge stands above and ranges over individual actions can we appreciate the distinct kind of universality that Aristotle attributes to practical wisdom. The confusion arises because Aristotle frequently speaks of experience as knowledge *of* particulars. For Aristotle, it is not the case that the person with ethical experience negotiates particular circumstances without a grasp of what they are doing. Moreover, this grasp must itself involve general terms that could apply in other similar situations.

As I argue below, on the picture developed by the Eleatic Visitor, by contrast to Aristotle's, so-called practical knowledge is essentially embodied in particular actions (258d8–e3), while it is left to a special branch of theoretical knowledge to direct and coordinate people who possess practical knowledge (259e8–260c5).[5] The political or royal art (*politikē; basilikē*) turns out to be an instance of this kind of theoretical knowledge, which is why the topic is introduced in the *Statesman* (260d11–261a2). Still, we should note that the complex structure of the Platonic dialogue leaves open the possibility that the initial distinction between practical and theoretical knowledge, or the further distinction between the kind of theoretical knowledge that is exercised solely in determining what is the case and the kind that directs others, might run aground when we try to locate politics.

It is enough for my purpose that Aristotle rejects the initial view proposed by the Visitor. There is good evidence from two key passages of *Nicomachean Ethics* VI that Aristotle had in mind the Visitor's view in developing his own conception of *phronēsis*, first in VI.8 where the relationship of *phronēsis* to political wisdom is explored and second in VI.10 where *phronēsis* is distinguished from comprehension (*sunesis*) by the fact that the latter does not prescribe action.[6] The close affinity between the later chapters of *NE* VI and the *Statesman* has generally been ignored. In this section, I will aim to illuminate the view of practical knowledge in the *Statesman* in order to bring out how Aristotle's own view of ethical knowledge differs from it.

As the Visitor notes at the beginning of the *Statesman* (258b6–11), forms of expertise or craft (*tekhnai*) had already been a topic of discussion for the interlocutors in the *Sophist*, to which the *Statesman* is a direct sequel. There, the sophist's knowledge or ability was defined (albeit in numerous and apparently incompatible ways) against the background of the various types of social

[5] I say more below about the terms 'practical' (*praktikē*) and 'theoretical' (*gnōstikē*), which, despite their familiarity to us, are used in a distinctive and potentially confusing way.

[6] I discuss the first of these texts extensively in Chapter 6 (§6.2, T21) and the second of them below (T23).

174 APPENDIX

practices and skills and professions that the term *tekhnē* can pick out (218b5–231e7). The main upshot of that exploration—to put it all too briefly—is that sophistry is not itself a profession or a practice in its own right but has only a shadow life of imitation and deception (232a1–7).

While it remains implicit in the Visitor's appeal at the beginning of the *Statesman* to that earlier discussion, we may surmise that Plato intends us to have a similar worry about politics and the statesman. After all, in Athenian discourse, political skill was closely associated with rhetoric. Moreover, while rhetoric and sophistry are sometimes distinguished in the dialogues (e.g., at *Gorgias* 465c3–7), Plato generally leads us to think that the sophists themselves professed to teach rhetoric.[7] The question for the interlocutors at the start of the *Statesman*, then, is very much the same that faced them in the *Sophist*: Where can politics be found in the web of intelligent activity that constitutes the life of the city, and can it be labeled a genuine form of expertise or skill itself?[8] Is it perhaps just sophistry in a different guise?

An important difference between the dialogues, however, is the more systematic basis the Visitor provides in the *Statesman* for a division of the various forms of expertise.[9] The highest-level division in the *Sophist* was between those kinds of expertise that are devoted to acquisition and those devoted to production (*Sophist* 219a8–c8)—i.e., getting versus keeping. This distinction turns on the type of characteristic effect of the relevant kinds of expertise, and more precisely, the way that things in the world are shaped by each sort of

---

[7] The historical question is a difficult one, and some modern scholars have identified Plato's framing as a hostile retrojection. See Michael Gagarin and Paul Woodruff, "The Sophists," in *The Oxford Handbook of Presocratic Philosophy*, ed. Patricia Curd and Daniel Graham (Oxford University Press, 2008), 365–382, esp. §III, "Did the Sophists Teach Rhetoric?"

[8] In this part of the dialogue, the Visitor moves back and forth between the words *tekhnē* and *epistēmē*. The words are clearly co-extensional, but the social character of expertise is highly relevant for the argument, so the division is perhaps best regarded as a division of *tekhnē*. I generally use the translation expertise (rather than craft or skill) for *tekhnē* to capture the very general notion at play. It is rather awkward—if not incoherent—to speak in English, for instance, of practical crafts as opposed to theoretical crafts. In contexts where the difference between *tekhnē* and *epistēmē* do not matter, I use the word 'knowledge' to range over both. For a thorough discussion of the relation of the two terms in Plato, see Emily Hulme, "Plato's Knowledge Vocabulary and John Lyons's *Structural Semantics*," *Oxford Studies in Ancient Philosophy* 61 (2022): 1–24. Hulme argues that *tekhnē* implies *epistēmē* but not vice versa.

[9] See Mary Louise Gill, *Philosophos: Plato's Missing Dialogue* (Oxford University Press, 2012), 177–185, for a discussion of the varying systematicity of the divisions in the *Sophist* and the *Statesman* and the contrasting lessons of the dialogues in the way that the sophist turns up in too many places in the divisions of the *Sophist* whereas the statesman has competition for his single place in the division of the *Statesman*. In *Philosophos* as a whole, Gill argues that the method of division in these dialogues functions (for us as readers of Plato) as a philosophical exercise that guides further inquiry and reflection.

APPENDIX 175

knowledge. Here, the close connection of *tekhnē* to productive crafts comes to the fore. By contrast, in the *Statesman*, the Visitor divides expertise into theoretical and practical branches, where theoretical knowledge is independent of action while practical knowledge is somehow possessed in performing the actions themselves (258d4–e7). This distinction is not about two kinds of effects in the world but rather about how knowledge can be joined to its effects in the first place. Therefore, the division in the *Statesman* is more fundamental than the one in the *Sophist*.

The distinction between theoretical and practical knowledge can seem so familiar to us (at least in its later, Aristotelian guise) that it is easy to miss what is surprising about the Visitor's division. Most importantly, it can seem as though the Visitor is saying that only practical knowledge has an effect on the world in the first place, whereas theoretical knowledge is somehow self-contained. The precise verbal descriptions of each kind of knowledge, however, belie this interpretation.[10]

Let us consider the details of the two descriptions together. The Visitor says of theoretical (*gnōstikē*) kinds of expertise, such as arithmetic, that they are "[1a] bare of actions and [1b] provide only knowledge (*gnōnai*)" (*Stsm.* 258d4–6). Practical (*praktikē*) kinds of expertise, by contrast, such as carpentry, "[2a] possess a knowledge that is intrinsically present, as it were, in actions, and [2b] bring to completion the bodies they have brought into being, which did not exist before" (258d8–e2). Each of these descriptions has two, parallel components, the first [1a, 2a] analyzing the relation of knowledge to actions (*praxeis*) and the second [1b, 2b] analyzing the characteristic effect of the exercise of that knowledge.

Of these four aspects, the one most liable to be confusing is [1a], the claim that theoretical kinds of knowledge are "bare" of actions. Because the parallel in [2a] claims that practical knowledge is, in a word, embodied, it may well seem that for theoretical knowledge to be bare of actions is for it to be wholly disembodied, which can lead us in turn to conclude (wrongly) that it has no effects in the world. Yet [1b] aims precisely to describe the effects of theoretical knowledge, and, as the Visitor's location of political expertise within the theoretical branch shows, these effects are in no sense self-contained. What, then, does it mean for a type of knowledge to be "bare" of actions, if it does not mean that it has no worldly effects?

---

[10] On how to understand this first division, see also Xavier Márquez, "Theory and Practice in Plato's *Statesman*," *Ancient Philosophy* 27: 31–53; Márquez, *A Stranger's Knowledge: Statesmanship, Philosophy, and Law in Plato's* Statesman (Parmenides, 2012), esp. Chapter 4; and Dimitri El Murr, "Theoretical, Not Practical: The Opening Arguments of Plato's *Politicus* (*Plt.*, 258e–259)," in *Plato's* Statesman *Revisited*, ed. Beatriz Bossi López and Thomas M. Robinson (De Gruyter, 2019), 55–72.

176 APPENDIX

Happily, Plato's use of the word "bare" (*psilos*) in other passages can point the way forward. Within the *Statesman* itself, the adjective *psilos* is used to describe speech without musical accompaniment (268b4). Elsewhere in the corpus and in other prose authors such as Aristotle, the adjective is used regularly to pick out epic poetry, by contrast to lyric poetry; that is to say, "bare" poetry is poetry composed without specific musical accompaniment in mind.[11] Of course, epic poetry *could* be performed with musical accompaniment, but the music in this case is, unlike the music that accompanies lyric poetry, inessential. Another instructive use is the Athenian Visitor's remark in the *Laws* that the soul of the sun is "bare" of the visible body with which we are directly acquainted (X.899a2). Of course, this remark cannot mean that the sun lacks a body; rather, the visible body is inessential to what the soul of the sun is, namely, an intellectual being. These two Platonic examples of the use of the adjective *psilos* suggests its meaning in our passage of the *Statesman*: to say that theoretical knowledge is bare of action is to assert that no *particular* actions are specified in its exercise. Theoretical knowledge, considered in itself, stands above particular actions.

The contrast between [1a] and [2a]—the different ways that theoretical and practical knowledge are related to action—should now be clearer, now that the idea that theoretical knowledge is bare of actions has been clarified. The Visitor is not characterizing theoretical knowledge as disembodied action, in the sense of not having actual effects in the world, but rather as non-bodily action, and hence standing above particular bodily actions.

My interpretation of the practicality of practical knowledge and its counterpart in theoretical knowledge to this point has been more suggestive than dispositive, inasmuch as I have been drawing primarily on contextual and philological considerations. A more conclusive reason in its favor—which I have already hinted at—is the fact that political skill will be identified as a kind of theoretical knowledge, and this, of course, is the most efficacious knowledge of all.

In fact, the division within theoretical knowledge that the Visitor makes highlights the efficacy of political skill. He establishes that one branch of theoretical knowledge, like mathematical knowledge, is devoted simply to making judgments, e.g., about odd and even numbers—such knowledge is called discerning (*kritikon*; 260b3–4). The other branch, which includes not only politics but also the overseer's or the master builder's skill in relation to building, not only produces judgments but also combines these with orders that guide the execution of further actions—such knowledge is called directive or commanding (*epitaktikon*). To highlight the way that efficacy and direct involvement in practice can come apart, the Visitor notes that an advisor can be said

---

[11] See Henry George Liddell, Robert Scott, Henry Stuart Jones, and Roderick McKenzie, *A Greek–English Lexicon*, rev. 9th ed. (Oxford University Press, 1995), s.v.

APPENDIX   177

to possess the royal art just as much as a king if the king simply follows what his advisor recommends (259a6–8). The force or efficacy involved in such knowledge is psychic, not bodily.

This further division leaves us with a more concrete picture of what practical knowledge comes to on the Visitor's picture. Practical knowledge cannot be individuated or identified simply in terms of what is done, e.g., a typical skilled action of a productive art, since these actions can also be governed by forms of directive knowledge. Rather, as [2a] makes clear, the Visitor conceives of practical knowledge as possessed *in* the actions, whereas theoretical knowledge stands above actions, either by concluding simply in judgment—which may or may not be put to further use in action—or by concluding in judgments that are orders for the execution of actions by others. The contrast between the master craftsman and an ordinary skilled worker implied by the passage as a whole is noteworthy. Both exercise knowledge that is concerned with the same actions, one by directing them and the other by actually performing them. Both are intelligent performances, but there is something essentially reflective about directive knowledge that may well be absent in practical knowledge. An ordinary worker needs to know techniques, but on the Visitor's account, he need not know anything more than that.

Together, these two divisions yield a threefold distinction among practical, discerning, and directive types of knowledge. The relevant contrast for us is between practical and directive knowledge, since both concern action. The activities of ordinary craftspeople in the city will generally be of the practical kind, concerned with the production and manipulation of bodies (including the bodies of the craftspeople themselves, but also with traditional craft-objects as in carpentry). Their activities are then further organized by higher, directive arts, culminating in political expertise, which, as the later stages of the discussion in the *Statesman* describe, will weave together all the activity of the city into a harmonious whole. Essential to the entire account is the idea that ordinary practical knowledge is unreflective know-how. It is this assumption that Aristotle's account of practical knowledge, both in the crafts and in ethics, resists.[12]

Throughout the Visitor's exposition of the various kinds of expertise, he and Young Socrates move freely between speaking about people and about the kinds of knowledge they have, that is, between experts and their expertise. Given the context, a discussion of politics and ideal rulership, one is inevitably reminded of the one person-one job principle of the *Republic*, on which the order and justice of the ideal city depend (II.369e3–370c2). But the

---

[12] Note: in reference to Aristotle, I will continue to speak about "practical knowledge" in this section as a wider category that includes considerably more than what the Visitor denominates as practical.

178 APPENDIX

assumption that a person is defined by their status as a craftsman runs quite deep in the classical Greek imagination.[13]

An implication of this view is that the division between practical and directive knowledge of actions is also a division between two classes of people. The master builder and the statesman, as possessors of directive knowledge, stand apart from those to whom they give orders. While the Visitor ends up rejecting the image of the herdsmen standing over a flock as the appropriate model for the (human) statesman (274e10–275a6), a distinction in class, if not in humanity, between the statesman and those he rules survives the shift to the weaving model in the second half of the dialogue (279a1 ff.).[14]

A further consequence we may draw out of this picture is that directive knowledge of a domain cannot be understood to develop directly from practical knowledge in that domain. What the person with practical knowledge has is contained within his actions. It might be possible for such a person to observe his own actions and how they fit into a larger context and thereby gain directive knowledge of them, but the actions—and the knowledge contained within them—would simply be an occasion for the acquisition of a knowledge entirely different in kind. Moreover, the possessor of directive knowledge need not first be acquainted with the techniques relevant to a given domain. In the case of the statesman, this task would be impossible, given the sheer variety of activities the statesman is responsible for organizing, which indeed constitute the whole life of the city. But even the master builder, on this picture, need not first be a menial laborer.

What matters instead to directive knowledge is learning *when* certain actions should be undertaken, the all-important *kairos* ("opportune moment").[15] While this knowledge still counts in an important way as knowledge of the same actions undertaken by one's subordinates, the possessor of directive knowledge is concerned with these actions in a different dimension. To use a bit of ordinary language: the person with directive knowledge is oriented to putting on actions, not (as the person of practical knowledge is) to pulling them off. Practical knowledge, then, on the Visitor's picture, is *limited* by its essentially embodied character.

---

[13] See Cameron Hawkins, "Artisans and Craftsman," *Oxford Classical Dictionary*, 4th ed. online (Oxford University Press, 2012).

[14] Gill comments that the later divisions seem to lead to an ever-more practical conception of political expertise (*Philosophos*, 181), but even if this is right (insofar as it leads to a tension between the herding model of political expertise and the initial division, which locates political expertise within theoretical kinds of knowledge), the tension cannot already be present in the first two cuts, which introduce us to what practical and theoretical knowledge are.

[15] See Melissa Lane, *Method and Politics in Plato's* Statesman (Cambridge University Press, 1998).

APPENDIX 179

For Aristotle, by contrast, the seeds of complete understanding are contained in ordinary practical knowledge. There is, further, no essential differentiation between those who possess each kind of knowledge, no epistemic division of labor. It may be, given a certain form of social organization, that some people's actions are organized by others. And the appropriateness of the latter's rule may well depend on their having a certain distinct kind of knowledge. But all the same it does not follow that two *kinds* of people must be involved, and mastery can—perhaps even must—first pass through the lesser kind of practical knowledge.[16]

The closest Aristotle comes to endorsing the Visitor's view is in his conception of the rule of the householder, who, among other tasks, organizes the productive activity of slaves within the household. But at the end of his meandering discussion of slavery and slave-mastery, Aristotle concludes that an overseer—who might very well be a slave—is more fit to organize the productive activity of the household (*Politics* I.7, 1255b32–40). That is because the real purpose of household activity is to supply the master with sufficient leisure to undertake the intrinsically choice-worthy activities of politics and philosophy, a purpose that would be defeated if the householder is too enmeshed in the productive activity of his slaves and subordinates.

Unlike the gentleman-farmer of Xenophon's *Householder (Oeconomicus)*, a refined version of the Athenian aristocratic ideal, Aristotle's householder is represented as better off for being removed from the day-to-day activity of the household he runs. Directive knowledge as such, then, drops out of Aristotle's picture of rule in favor of a sharp divide between a productive sphere where the activities of menial laborers and their supervisors takes place and a practical sphere where the intrinsically choice-worthy activities of free, adult men is pursued.[17]

Aristotle argues, of course, for different kinds of division of labor within and between these spheres, with slaves and menial laborers firmly placed outside the political life of the city, for instance, but these divisions of labors are teleologically grounded. In the absence of any distinction between production and

---

[16] Of course, it may nevertheless be true that some people only reach a lower degree of attainment as a matter of fact, which generates a different type of epistemic class distinction. We can find such a view implicit in *Metaphysics* Alpha.1, where, as I noted in Chapter 1 (§1.2.1), Aristotle describes manual workers as acting mindlessly the way that fire does. My claim here, which I develop more fully in Chapter 2, is that, on Aristotle's considered view, ground-level knowledge in a domain—including ordinary practical knowledge—should not be characterized in this way.

[17] Women's position in this division is, as often with Aristotle's political views, ambivalent. He insists that women and slaves must be functionally differentiated, but even free women's activities fall on the side of the preservation of life not the pursuit of living well. Like slaves, women are simply those without whom the city could not be, by contrast to free adult men (and in a qualified sense, their male children), who are genuinely the parts of the city (*Politics* VII.8, 1328a21–37).

180 APPENDIX

action, the Eleatic Visitor in Plato's *Statesman* hews instead to a distinctly epistemic model of the division of labor, which applies in any domain where practical knowledge is possible. Such practical knowledge is never autonomous and always requires governance from a higher directive form of knowledge precisely because it is mere know-how. Despite Aristotle's agreement with the Visitor that political expertise is a single kind of knowledge that is supreme in the city and organizes all human life, he allows for a considerably more robust conception of ordinary practical knowledge.

As I argued in Chapter 2, Aristotle is committed to the view that experience is the starting point for the acquisition of practical understanding. In the crafts, it is relatively straightforward to see how this process would unfold, even without a detailed picture of what kind of knowledge experience is. Aristotle's favorite example is medicine. The book learning that describes the causes that promote and damage health is of no use to a would-be doctor unless they also grasp how to connect these causes to the perceptible features about health and disease that only experience makes intelligible *as* marks of health and disease.

But experience and the general principles that books of medical knowledge aim to describe are not fully distinguishable components of the doctor's complete understanding. It is *from* experience, which points implicitly to underlying causal facts, that medical understanding comes to be, and such understanding is the single capacity to heal on the basis of a causal *and* experiential grasp of health. Moreover, the person with medical experience (whom I shall refer to as the empiric doctor) is trying to do just what the doctor tries to do—to heal—not something else.

Just for these reasons, experience cannot be a matter merely of having know-how, in the sense of a set of techniques that are deployed on the basis of a merely intuitive grasp of what to do that is not itself autonomous. It is not the fine motor skills of the surgeon that count as her experience. Instead, it is her knowledge of how to apply these skills to carry out a successful surgery. Such knowledge more closely resembles the directive knowledge described by the Visitor in the *Statesman* than it does practical knowledge. For it, just like the understanding that constitutes true medical expertise, is a knowledge of *when* to do something. It is just that experience does not already include a grasp of *causes*, that is, of *why* acting thus-and-so is appropriate, given the underlying nature of the situation.

Recall that the Visitor's conception of practical knowledge locates the knowledge, in some sense, *in the actions performed*. Above, I understood this point to mean not only that practical knowledge was concerned with techniques but also that it was not reflective. One may object, then, that Aristotle's association of a knowledge of causes with the product of inquiry implies that experience, equally, is unreflective. Here, again, we encounter the pernicious conflation of reflective awareness with an inward act of the mind that is directed to what a person knows. The person with experience is reflectively aware insofar as

APPENDIX 181

they *discriminate* among different kinds of situations in order to apply their experience. They might not, of course, have engaged in any course of inquiry that seeks to determine the causes that underlie the experience they have. Nevertheless, acting from experience is not acting mindlessly.

In appreciation of this distinction, we are helped by an idea that is brought to the fore in the explicitly political context of the *Statesman*: for the Visitor, the ordinary practical knowledge possessed by craftsmen fails to be autonomous. We may supply, though it is not entirely evident from the text, the thought that, for its successful exercise, such knowledge must be guided by a relevant directive expertise. In Aristotle's reckoning, experience, inasmuch as it approximates the complete success of full expertise, can achieve a modicum of success in its own domain, even apart from guidance from above. Moreover, a single knower advances from mere experience toward full expertise, and when expertise is achieved, its exercise is hardly a matter of a person commanding themselves.

This last point of disagreement between Aristotle and the Visitor comes to the fore in an important passage of *NE* VI.10 where Aristotle draws on the Visitor's terminology to describe practical wisdom as directive or commanding (*epitaktikē*). Tellingly, the main contrast here is not with either theoretical knowledge or a subordinate form of practical knowledge but rather with a distinct practical virtue, namely, comprehension (*sunesis* or *eusunesia*), which is described in its turn as discerning (*kritikē*):

> [T23] Comprehension concerns neither the eternal and unmoved nor whatever might come to be but rather what one might be at a loss over and deliberate over. For that reason it concerns the same things that practical wisdom does, though comprehension and practical wisdom are not the same. Why? Practical wisdom is commanding (*epitaktikē*). For its goal is what one ought or ought not do. Comprehension, on the other hand, is discerning (*kritikē*). (*NE* VI.10, 1143a4–10)

Here, Aristotle puts a version of the Visitor's distinction between the two kinds of theoretical knowledge to use in order to distinguish two practical virtues. For my present purposes, what matters is that the fact that *phronēsis* is commanding is explained in terms of *achieving* what one should do or not as opposed to merely recognizing it. To be commanding is not for practical wisdom to command *another* to perform an action but to be *authoritative*, that is, to offer the basis on which other activities are pursued.[18] Of course, practical wisdom is equivalent to political expertise for Aristotle, which does, as he notes at the outset of the *Nicomachean Ethics*, issue commands to other kinds of expertise and prescribes the extent to which they should be used by others

---

[18] I explore this thought in Chapter 3 (§3.1) in my discussion of the Independent Agency Criterion.

182 APPENDIX

in the political community (I.2, 1093a28–b7). Nevertheless, Aristotle has widened the sense of 'commanding' (*epitaktikē*) to go beyond the relational scenario envisioned by the Visitor.

Practical wisdom, to sum up, is hands-on, even as it is reflective in a way that goes beyond experience. This mark is the second of the four I identified in the Introduction as central to Aristotle's conception of practical wisdom as practical understanding. *Phronēsis*, just as much as ethical experience, is exercised in bringing about particular virtuous actions.

A.2 Ordinary practical knowledge as prudence

One may object that the view of ethical experience I have attributed to Aristotle, by contrast to both the deflationist view of ordinary practical knowledge as mere opinion and the Visitor's view of it as know-how, makes his conception of ordinary practical knowledge too closely resemble practical wisdom itself. After all, if experience is a reflective kind of knowledge, which enables its possessor to hit the mark with respect to virtuous action reliably, has not the distinction in kind been reduced to a distinction merely in degree? We can get some traction on how to respond to this objection by considering Aristotle's own view of the relationship between knowledge and practical success in the *Eudemian Ethics*.

One undisputed fact about practical wisdom is that it is the state of soul whereby a person achieves practical success, i.e., whereby they live successfully. What is it to live successfully? One mark that Aristotle attributes to the happy person—the person whose whole life is fully successful—is that they lack none of the most important good things. But some of these important good things are present in other lives, even in the absence of happiness. This insight opens up a different way of thinking about different grades of practical knowledge. On such a view, which I will argue we find in *EE* VIII.3, only the fully virtuous and practically wise person is reliably able to achieve complete practical success (bracketing the effects of fortune), whereas those with more ordinary practical knowledge achieve practical success that is above a certain threshold but is nevertheless incomplete.

There appears to be in Aristotle's view of what is good in human life a relevant threshold: organizing one's life according to virtue. For less-than-virtuous people, having things that are good, taken in isolation, can actually be an impediment to the success of their lives. Wealth combined with lack of moderation, for instance, is positively dangerous. (I discussed this example in Chapter 1, §1.4, as it arises in the discussion of the 'for the most part' character of ethics in *Nicomachean Ethics* I.3, but it recurs in a new context in *EE* VIII.3, which I go on to discuss below.)

APPENDIX   183

On the most extreme (perhaps Socratic) version of this view, nothing is really good unless it is possessed by the person of complete virtue and wisdom (e.g., *Euthydemus* 280d7–281b4). This extreme version is hard to sustain in the face of important parts of our first-order ethical thinking. By contrast, Aristotle's theory makes room for the common view that success in life comes in degrees and does not belong solely to the fully virtuous person. In other words, while vice can certainly turn good things against you, there still exist aspects of success that are independent of virtue and vice. For example, less-than-virtuous people can have friendships, even if they are not of the best or "complete" kind (*NE* VIII.3–4, 1156a7–b12), and friendship is the best of the external goods (IX.9, 1169b7–9). These friendships genuinely improve the lives of such people. Likewise, it is true to say that less-than-virtuous people are, generally speaking, better off with health rather than sickness and wealth rather than poverty, even though their lack of good character can turn these advantages to disadvantages in certain circumstances.[19]

In his different ethical treatises, Aristotle countenances different versions of this basic framework about what is good for us and our knowledge of it. In the remainder of this section, I take up the view presented in *Eudemian Ethics* VIII.3, where he argues that only people who possess the virtues—at least to some degree—are capable of pursuing and keeping what is good, but that they do not necessarily possess the complete virtue of nobility (*kalokagathia*), which ensures complete success in life. My aim is to show how this view in the *Eudemian Ethics* differs from the conception of ordinary practical knowledge as ethical experience that he develops in the *Nicomachean Ethics*.[20]

The special and elevated status of nobility introduces a class of people into Aristotle's *Eudemian* theory—the decent—who are equipped with a kind of practical knowledge and are able to avoid certain kinds of failure and folly, even though they fail to understand what is most important in human life,

---

[19] Stoic axiology, in which there are two kinds of value—ethical value, on the one hand, and preferred and dispreferred indifferents, on the other hand—can be seen as an attempt to recover the Socratic insight about the categorical supremacy of virtue (or wisdom) while accounting for the role of other goods in choice and avoidance, as Aristotle's theory also manages to do.

[20] I note that the textual complexity of the *EE* passage and the fraught question of the relationship between the ethical treatises recommend some caution in making use of *EE* VIII to aid in the interpretation of the *NE*. Let me state that what is important for my purposes is only the general drift of the *EE* passage and the categories it implies. Moreover, nothing in my interpretation of the *NE* hangs directly on reading the *EE* passage correctly. Still, I hold that it is useful to reflect on a way of thinking about practical success and knowledge, which is evinced in the *EE* but is clearly distinct from the way Aristotle discusses ethical experience in the *NE*. Indeed, it is not essential to my argument that Aristotle has changed his mind across the two treatises, only that he takes up a different way of thinking about ordinary practical knowledge in the *NE*. Thanks to Marta Jimenez for urging me to make these points explicit.

184 APPENDIX

namely, noble action taken on its own. Since noble actions themselves require the possession of external goods of various kinds, e.g., wealth to be generous to others, the ability to navigate life in the way decent people do makes a contribution to the practical knowledge of the noble man. Moreover, the good things thereby achieved do not spoil the lives of decent people because they lack the vices. I will call the ordinary practical knowledge attributed to the decent by Aristotle in *EE* VIII.3 *prudence*, though he does not give it a distinct name in that text, since his focus is not on practical epistemology.[21]

By taking up this neglected Aristotelian text, I will show an important difference between its view of the prudence of decent people and the *Nicomachean* conception of ethical experience as the precursor to practical wisdom. More specifically, I will argue that, in the *Eudemian Ethics*, the complete practical knowledge of the noble man includes a subject matter that mere prudence does not, namely, how to understand the relationship between the various goods—virtue, virtuous actions, and the external goods—within the whole of a human life. On this view, one can be decent while mistaking the superiority of virtue to these external goods, a condition that Aristotle, strikingly, attributes to the Spartans (1248b37–49a3). By contrast, in the *Nicomachean* theory, both experience and practical wisdom have a single subject matter: the good for human beings. We must appreciate this point in order to see why it is that *phronēsis* should count as practical *understanding* of the human good, the third of the four marks I described in the Introduction.

In *Eudemian Ethics* VIII.3, the last of a disjointed and likely incomplete series of essays that conclude the treatise, Aristotle sets out to describe the complete virtue that belongs to the *kaloskagathos*, the noble man. This figure possesses *phronēsis* as one among the most important intellectual virtues, but it should be understood as an ethical exemplar distinct from the *phronimos* that is the focus of the (bulk of the) *Nicomachean Ethics*. In particular, while *phronesis* guarantees the unity of the virtues of character, nobility (*kalokagathia*) entails possessing all the intellectual virtues as well (*EE* VIII.3, 1248b8–16).[22]

---

[21] This translation might catch readers off guard, but I intend here to recover the ordinary sense of this English word. In the Latin tradition from Cicero onwards, *prudentia* was used to translate *phronēsis*, mediated by the Stoic notion of *pronoia* (providence). (On the role of Stoic thought in facilitating this transition, see Sophie Aubert-Baillot, "De la φρόνησις à la prudentia," *Mnemosyne* 68, no. 1 [2015]: 68–90.) The special connection of prudence, in modern English, to the use of external goods, such as money, is further reason to adopt it here.

[22] For this point and a thorough account of the place of *kalokagathia* in the argument of the *EE* see Giulia Bonasio, "*Kalokagathia* and the Unity of the Virtues in the *Eudemian Ethics*," *Apeiron* 53, no. 1 (2019), 27–57. I am grateful, also, to Bonasio for several fruitful conversations on this and related aspects of the *EE* and am indebted to her views in what follows in this section.

APPENDIX   185

Because the noble man is distinguished by his possession of *all* the virtues, character and intellectual virtues alike, the question arises how this unity of the virtues manifests itself, that is, how it shapes the outlook and behavior of the noble man. Aristotle gives a striking answer to this question—striking, at least, to readers more familiar with the *Nicomachean Ethics*—in the following passage.

[T24] Now, the good man is the one for whom naturally good things are good. For the things people compete over and which are thought to be the greatest goods, honor and wealth and excellences of the body and good fortune and power—these are naturally good but can be harmful for some people because of their character. For neither the foolish man nor the unjust nor the licentious one could ever benefit from employing these [goods], just as the sick man cannot benefit by taking the same nourishment as the healthy nor the feeble or maimed by employing the adornments of the healthy and whole.

But the noble man is the one for whom the things that are noble from among the goods belong for their own sake and who is capable of achieving through action the things that are noble for their own sake. What is noble are the virtues and actions on the basis of virtue. (*EE* VIII.3, 1248b26–37)

The question of the relationship between the *kaloskagathos* and the *phronimos* as ethical exemplars is, of course, complicated because of the disputed status of the common books (*NE* V–VII = *EE* IV–VI). The *Eudemian Ethics* must have contained *some* discussion of the intellectual virtues, perhaps even one largely similar to the one we possess as *NE* VI (*EE* V). My working hypothesis, consistent with the majority view of the scholarship, is that *NE* VI represents a later edition of an originally *Eudemian* treatise on the intellectual virtues. For a recent assessment focused on the intellectual excellences, see Christopher Rowe, "Sophia in the *Eudemian Ethics*," in *Investigating the Relationship between Aristotle's* Eudemian *and* Nicomachean Ethics, ed. Giulia Di Basilio (Routledge, 2022), 122–136.
To be sure, some aspects of the Common Book that we have seem to point forward to something like *EE* VIII: most notably, the discussion in VIII.3 of the limit to which the noble man looks seems at first glance to correspond better to the question raised about the limit to which practical wisdom looks in *NE* VI.1 (*EE* V.1). But the majority of the book, and especially its final two chapters (*NE* VI.12–13 = *EE* V.12–13), points to the concluding discussion of happiness and its two forms that is unique to *NE* X. As I have argued elsewhere, Chapters 12 and 13 can be understood to provide a different and equally conclusive answer to the issue of the limit raised in Chapter 1, which in turn supports the idea that the revision of the book on the intellectual virtues went in the direction of the *Nicomachean Ethics*, since these concluding chapters form a fulcrum in the comparatively well-organized argument of the *NE*, binding the discussion of happiness and the virtues together, whereas they fit unevenly in the *EE*, which fails to return to the subject of happiness altogether (Jagannathan, "Right Reason and Practical Truth," in *Practical Reason, Knowledge, and Truth*, ed. Jennifer Frey and Christopher Frey [Oxford University Press, 2024]).

186 APPENDIX

What is surprising in this passage is that those not in possession of nobility (*kalokagathia*) may well be considered good, i.e., they may well possess the virtues of character.[23] As Aristotle goes to on explain, what such people lack is a determination to exercise their virtues for the sake of what is noble (1248b34–49a7). As a result, in their actions, they may well acquire what is good for themselves, but they fail to achieve what is noble. As I noted above, I will call these people "the decent," since they possess virtue in an incomplete way.

The operative contrast in **T24** is between acting for the sake of what is noble and acting for other ends, especially the sorts of ends that are desirable goods or advantages in life (which Aristotle refers to, here and elsewhere in the *EE*, as "natural goods"). It is hard to imagine someone in possession of a virtue acting out of malice or spite, but it is possible to countenance a virtuous person who lacks the correct organization of ends and instead performs a virtuous action in some circumstance not for the sake of what is noble but instead, e.g., to preserve their social standing.

It may seem that Aristotle is saying that such decent people act *purely* in order to achieve these advantages, which would mean they have only a simulacrum of virtue. For true courage is distinguished from civic courage and mercenary courage precisely because the truly courageous person acts for the sake of what is noble *rather than* acting for the sake of honor or wealth (*NE* III.7, 1115b20–24; *EE* II, 1230a27–29). On this view, the decent would be distinguished from the noble by an important motivational shortcoming, their character representing at best an imitation of real virtue.

Note, however, that Aristotle attributes good character to the decent, which suggests they have more than a simulacrum of virtue. A more plausible alternative, then, is to locate the error of decent people primarily in what we can call their *outlook*. We can imagine someone who chooses virtuous actions in a given context because they are virtuous and not for some extrinsic gain, but who, all the same, looks upon that choice with regret outside the situation of choice because they would rather have some of the advantages that such actions make them give up. Let us label this sub-type of the decent as "the long-suffering virtuous person."[24]

---

[23] Note that this suggests a different view of the unity between *phronesis* and the virtues of character than we find in *NE* VI.12–13 (*EE* V.12–13), which in turn allows for some of the possibilities I discuss below. See the previous note for my view of those chapters.

[24] The long-suffering are very likely not the only kind of decent people there could be. We might think also of people who have disciplined themselves to the virtues of character but have not yet acquired any particular view on what the virtues are ultimately *for*. We could call these people "the comme-il-faut virtuous." Perhaps such a state of character corresponds roughly to what, in one passage, Aristotle calls "habituated virtue" (*NE* VII.8 = *EE* VI.8, 1151a18).

APPENDIX 187

The long-suffering virtuous person is not a mercenary whose virtue is an illusion, like the person who does what is required by courage or moderation only when it is convenient or when others are watching. Nor are they merely self-controlled (enkratic); for we can suppose they experience no situational-internal motivational conflict. Nevertheless, in organizing their lives, they place the wrong importance on the virtues, failing to see them as among the most valuable things human beings can have and their exercise as the best thing human beings can achieve.

An important point about the relationship between practical reason and the virtues of character already arises from this investigation of what the decent person is like. If we construe the function of practical reason as selecting means to fully determinate ends that are given at the outset of deliberation, a failure to have the right outlook—the right prioritization and organization of one's ends—is consistent with a kind of excellence in practical reason. After all, what the wise and the decent alike have is what I labeled *prudence* above, and such prudence really does enable the decent to navigate aspects of life successfully. All the same, by Aristotle's lights, it falls short of genuine practical wisdom precisely because knowing how to prioritize and organize one's ends is an important part of good practical reasoning. We should not, therefore, identify excellence in practical reasoning purely with the selection of means to determinate or given ends, even supposing the ends to be worthwhile ones.

Indeed, one's outlook bears directly on the actions one goes on to take. Moreover, our attraction and attachment to certain ends is shaped by the kinds of activities we pursue, a point Aristotle emphasizes in his account of habituation (e.g., *NE* II.1, 1103a34–b25), which leads to a sort of feedback loop even in relatively mature people. Practical regret, even of a relatively idle or wistful sort, cannot be fully insulated from our habits and inclinations. Hence, a decent person's impaired outlook makes them fall short of both practical wisdom and full practical success in life.

The heart of this point is in fact already contained in Aristotle's first observation about the good and the noble, where he describes what is noble as a *subset* of the intrinsically choice-worthy goods: "Among the good things there are goals which are choice-worthy just for their own sake. Among these are what is noble, which are all praiseworthy because of what they are. For those things from which praiseworthy actions come and are themselves praiseworthy [are noble], justice and [just] actions and moderate [actions], since moderation too is praiseworthy" (VIII.3, 1248b18–22). Since noble things are among the most important of good things, no one could pursue the good fully (and thereby be practically successful) and not also pursue the noble. Pursuing what is noble requires having the right outlook, the outlook that belongs to the supreme virtue of nobility.

All the same, as I have emphasized above, in *EE* VIII.3, Aristotle is evidently comfortable with according virtue (goodness of character) to some

188 APPENDIX

people who fall short of nobility. The most intriguing example of such people that he provides are the Spartans, who in a familiar—and, as we might put it, Athenocentric—trope were supremely disciplined in military matters but fell short of virtue in other regards. Here, their error is described as follows:

> [T25] There is a certain political condition [of soul] (*hexis politikē*), which the Spartans have or which others like them would have. This state is of the following sort: there are some who suppose one must have virtue but for the sake of the natural goods. That is why they are good (since they have what is naturally good) but they are not noble and good men. For noble things do not belong to them in their own right.[25] (1248b37–49a3)

Aristotle refers to the character of the Spartans as a political condition, either because it is a kind of civic virtue (as opposed to virtue in the proper sense) or, more likely, because it is a product of the famed Lycurgan constitution.[26] In any case, the Spartans have enough virtue to avoid the kinds of failure and folly attributed to the less than virtuous earlier in the passage. Still, they fail to have nobility because they do not pursue virtue for the right reason; their outlook is misguided.

Let us turn now to the implications for Aristotle's practical epistemology of this *Eudemian* account of different levels of virtue. The difference in outlook between decent people and the exemplary noble man corresponds to two ways of knowing and pursuing what is good. The decent person will reliably secure practical success by using their prudence to get and keep natural goods. The noble person will, by contrast, use their grasp of what is noble to guide their pursuit of the natural goods and noble action itself. Aristotle does not here say that this grasp of what is noble is part of practical wisdom, but his interest in setting out in *EE* VIII.1 how practical wisdom is superior to other kinds of knowledge and how it, like the virtues of character, cannot be misused suggests that he would endorse this claim in this context.

At this point, we should take note of how the aesthetic dimension of what is "noble" (*kalon*)—which can also be rendered into English as "fine," "attractive," or "beautiful"—comes to the surface in the *EE* VIII.3 passage, as it does

---

[25] As in much of *EE* VIII there are textual difficulties in this passage, some significant. I have generally followed the text of Susemihl here but retain the manuscripts *hoion* at 1248b38. The extremely puzzling *agrioi* (savage) in the manuscripts at 1249a1 can perhaps be salvaged (which would be preferable according to the *lectio difficilior* principle), but to avoid a lengthy defense of this reading, I here follow Susemihl and most other modern editors, who emend the word to *agathoi* (good). Either way, the passage is clear that the Spartans have (some) virtue while lacking nobility because they prefer the natural goods to noble action.

[26] Aristotle discusses the shortcomings of Spartan education and related aspects of constitutional design in *Politics* VII.14, 1333b11–20.

APPENDIX   189

quite regularly in the Aristotelian corpus.[27] Indeed, Aristotle regularly uses perceptual language to talk of our access to the *kalon*. In one place, he even speaks of how well-brought-up people have had a *taste* of the noble, unlike the masses (*NE* X.9, 1179b7–16). In these passages, Aristotle characteristically connects an appreciation of what is noble to having a good character or being well-brought up.

What is more unusual about the *EE* VIII.3 passage is the additional emphasis on the *refinement* needed to appreciate what is noble as noble. Such refinement is not simply a matter of picking up on the attractiveness of what is noble or not, as is suggested in the other passages. After all, even decent people appreciate the value of virtuous action, in a sense. But this appreciation is limited; such people see the goodness—the advantage or utility—of the virtues but not their real splendor. When something is not only good but also noble, as the virtues and their exercises are, there are, then, two corresponding ways of registering its value.

As I showed above, these capacities for knowing the value of virtue arise from the differing outlooks of the decent and the noble. Aristotle's strongly realist ethics entails that the merely decent *fail to see* an important dimension of value and to organize their pursuits accordingly. Indeed, the prudence possessed by decent people is transformed when it begins to approximate the grasp that belongs properly to noble people. It is not simply that they acquire a grasp of a new subject matter.

Nevertheless, the epistemology of value is strongly parallel in the case of what is good and what is noble. Specifically, Aristotle seems to assume in *EE* VIII.3 that responding appropriately to value in the world is a matter chiefly of recognizing what is valuable and acting in order to *acquire* this value for oneself. Throughout the passage, he speaks of good things being good *for* the good (i.e., decent) person and not for the less-than-virtuous person and, likewise, noble things being noble *for* the noble person but not for others.

This conception of value and its pursuit is not alien to the *Nicomachean Ethics*, but it is not Aristotle's favored framework there. The most prominent example of its deployment there is the well-known remark, in the discussion of self-love in *NE* IX.8, that the virtuous person will sacrifice other goods, even their very life, in order to keep what is noble for themselves (1169a31–b1). Generally, however, Aristotle speaks of pursuing goods in teleological and non-subjective terms, where some ends are valuable in their own right and these in turn confer value to actions in pursuit of them.[28]

---

[27] For comment on this dimension of nobility, see Gabriel Richardson Lear, "Aristotle on Moral Virtue and the Fine," in *The Blackwell Guide to Aristotle's* Nicomachean Ethics, ed. R. Kraut (Blackwell, 2006), 116–136, esp. 122–123.

[28] See Sukaina Hirji, "What's Aristotelian about Neo-Aristotelian Virtue Ethics?," *Philosophy and Phenomenological Research* 98 (2019): 671–696, for a discussion of this basically consequentialist picture of value in Aristotle.

190 APPENDIX

While there is much more that one could say about the distinctive episte-mology of value in the *EE* VIII.3 passage, what I am interested in here is the relationship between ordinary practical knowledge—the prudence that the decent have—and the more exalted grasp that belongs to noble people alone. The transition from decency to nobility would involve a kind of discontinuity, a transformation or refiguring of what one has grasped before. Indeed, there is a strong resemblance between this *Eudemian* view of moral development and the Stoic theory of appropriation or affiliation (*oikeiōsis*), where our attach-ment to the advantages is transformed when we become acquainted with what is noble and its strictly superior value.[29]

Since what is noble is a subclass of good ends, there is certainly a sense in which what the decent know and what the noble know is closely connected. A successful human life, properly understood, will involve the pursuit of both good and noble things. Still, it would be misleading to say that nobility involves a deeper knowledge *of the very same things* that decent people grasp, since the latter fail to see the distinctive value of noble actions, taken in them-selves. On the *EE* VIII.3 account, then, ordinary practical knowledge is not only transformed but also transcended when one acquires full excellence with respect to practical reason.

Like Plato, Aristotle is famously and evidently an elitist in his ethical and political theory.[30] It is tempting, therefore, to attribute to him the view that those who fall short of complete virtue entirely lack the capacity to achieve practical success in life. In the terms of the view in *EE* VIII.3 that I have been exploring, this sort of elitism certainly applies to the difference between those who are good and those who lack virtue altogether. It does not, however, apply to the gap between those who are merely good—the decent—and the noble, who possess the full measure of human excellence. Even the decent achieve some practical success by securing what is naturally good and by avoiding ruin. What they lack should be understood as a sort of refinement, an appre-ciation for what is noble that would reorient their practical pursuits to value noble action above all.

We may contrast this picture with the *Nicomachean* account of ordinary practical knowledge as ethical experience. As I argue in Chapter 2, those with ethical experience have a practical grasp of the kinds of actions that are appro-priate to different sorts of circumstances, accompanied by the motivation to

---

[29] The affinity is especially pronounced when we consider the version of the theory of *oikeiōsis* in Cicero, *De finibus* III, where the main speaker Cato emphasizes the discon-tinuity that occurs when one comes to be acquainted with what is noble (the *honestum*). See especially *De finibus* III.21. For a teleological analysis of the Stoic theory, see Jacob Klein, "The Stoic Argument from *Oikeiōsis*," *Oxford Studies in Ancient Philosophy* 50 (2016): 143–200.

[30] See Chris Bobonich, "Elitism in Plato and Aristotle," in *The Cambridge Companion to Ancient Ethics*, ed. Chris Bobonich (Cambridge University Press, 2017), 298–318.

APPENDIX 191

choose these actions (since experience is acquired by being well-brought-up, i.e., habituated properly). In light of what Aristotle says about the virtues of character, we must suppose, further, that this motivation includes an appreciation, however inchoate or uncertain, of what is noble. It is not only the person with complete virtue but also the ethical learner who orients their actions to this end.[31] What such a person lacks, instead, is an understanding of the human good that would explain *why* these actions are appropriate.

While Aristotle retains his commitment in both ethical treatises to the thesis that the advantages can be the source of disaster for human beings, due either to circumstances or to a lack of virtue on the part of the agent, he seems to have changed his mind about the way that good motivation and excellence in the rational pursuit of human goods come together. The very notion of the natural goods seems to drop out of view (apart from the Common Books, notably the first: *NE* V = *EE* IV) in the *Nicomachean* account, though such goods remain indispensable conditions for happiness. Moreover, habituation is emphasized as the essential process of moral development, which both reshapes motivation and equips the moral learner with the starting points for developing practical wisdom, which, I have argued, should be understood as a dimension of ethical experience. As a result, there is no room for the category of the decent in the *Nicomachean* typology of character. Most importantly, for my purposes, practical wisdom is represented as the corresponding end-stage of a process of acquiring excellence in deliberation that begins with ethical experience.

Plausibly, this shift in Aristotle's thinking is what explains the change in ethical exemplar between the two treatises—from the noble man of the *Eudemian Ethics* to the practically wise man of the *Nicomachean*. The residue of this change is the idea that greatness of soul is the crown of the virtues of character (IV.3, 1124a1–4). Indeed, it is only in this passage of *NE* IV where nobility appears explicitly as a trait in the *NE*. Even if nobility belongs to someone in full possession of the character virtues and practical wisdom, it is no longer figured, as it was in *EE* VIII.3, as the *sum total* of the virtues.

Two features of ethical experience are brought out particularly clearly through this contrast. First, experience is ground-level practical knowledge *concerning the human good*, not just concerning the advantages. Second, experience contains within itself the seeds of the understanding that constitutes full practical wisdom. Experience is not transcended but is instead included in the knowledge of the practically wise person, since even understanding must reach to the particulars to be efficacious.

---

[31] See Marta Jimenez, "Aristotle on Becoming Virtuous by Doing Virtuous Actions," *Phronesis* 61 (2016): 3–32, on how the motivation of ethical learners should be understood in the context of *NE* II.4.

192 APPENDIX

A.3 Some philosophical lessons

My exploration, in Chapter 1 and in this Appendix, of Aristotle's conception of ordinary practical knowledge in the *Nicomachean Ethics* and how it differs from those we find in Isocrates, in Plato's *Statesman*, and finally in the *Eudemian Ethics* has been intended chiefly to bring out aspects of that view that would otherwise be obscured. While there are traces of the first two views in the text of the *NE* itself, and it is natural to compare Aristotle's two ethical treatises, the specific points of intellectual history have been less important to me than an exploration of the possibility space of views within which Aristotle himself might be taken to work. Still, to the extent that influence can be traced (in the case of the Isocratean and Platonic texts) or development charted (between the two Aristotelian ethical treatises), I hope that I have made more plausible the outlines of the view I develop more fully in the rest of this book.

At the same time, I have also tried to demonstrate the philosophical stakes that lie behind Aristotle's conception of ethical experience as ordinary practical knowledge in the *NE*. This conception has a number of surprising features that distinguish it from alternatives that are not only actually attested in fourth-century Greek philosophical writing but that also have intelligible analogs in our own reflection on practical reasoning and ethical knowledge.

For convenience, I briefly summarize here what I take to be the main philosophical lessons of this inquiry. First, as I argued in Chapter 1, ethical experience is not mere opinion, it is a form of genuine knowledge—and, indeed, Aristotle begins his inquiry in the *Nicomachean Ethics* from the thought that such knowledge of what we should do is a possibility for human beings. Second, as I showed in §A.1 of this Appendix, ordinary practical knowledge is not know-how as opposed to a more reflective or propositional mode of knowledge. The person with experience has a reflective grasp on what they are doing. Third and finally, as I showed in §A.2 of this Appendix, experience is not (mere) prudence, that is, the ability to get by in life in the absence of the right prioritization of one's ends. Instead, it is itself knowledge that concerns the human good as such and hence can serve as the basis for ethical understanding.

Bibliography

Achtenberg, Deborah, *Cognition of Value in Aristotle's Ethics: Promise of Enrichment, Threat of Destruction*. State University of New York Press, 2002.

Ackrill, John, "Aristotle on *Eudaimonia*." In Amélie Oksenberg Rorty, ed., *Essays on Aristotle's Ethics*. University of California Press, 1980, 7–33.

Anagnostopoulos, Georgios, *Aristotle on the Goals and Exactness of Ethics*. University of California Press, 1994.

Angier, Tom, *Technē in Aristotle's Ethics: Crafting the Moral Life*. Continuum, 2010.

Annas, Julia, *Intelligent Virtue*. Oxford University Press, 2011.

Annas, Julia, *Virtue and Law in Plato and Beyond*. Oxford University Press, 2017.

Anscombe, Elizabeth, *Intention*. 2nd ed. Blackwell, 1963.

Apfel, Lauren, *The Advent of Pluralism: Diversity and Conflict in the Age of Sophocles*. Oxford University Press, 2011.

Aubert-Baillot, Sophie, "De la φρόνησις à la prudentia." *Mnemosyne* 68, no. 1 (2015): 68–90.

Bobonich, Chris, "Elitism in Plato and Aristotle," In Chris Bobonich, ed., *The Cambridge Companion to Ancient Ethics*. Cambridge University Press, 2017, 298–318.

Bonasio, Giulia, "*Kalokagathia* and the Unity of the Virtues in the *Eudemian Ethics*." *Apeiron* 53, no. 1 (2019), 27–57.

Brewer, Talbot, *The Retrieval of Ethics*. Oxford University Press, 2009.

Broadie, Sarah, *Ethics with Aristotle*. Oxford University Press, 1991.

Broadie, Sarah, "Practical Truth in Aristotle." *American Catholic Philosophical Quarterly* 90 (2016): 281–298.

Bronstein, David, *Aristotle on Knowing and Learning: The Posterior Analytics*. Oxford University Press, 2016.

Burnet, John, *The Ethics of Aristotle*. Methuen, 1900.

Cohoe, Caleb, "Knowing in Aristotle Part 1: *Epistēmē, Nous*, and Non-Rational Cognitive States" and "Knowing in Aristotle Part 2: *Technē, Phronēsis, Sophia*, and Divine Cognitive Activities." *Philosophy Compass* 17, no. 1 (2022), e12801 and e12799. Part 1: https://compass.onlinelibrary.wiley.com/doi/epdf/10.1111/phc3.12801. Part 2: https://compass.onlinelibrary.wiley.com/doi/epdf/10.1111/phc3.12799

Cooper, John, *Reason and Human Good in Aristotle*. Harvard University Press, 1975.

Curzer, Howard, "Rules Lurking at the Heart of Aristotle's Virtue Ethics." *Apeiron* 49 (2016): 57–92.

194 BIBLIOGRAPHY

Denyer, Nicholas, "The Political Skill of Protagoras." In Verity Harte and Melissa Lane, eds., *Politeia in Greek and Roman Philosophy*. Cambridge University Press, 2014, 155–167.

Depew, David, "The Inscription of Isocrates into Aristotle's Practical Philosophy." In Takis Poulakos and David Depew, eds., *Isocrates and Civic Education*. University of Texas Press, 2004, 157–185.

Devereux, Daniel, "Particular and Universal in Aristotle's Conception of Practical Knowledge." *Review of Metaphysics* 39 (1986): 483–504.

Dixsaut, Monique, "De quoi les philosophes sont-ils amoureux? Sur la phronèsis dans les dialogues de Platon." In Monique Dixsaut, ed., *Platon et la question de la pensée: études platoniciennes*. J. Vrin, 2000, 93–119.

Dreyfus, Hubert, "Overcoming the Myth of the Mental: How Philosophers Can Profit from the Phenomenology of Everyday Expertise." *Proceedings and Addresses of the American Philosophical Association* 79 (2005): 47–65.

Gadamer, Hans-Georg, *Truth and Method*. 2nd ed. Sheed and Ward, 1989.

Gagarin, Michael, and Paul Woodruff, "The Sophists." In Patricia Curd and Daniel Graham, eds., *The Oxford Handbook of Presocratic Philosophy*. Oxford University Press, 2008, 365–382.

Gasser-Wingate, Marc, *Aristotle's Empiricism*. Oxford University Press, 2021.

Gill, Mary Louise, *Philosophos: Plato's Missing Dialogue*. Oxford University Press, 2012, 177–185.

Gomme, Arnold Wycombe, Theodore John Cadoux, and P. J. Rhodes, "Cleon." *Oxford Classical Dictionary*. 4th ed. Oxford University Press, 2012.

Gregorić, Pavel, and Filip Grgić, "Aristotle's Notion of Experience." *Archiv für Geschichte der Philosophie* 88 (2006): 1–30.

Hansen, Mogens Herman, "*Nomos* and *Psephisma* in Fourth-Century Athens." *Greek, Roman, and Byzantine Studies* 19, no. 4 (1978): 315–350.

Harbin, R. Kathleen, "The Practical Syllogism and Practical Cognition in Aristotle." *Archiv für Geschichte der Philosophie* 104 (2022): 633–662.

Hawkins, Cameron, "Artisans and Craftsman." *Oxford Classical Dictionary*. 4th ed. Oxford University Press, 2012.

Henry, Devin, and Karen Margrethe Nielsen, eds., *Bridging the Gap between Aristotle's Science and Ethics*. Cambridge University Press, 2015.

Hirji, Sukaina, "Acting Virtuously as an End in Aristotle's *Nicomachean Ethics*." *British Journal for the History of Philosophy* 26 (2018): 1006–1026.

Hirji, Sukaina, "What's Aristotelian about Neo-Aristotelian Virtue Ethics?." *Philosophy and Phenomenological Research* 98 (2019): 671–696.

Hulme, Emily, "Plato's Knowledge Vocabulary and John Lyons's *Structural Semantics*." *Oxford Studies in Ancient Philosophy* 61 (2022): 1–24.

Hursthouse, Rosalind, *On Virtue Ethics*. Oxford University Press, 1999.

Hursthouse, Rosalind, "Practical Wisdom: A Mundane Account." *Proceedings of the Aristotelian Society* 106 (2006): 285–309.

Hursthouse, Rosalind, "What Does the Aristotelian *phronimos* Know?" In Lawrence Jost and Julian Wuerth, eds., *Perfecting Virtue: New Essays on Kantian Ethics and Virtue Ethics*. Cambridge University Press, 2011, 38–57.

BIBLIOGRAPHY 195

Inglis, Kristen, "Philosophical Virtue: In Defense of the Grand End." In Ronald Polansky, ed., *The Cambridge Companion to Aristotle's* Nicomachean Ethics. Cambridge University Press, 2014, 263–287.

Irwin, Terence, "Aristotle on Reason, Desire and Virtue." *Journal of Philosophy* 73 (1975): 567–78.

Irwin, Terence, "Ethics as an Inexact Science: Aristotle's Ambitions for Moral Theor." In Brad Hooker and Margaret Little, eds., *Moral Particularism*. Oxford University Press, 2000, 100–129.

Irwin, Terence, *Aristotle: Nicomachean Ethics*. 2nd ed. Hackett, 2000.

Irwin, Terence, *The Development of Ethics*. Vol. 1. Oxford University Press, 2007.

Jagannathan, Dhananjay, "'Every Man a Legislator': Aristotle on Political Wisdom." *Apeiron* 52, no. 4 (2019): 1–20.

Jagannathan, Dhananjay, "Reciprocity and Political Justice in Aristotle's *Nicomachean Ethics* Book V." *Archiv für Geschichte der Philosophie* 104 (2022): 53–73.

Jagannathan, Dhananjay, "Right Reason and Practical Truth." In Jennifer Frey and Christopher Frey, eds., *Practical Reason, Knowledge, and Truth: Essays on Aristotelian Themes*. Oxford University Press, forthcoming.

Jagannathan, Dhananjay, "A Defense of Aristotelian Justice." *Ergo*, forthcoming.

Jimenez, Marta, "Aristotle on Becoming Virtuous by Doing Virtuous Actions." *Phronesis* 61 (2016): 3–32.

Jimenez, Marta, "*Empeiria* and Good Habits in Aristotle's Ethics." *Journal of the History of Philosophy* 57 (2019): 363–389.

Johansen, Thomas Kjeller, ed., *Productive Knowledge in Ancient Philosophy: The Concept of Technê*. Cambridge University Press, 2021.

Karbowski, Joseph, *Aristotle's Method in Ethics*. Cambridge University Press, 2019.

Klein, Jacob, "The Stoic Argument from *Oikeiōsis*." *Oxford Studies in Ancient Philosophy* 50 (2016): 143–200.

Kontos, Pavlos, *Aristotle on the Scope of Practical Reason: Spectators, Legislators, Hopes, and Evils*. Routledge, 2021.

Kosman, Areyh, "Aristotle on the Virtues of Thought" in *Virtues of Thought: Essays on Plato and Aristotle*. Harvard, 2014, 280–298.

Kraut, Richard, *Aristotle on the Human Good*. Princeton University Press, 1989.

Kraut, Richard, "In Defense of the Grand End." *Ethics* 103 (1993): 361–374.

Kupreeva, Inna, "Galen's Empiricist Background: A Study of the Argument in On Medical Experience." In Matyáš Havrda, ed., *Galen's Epistemology: Experience, Reason, and Method in Ancient Medicine*. Cambridge University Press, 2022, 32–78.

Laks, André, and Most, Glenn, *Early Greek Philosophy*. 9 vols. Harvard University Press, 2016.

Lane, Melissa, *Method and Politics in Plato's Statesman*. Cambridge University Press, 1998.

LeBar, Mark, "After Aristotle's Justice." *Oxford Studies in Normative Ethics* 10 (2020): 32–55.

Liddell, Henry George, Robert Scott, Henry Stuart Jones, and Roderick McKenzie, *A Greek–English Lexicon*. Rev. 9th ed. Oxford University Press, 1995.

196 BIBLIOGRAPHY

Lorenz, Hendrik, and Benjamin Morison, "Aristotle's Empiricist Theory of Doxastic Knowledge." *Phronesis* 64, no. 4 (2019): 431–464.

Lyons, John, *Structural Semantics: An Analysis of Part of the Vocabulary of Plato.* Blackwell, 1963.

MacDowell, D. M., "Epikerdes of Kyrene and the Athenian Privilege of Ateleia." *Zeitschrift für Papyrologie und Epigraphik* 150 (2004): 127–133.

Malink, Marko, "Aristotle on Circular Proof." *Phronesis* 58 (2013): 215–248.

Márquez, Xavier, *A Stranger's Knowledge: Statesmanship, Philosophy, and Law in Plato's Statesman.* Parmenides, 2012.

Márquez, Xavier, "Theory and Practice in Plato's *Statesman*." *Ancient Philosophy* 27 (2007): 31–53.

McDowell, John, "Deliberation and Moral Development in Aristotle's Ethics." In Stephen Engstrom and Jennifer Whiting, eds., *Aristotle, Kant, and the Stoics: Rethinking Happiness and Duty.* Cambridge University Press, 1998, 19–35.

McDowell, John, *The Engaged Intellect: Philosophical Essays.* Harvard University Press, 2009.

McDowell, John, "Virtue and Reason." *The Monist* 62 (1979): 331–350.

Migeotte, Léopold, "Ateleia." In Roger S. Bagnall, et al., eds., *The Encyclopedia of Ancient History.* Wiley, 2013.

Moss, Jessica, *Aristotle on the Apparent Good: Perception, Phantasia, Thought, Desire.* Oxford University Press, 2012.

Moss, Jessica, *Plato's Epistemology: Being and Seeming.* Oxford University Press, 2021.

Moss, Jessica, "Right Reason in Plato and Aristotle: On the Meaning of *Logos*." *Phronesis* 59 (2014): 181–230.

Moss, Jessica, "'Virtue Makes the Goal Right': Virtue and Phronesis in Aristotle's Ethics." *Phronesis* 56 (2011): 204–261.

Müller, Jörn, "Ethics as a Practical Science in Albert the Great's Commentaries on the *Nicomachean Ethics*." In Walter Senner et al., eds., *Albertus Magnus. Zum Gedenken nach 800 Jahren: Neue Zugänge, Aspekte und Perspektiven.* Akademie Verlag, 2001, 275–285.

Müller, Jorn, *Natürliche Moral und philosophische Ethik bei Albertus Magnus.* Aschendorff, 2001, 325–358.

Murr, Dimitri El, "Theoretical, Not Practical: The Opening Arguments of Plato's *Politicus. Plt*, 258e–259." In Beatriz Bossi López and Thomas M. Robinson, eds., *Plato's Statesman Revisited.* De Gruyter, 2019, 55–72.

Nussbaum, Martha, "Aristotelian Social Democracy." In R. Bruce Douglass, Gerald M. Mara, and Henry S. Richardson, eds., *Liberalism and the Good.* Routledge, 1990, 203–252.

Nussbaum, Martha, "The Discernment of Perception: An Aristotelian Conception of Private and Public Rationality." In Martha Nussbaum, ed., *Love's Knowledge: Essays on Philosophy and Literature.* Oxford University Press, 1990, 54–105.

Nussbaum, Martha, *The Fragility of Goodness: Luck and Ethics in Greek Tragedy and Philosophy.* Cambridge University Press, 1986.

BIBLIOGRAPHY 197

Nussbaum, Martha, "Nature, Function, and Capability: Aristotle on Political Distribution." *Oxford Studies in Ancient Philosophy* suppl. vol. (1988): 145–184.

Ober, Josiah, *Political Dissent in Democratic Athens: Intellectual Critics of Popular Rule.* Princeton University Press, 1998.

Olfert, Christiana, *Aristotle on Practical Truth.* Oxford University Press, 2017.

Owen, G. E. L., "*Tithenai ta phainomena.*" In S. Mansion, ed., *Aristote et les problems de méthode.* Publications Universitaires de Louvain, 1961, 83–103.

Pakaluk, Michael, "The Great Question of Practical Truth." *Acta Philosophica* 19 (2010): 145–162.

Perelmuter, Zeev, "Nous and Two Kinds of *Epistêmê* in Aristotle's *Posterior Analytics.*" *Phronesis* 55, no. 3 (2010): 228–254.

Price, A. W., *Virtue and Reason in Plato and Aristotle.* Oxford University Press, 2011.

Reeve, C. D. C, *Aristotle. Politics. A New Translation.* Hackett, 2017.

Reeve, C. D. C, *Practices of Reason.* Clarendon Press, 1992.

Richardson Lear, Gabriel, "Aristotle on Moral Virtue and the Fine" in R. Kraut, ed., *The Blackwell Guide to Aristotle's* Nicomachean Ethics. Blackwell, 2006, 116–136.

Richardson Lear, Gabriel, *Happy Lives and the Highest Good.* Princeton University Press, 2004, 17–19.

Riesbeck, David, *Aristotle on Political Community.* Cambridge University Press, 2016.

Rosler, Andres, *Political Authority and Obligation in Aristotle.* Oxford University Press, 2005.

Ross, W. D., *Aristotelis Politica.* Clarendon Press, 1957.

Rowe, Christopher, "Sophia in the *Eudemian Ethics.*" In Giulia Di Basilio, ed., *Investigating the Relationship between Aristotle's* Eudemian *and* Nicomachean Ethics. Routledge, 2022, 122–136.

Russell, Daniel, *Practical Intelligence and the Virtues.* Oxford University Press, 2009.

Sauvé Meyer, Susan, "Living for the Sake of an Ultimate End." In Jon Miller, ed., *Aristotle's* Nicomachean Ethics: *A Critical Guide.* Cambridge University Press, 2011, 47–65.

Schofield, Malcolm, "Sharing in the Constitution." *The Review of Metaphysics* 49, no. 4 (1996): 831–858.

Scott, Dominic, *Listening to Reason in Plato and Aristotle.* Oxford University Press, 2020.

Segvic, Heda, "Deliberation and Choice in Aristotle." In Myles Burnyeat, ed., *From Protagoras to Aristotle: Essays in Ancient Moral Philosophy.* Princeton University Press, 2009, 144–171.

Sherman, Nancy, *The Fabric of Character: Aristotle's Theory of Virtue.* Oxford University Press, 1991.

Sjoerd Hasper, Pieter, and Joel Yurdin, "Between Perception and Scientific Knowledge: Aristotle's Account of Experience." *Oxford Studies in Ancient Philosophy* 47 (2014): 119–150.

Too, Yun Lee, *A Commentary on Isocrates' Antidosis.* Oxford University Press, 2008.

Vogt, Katja, *Belief and Truth: A Skeptic Reading of Plato.* Oxford University Press, 2013.

198 BIBLIOGRAPHY

Walker, Matthew, *Aristotle on the Uses of Contemplation*. Cambridge University Press, 2018.

Walsh, Moira, "The Role of Universal Knowledge in Aristotelian Moral Virtue." *Ancient Philosophy* 19 (1999): 73–88.

Wiggins, David, "Deliberation and Practical Reasoning." In Amélie Oksenberg Rorty, ed., *Essays on Aristotle's Ethics*. University of California Press, 1974, 221–240.

Winter, Michael, "Aristotle, *hōs epi to polu* Relations, and a Demonstrative Science of Ethics." *Phronesis* 42 (1997): 163–189.

Wolfsdorf, David, "'*Sophia*' and '*Epistēmē*' in the Archaic and Classical Periods." In Nicholas D. Smith, ed., *Knowledge in Ancient Philosophy: The Philosophy of Knowledge: A History*. Vol. 1. Bloomsbury, 2019, 11–29.

Woodruff, Paul, "*Euboulia* as the Skill Protagoras Taught." In J. M. van Ophuijsen, M. van Raalte, and P. Stork, eds., *Protagoras of Abdera: The Man, His Measure*. Philosophia Antiqua. Vol. 134. Brill, 2013, 179–193.

General Index

For the benefit of digital users, indexed terms that span two pages (e.g., 52–53)
may, on occasion, appear on only one of those pages.

Albert the Great (Albertus Magnus),
117
Aquinas, 81n.5
Aristophanes, 137–38

cleverness (*deinotēs*), 22–23, 33–
34, 127–28
contingency, 5–6, 10, 71–72, 115

Demosthenes, 166–67

education, *see paideia* (education)
empeiria (experience), 35–74, 171
empiricism, 35–36n.1, 49n.8
epistēmē (scientific knowledge),
9, 13n.21, 52, 64n.16,
93n.20, 101–20
ethical inquiry, 40–41, 113–14,
117
euboulia (deliberative excellence),
126–28
eudaimonia (happiness), 1, 86n.12,
89n.17, 117–18, 123–24, 147–
49, 154, 182
Eudemian Ethics, 9–10, 76n.2, 83n.8,
131n.17, 182–91
eupraxia (acting successfully), 5, 89–
90, 98, 145, 146
experience, *see empeiria*
(experience)

Foot, Philippa, 72–73

Gadamer, Hans-Georg, 1–2n.1

habituation, 36, 37n.2, 43–44, 58–
59, 191
happiness, *see eudaimonia*
(happiness)

Isocrates, 21–23, 24–26

Justice, 130–43

kalokagathia (nobility), 1, 184–91

legislation, 59–61, 65–66, 77, 124n.6,
154–56, 158, 164–67

medicine, 38–39, 47–51, 62–63,
88–89, 180

nature
natural normativity, 30, 111–12
in relation to virtue, 58

Ockham, 4n.3

paideia (education), 10–11, 24,
27, 38–39
Plato, 4n.5, 22n.3, 26n.8, 27, 41, 45–
46, 59, 60n.15, 65n.19, 70–71,
73, 76–77, 76n.2, 89n.16, 114,
123, 136, 155–56, 165–66, 168–
69, 173–82

200 GENERAL INDEX

politikē (political wisdom), 6, 151–69
practical syllogism, 54, 109–10n.12
practical truth, 44–45, 92–100
principles, 30–32, 50, 52, 55, 64–65,
    107–11, 114–16, 123–25, 145–46
Protagoras, 22, 28

right reasoning (*orthos logos*), 77–78,
    82–83, 97, 139n.25

sophia (theoretical wisdom), 9,
    25n.7, 76–77, 84–85, 86, 90,
    92–93, 104–6

sunētheia (familiarity), 66–67

tekhnē (craft), 8, 38–39, 48–49, 64–
    65, 70–74, 91, 93, 103n.4, 145,
    172, 173–75, 177–78
Theognis, 59n.14
theoretical wisdom, *see sophia*
    (theoretical wisdom)

universals, 54–55, 67, 144–50

Xenophanes, 26n.8
Xenophon, 179

Index of Quoted Passages

For the benefit of digital users, indexed terms that span two pages (e.g., 52–53)
may, on occasion, appear on only one of those pages.

Aristotle *Nicomachean Ethics*
  I.3, 1094b14–22 [T2], 29
  I.3, 1094b27–95a6 [T4], 38
  I.4, 1095a30–b7 [T3], 31–32, 40
  I.4, 1095a25–26, 120
  II.2, 1104a3–10 [T17], 112–13
  II.6, 1106b36–1107a2, 4
  III.8, 1116b3–8 [T11], 69–70
  VI.1, 1139a6–14 [T18], 114
  VI.2, 1139b12–13, 92–93
  VI.2, 1139a22–33 [T14], 96
  VI.5, 1140a33–b2 [T15], 107
  VI.5, 1140b4–20 [T20], 144–45
  VI.7, 1141b14–21 [T5], 45, 51–52, 53, 104
  VI.8, 1141b23–24, 152
  VI.8, 1141b24–33 [T21], 155
  VI.10, 1142b17–33 [T18], 126
  VI.10, 1143a4–10, 181
  VI.11, 1143a32–b5 [T16], 108
  VI.12, 1143b18–28 [T13], 88
  VI.12, 1144a1–3, 90
  VI.13, 1145a6–11 [T12], 84
  X.9, 1180a34–b16 [T6], 62
  X.9, 1180b16–28 [T7], 63, 164
  X.9, 1181a9–14 [T8], 66

X.9, 1181a19–23 [T9], 66
X.9, 1181a23–b12 [T10], 67–68
X.9, 1181b15, 168
Aristotle, *Eudemian Ethics*
  VIII.3, 1248b18–22, 187
  VIII.3, 1248b26–37 [T23], 185
  VIII.3, 1248b37–49a3 [T24], 188
Aristotle, *Politics*
  III.4, 1276b27–34 [T21], 159–61
  III.4, 1277b13–16, 161

Homer, *Iliad*
  9.443, 25

Isocrates, *Antidosis*
  15.271 [T1], 24–25

Plato
  Protagoras 318e5–319a2, 25n.6
Protagoras
  DK B1, 28

Xenophanes
  DK B2, 26n.8
  DK B34, 26n.8